CHINESE CIVILIZATION AND BUREAUCRACY
Variations on a Theme

Sponsored by The East Asian Research Center, Harvard University and The Council on East Asian Studies, Yale University

CHINESE

CIVILIZATION

AND

BUREAUCRACY

Variations on a Theme

by Etienne Balazs

Translated by H. M. Wright
Edited by Arthur F. Wright

New Haven and London
Yale University Press

PREFACE

When Etienne Balazs visited the United States in 1962, we proposed to him the publication of a collection of his writings. We managed to overcome his native modesty, and agreement was reached on a plan. The selection of writings was initially his, and the final table of contents received his approval just a week before his sudden death in November 1963.

This volume is only a selection from Professor Balazs' voluminous publications. Other important monographs and studies are mentioned in the Introduction which follows. A complete bibliography and a memoir are being prepared by Professor Paul Demiéville for publication in *T'oung Pao*, volume 51 (1964).

We were extremely fortunate in being able to enlist the services of Mrs. Hope M. Wright as translator of this collection. Mrs. Wright was trained in Chinese studies at the University of London, was a close friend of Professor Balazs, and is an experienced professional translator. She had the advantage of frequent consultation with the author in the course of her work. On certain technical problems she received generous help from members of the faculty of the School of Oriental and African Studies, University of London. Mrs. Shu-chü Chang of New Haven provided the calligraphy for the glossary-index and Mr. James Millinger of Yale prepared the chronological table. We acknowledge with gratitude the permissions granted by the editors of numerous journals to reprint these studies. Details on the original publications are given in the first footnote of each chapter.

This volume was planned with the hope of bringing to the attention of the English-reading public, both lay and professional, the ideas and insights of one of Europe's greatest scholars of China. Now it must also serve as a memorial to a man whose character and scholarship were as great an inspiration to us and our students as to his colleagues and students in Europe.

The publication of this volume has been jointly sponsored by the East Asian Research Center, Harvard University, and the Council on East Asian Studies, Yale University. We hope it may be received as a worthy salute to a great scholar and as a symbol of international co-operation in the study of Chinese civilization.

April 1964   John King Fairbank
                                                 Harvard University
                                                 Arthur Frederick Wright
                                                 Yale University

CONTENTS

INTRODUCTION

Etienne Balazs was at the time of his death in 1963 a major figure in the world community of Chinese scholars. For thirty years he had been concerned with the study of Chinese civilization, and the essays in this volume are representative of his principal interests. The title given to this collection was his, and it is suggestive of the ambivalence of his views of Chinese civilization. On the one hand, he admired the great achievements of the Chinese: the creation of the most enduring political order in human history, the brilliance of their art and literature, the ingenuity and resourcefulness of the builders and reformers of three millenia who dealt with the whole range of problems of man and society and often reflected brilliantly upon them. On the other hand he was sensitive to the human cost of these achievements: the oppressions of orthodoxy, the authoritarianism of the traditional family and the educational system, the totalitarian strain that found expression in law, government, and the instruments of social control. This ambivalence toward Chinese civilization is reflected in the scope and the tone of Balazs' scholarly writings. There is a pervasive skepticism about elite myths, especially about the symmetrical holistic image of the civilization that its defenders held up to themselves. There is the highly developed ability to see through the formal verbiage of state ideology and public documents to the realities of power and interest. There is deep empathy for those thinkers who were the victims and the critics of the traditional order.

These views may be explained in part by reference to Balazs' biography. He was born in Hungary in 1905 and developed out of his studies of philosophy an interest in Taoism and Buddhism. He went to Berlin University for advanced study and enrolled in the seminar of the late Otto Franke. There he put aside for the time being his interests in Chinese thought and, characteristically, chose to write his dissertation on a subject that lay outside the concerns of traditional Sinology and the political-historical interests of his guiding professor. This was his study of the economic history of the T'ang period, A.D. 618–906.[1] It remains an astonishing achievement—the pioneer Western work on Chinese economic history written before this field had begun to be developed by Chinese and Japanese scholars. Some of the organizing ideas for this study were from Marx, others from Max Weber, but what strikes the reader today is its original analysis of key problems and its critical use of a great variety of traditional sources for new purposes.

In the years immediately following his dissertation work, Balazs turned to the study of key thinkers, and it is in this period that he wrote three of the articles in the present volume: the study of Ts'ao Ts'ao's poems, the essay on the anti-Buddhist Fan Chen and the study of the reformer Li Kou (Chapters 11, 15, 16). Also at this time he published a translation and study of inscriptions, mainly Buddhist, from the collection of Baron von der Heydt.[2] These writings, for all their brilliance, had no immediate sequels. These were the years of the rise of Hitler, and Balazs worked actively in the anti-fascist movement. In the late thirties he fled to France. When Paris fell to the Nazis, he fled again, this time to the small village of Meauzac in the then unoccupied south. There he and his family lived "underground"; he worked as a farm laborer and went into hiding during frequent police raids. One who knew him then writes of their life: "In Meauzac, where there were five refugee families, the whole village took pride in sheltering and protecting those refugees and often literally stood watch for them. The gendarmes usually closed their eyes . . . but some were known for their zeal, and one could never predict. The psychological pressure and uncertainty were great. During those years Balazs was much admired for his steadfastness that allowed him to

1. "Beiträge zur Wirtschaftsgeschichte der T'ang-Zeit," *Mitteilungen des Seminars für Orientalische Sprachen*, 34 (1931), 1–92; 35 (1932), 1–73; 36 (1933), 1–62.
2. *Die Inschriften der Sammlung Baron Edouard von der Heydt* (Berlin, 1932).

pursue some research in spite of fatigue and strain . . ."[3] It was only after the end of World War II that he began to publish again, and his first major article was the striking study of intellectuals in an age of war and social chaos that appears as Chapter 14 of this collection.

At long last Balazs found in the postwar years a setting and a position suited to his talents. The Sixth Section of the École Pratique des Hautes Études (Sorbonne) devoted to economic and social studies was established in 1947, and he was subsequently appointed to the new chair for the economy and society of ancient China. For the next fifteen years he worked with great intensity in teaching, research, and organization. In 1953 and 1954 he published his notable studies of the economic and legal history of the Age of Disunion, c. A.D. 200–600,[4] and in the following years the articles which appear in Parts I and II of this volume. Out of discussions with his European colleagues he developed, beginning in 1954, a large-scale collaborative project whose aim was to produce an encyclopedic manual of the history of the Sung Dynasty (960–1279). He stated the rationale of this enterprise in his first circular to his collaborators: "This project proceeds from the very simple idea that a modern scientific inventory of the most voluminous history of mankind is impossible without (a) efficient working tools, practical and meeting the demands of Western scholarship, and (b) coordination of individual researches."[5] Some useful publications ap-

3. Letter from Professor Konrad Bieber of Connecticut College to the editor, dated March 4, 1964. Quoted with the writer's kind permission.

4. *Le Traité Economique du Souei-chou* (Leiden, 1953); also appeared in *T'oung Pao*, 42 (195), 113–329. *Le Traité Juridique du Souei-chou* (Leiden, 1954) is Volume IX of the Bibliothèque de l'Institut des Hautes Études Chinoises. Because the two monographs from the *History of the Sui Dynasty* are in fact retrospective accounts of the preceding period of disunion, the chronological scope of the studies is roughly A.D. 200–600. The two treatises, together with a third—the treatise on law of the *Chin-shu*—are being prepared by Balazs' European colleagues for publication in a single volume. The volume will also contain an index to the treatises, a memoir, and a bibliography of Balazs' writings.

5. "Projet Provisoire d'un *Manuel de l'Histoire des Song*" dated Paris, September 25, 1954. The following excerpt from the circular recalls the wit and gusto of Balazs' communiqués: "La question éternelle: où trouver les fonds nécessaires pour la mise en oeuvre d'un tel projet—primauté de l'oeuf ou de la poule—posée à différentes personnes, paraît recevoir toujours la même réponse: fournir d'abord le travail bénévole qui, par ses premiers résultats tangibles, engendrera les capitaux. Si cette façon de voir est chimérique ou ideéaliste l'avenir le montrera. Essayons! Qu'est-ce que nous avons à perdre—nous autres sinologues qui ne pouvons pas contribuer à la fission nucléaire—que notre temps et notre force? Ils ne valent pas cher. Donc rémunération des travaux: pour le moment zéro, plus tard on verra."

peared under the Project's auspices; one of the most valuable was the detailed and fully documented map of Sung commercial and industrial life developed by Balazs himself.[6] In the work of the Sung Project, in his own research and teaching, and in his efforts to bring Chinese civilization into the intellectual life of Europe, Balazs was a tireless and creative innovator. When a Western scholarship of China emerges that is mature, responsible, and wise, much of the credit will be his.

It will be seen that Balazs lived most of his life in the midst of crisis: the Great Depression, the rise of fascism, the upheavals of World War II, the emergence of Communist states, the Cold War, the political crises of postwar France. He lived through times of upheaval, not as a detached observer, but as a man deeply concerned and deeply engaged. He had in full measure what Marc Bloch called the master quality of a historian: the faculty of understanding the living. In Balazs this faculty was made up of the compassion born of searing experience and great analytical gifts—the capacity to abstract significant trends and forces from the stream of events. He was intensely conscious of the power of present experience to shape the scholar's view of the past. He remarked that if the great Sinologue Edouard Chavannes had lived into the second half of the twentieth century, he would have seen more dimensions of tragic meaning in the letter which China's greatest historian wrote in the first century B.C. to his friend, a letter "which denounced the autocratic state for the humiliations inflicted upon its subjects and discussed with great lucidity the problem of whether to commit suicide under a despotism." Balazs believed that Western experience in the twentieth century could "bring us to a better understanding of the past history of China, which in turn may throw light upon those deep-seated and alarming tendencies —totalitarian, state-centered, bureaucratic—that are to be discerned as we move toward a unified world, everywhere pulsating with the same rhythm." For Balazs, the emergence in Peking of a new centralized autocratic state cast light backward on the phenomena he had studied and threw shadows forward on the future of mankind. Chinese history was seen, more clearly than ever before, as neither exotic nor

6. "Une Carte des Centres Commerciaux de la Chine à la Fin du XI⁰ Siècle," *Annales: Économies Sociétés Civilisations*, *4* (October–December 1957), 587–93, Introduction by Professor Fernand Braudel.

irrelevant but as integral to the history and destiny of mankind. The study of Chinese history and civilization was validated in new ways: not only could it help to liberate the Western mind from its old parochialisms, it could also lead to deeper understandings of the present and the future. This outlook and these concerns find expression in the themes which run through the essays in this volume.

This view of what the study of China could mean colored Balazs' attitudes toward the organization of learning. He hoped that the traditional isolation of Chinese studies—reiterated in academic bodies and time-worn practices—would end and that knowledge of the Chinese experience would become accepted as necessary for all types of scholarly inquiry. And, in his view, this could come about only if Chinese studies became more vigorous, more creative, and more attuned to the major intellectual concerns of the modern world. Though he admired the great French scholars of China—Marcel Granet, Paul Pelliot, Henri Maspero, and his friend Paul Demiéville—he was sharply critical of many aspects of traditional Sinology; its concentration on antiquity and the Classics, its lack of concern for basic problems of social and cultural history, its penchant for marginalia, which he described as "disquisitions on philological trifles, expensive trips in abstruse provinces, bickering about the restitutions of the names of unknown persons and other delightfully antiquated occupations." [7] At the same time he was on guard against many "modernizing" influences which he saw as threats to a mature and responsible Chinese scholarship: ideological axe-grinding, the grand systems that claimed to explain everything, "the immoderate use of academic highbrow jargon," jejune comparativism. In 1957 he spoke hopefully of postwar developments in Europe:

A new orientation, tending more and more towards the study of Modern China, is particularly seen in the attention given to problems of economic, social and institutional history in the post-T'ang period (after 900 A.D.). The increasing interest in New China on the one hand, and the general tendencies developing in the humanistic sciences on the other, are not without repercussions in the domain of Chinese studies where the specialists will no longer

7. Review of John K. Fairbank, ed., *Chinese Thought and Institutions* (Chicago, 1957) in *Journal of Asian Studies, 19* (1960), 321.

be able to confine themselves to some eccentric corner of their private curiosities. The preceding generation's preoccupations with external forms, with the unique event and marginal contacts is giving way to the desire to seize structures, the content and the significant facts and relations.[8]

Balazs' own concern with the structure of Chinese society centers on the scholar-official class in its complex relations with the system it dominated. He is at once deeply impressed by the achievements and the powers of survival of this class and repelled by the tyrannies it resorted to. Those accustomed to the bland and smiling face which Chinese elite culture presents in many writings may well be shocked by what they find in these essays. But historical realities are inevitably less symmetrical and less appealing than myths. Balazs sees the basic reason for the milennial survival of the scholar-official class in its monopoly of certain basic functions, notably recording and callelation, management of large-scale public works, control of agricultural production and distribution, the staffing of government offices great and small. He calls attention to the many devices by which the scholar-officials defended their monopoly. One of the most important was their control of education, their successful defense down the centuries of the principle of a general and humane education as the only proper preparation for public service. This was a principle which they never renounced, for to admit a specialist with some technical skill to the elite was at once to open its doors too wide and to destroy the carefully guarded homogeneity of elite culture.

Balazs calls attention to many of the policies and stratagems which scholar-officials used to maintain their dominant position. One was their use of law. Although official Confucianism always condemned the excesses of the classical Legalists, Confucian officials were never slow to resort to law—often of draconian severity—as a means of ensuring social stability. As Balazs says, "Confucianists and Legalists are (and always were) in agreement on the necessity to proceed against the lower classes with all the rigor of the law. Where they disagreed was on the question of raising the law to universality [as the Legalists would] so that it applied indiscriminately to the nobility and the lower

8. "The Present Situation of Chinese Studies in France," a paper read at the International Symposium on the History of Eastern and Western Cultural Contacts (Tokyo and Kyoto, October 28–November 5, 1957, mimeo.), p. 2.

classes, the rulers and the ruled. It was not legality in itself which divided the two parties, but equality before the law." [9] The Confucian scholar-officials also took over from Legalism that very economical device for social control, the mutual responsibility group (*pao-chia*). Whatever moral scruples they may have had about a profoundly amoral institution were outweighed by its proven effectiveness in enforcing conformity.

Imperial edicts inspired and written by scholar-officials ordained countless measures for the control of groups that might challenge the established balance of power. In Chapter 4 Balazs deals with official control of commercial activity; there and elsewhere he shows how the scholar-official class, by means of taxation, the creation of state monopolies and political pressure, managed to keep a bourgeoisie from developing to challenge their power. Balazs also stresses the heavy controlling hand of the scholar-officials in the regulation of fairs, guilds, and city life, especially before A.D. 1000. Added to these legal and quasi-legal devices were nepotism and corruption. Nepotism, which found ultimate justification in the Confucian ethic, helped to assure the survival of scholar-official families while corruption could be used for the same purpose and as an unofficial instrument for milking and thus weakening upstart economic groups.

The role of scholar-officialdom in shaping the economic history of China is another theme which, begun in his early study, runs through the essays in this collection. He views the elite's perennial insistence on the primacy of agriculture and the moral superiority of rural life as in part the demagogic manipulation of myth-symbols and in part the expression of class interest. The elite's paternal concern for the peasant and his livelihood is reiterated ad nauseam in tens of thousands of memorials to the throne, yet Balazs shows that most agrarian reform measures were designed primarily to ensure the state more stable revenues from the land tax—the mainstay of a political order whose principal beneficiaries were the scholar-officials. Again, Balazs insists that the merchant, whose mode of life was always denounced by official ideologues as amoral and unproductive, had certain ties of

9. *Le Traité Juridique du Souei-chou,* p. 9. See also Appendix III of the same volume, pp. 195–206, which contains a critical translation of a recorded discussion between two sixth-century officials on the most effective use of torture to exact confessions.

mutual interest with the literati—often expressed through bribery in return for short-term concessions—and a better chance to enter the elite than the sons of the peasant. Nevertheless the merchants as a class were never allowed to develop an independent position; they might gain temporary concessions, but they had no rights or immunities, and their fortunes and their enterprises could be taken over the moment they seemed about to become a class and thus a threat to the time-honored system. Private capitalism initiated countless enterprises, but these tended inevitably to be taken over by the state. Thus China entered the modern world with few traditions of private enterprise but with long and varied experience in state capitalism.

Balazs' interest in institutions led him to consider Confucianism mainly as an ideology, that is, a system of ideas used to rationalize and justify a system of power. In speaking of the cardinal virtue of Confucianism, *hsiao,* "obedience," often mistakenly translated as "filial piety," he stressed the effects of the inculcation of this value by indoctrination and punitive laws on the development of Chinese society, and he seems to have agreed with the late Wu Yü that the effect had been "to turn China into a great factory for producing an obedient populace." [10] He was not interested in the schools of Confucianism or in the history of Confucian scholarship. For him the Classics were interesting as repositories of value statements that could be, and were, put to ideological use. He once proposed that the vast bulk of the Classics and their commentaries could be rendered into a codex of key passages used again and again to justify one position or another in discussions of recurrent questions of state policy.[11] His judgments of Confucians and Confucianism may at times seem harsh, but they are a useful corrective to the bland and pompous exercises in self-justification that appear in many Chinese sources and in Western writings reflecting them.

In his consideration of the Chinese historical records, Balazs was

10. *Le Traité Juridique du Souei-chou,* p. 144. Wu Yü (1872–1950?) is discussed in W. Franke, "Der Kampf der Chinesischen Revolution gegen den Konfuzianismus," *Nachrichten der Gesellschaft für Natur- und Völkerkunde Ostasiens* (Hamburg), 74 (1953), 3–9.

11. *Le Traité Juridique du Souei-chou,* pp. 220–27. Balazs here explores the possibilities of codifying the *effective* passages from the Classics by grouping the *loci classici* used generation after generation to argue, on the one hand, for indulgent laws and, on the other, for severe laws.

always concerned to get behind the façade of moralistic verbiage and to discover those rare surviving documents that speak frankly and directly on the real interests that lay behind a decision or a policy. The reader will find at the beginning of Chapter 10 a summary of Balazs' views of the traditional histories, their strengths and their limitations. That essay makes the case that the histories were written by officials for officials and that the limitations imposed by Confucian ideology account for the most serious shortcomings of the traditional records. The case is strongly argued, but, as I have pointed out elsewhere, it tends to ignore the occurrence among some of the greatest Chinese historians of motivations that appear to be common to historians everywhere, particularly the inspiration of the great and universal question: how has this come out of that?[12] One may think that Balazs views historical compilation too much as an instrument of the dominant class. Yet one cannot deny the justness of his remarks on the great institutional compilations of the last two dynasties: "The many editions . . . conjure up a striking picture of the cumbrous, gigantic machinery of government, with its red tape, its hitches, and yet, despite these, its efficient functioning. No trace of the great steam-roller's many victims can be found here. . . ."

The reader will notice that the essays in history and thought are concentrated heavily on the period of the break-up of the first Chinese empire of Han and the Age of Disunion which followed it. No doubt Balazs was initially drawn to this chaotic period by his early interest in Taoism and Buddhism—traditions that played a dominant role in its intellectual and religious life. Further he was attracted by the critics, the dissenters, the colorful anarchists of the time whose ideas ranged more widely than did those of Confucian thinkers in more stable periods. These may have been some of the things that led him into the study of a period long neglected by both the traditionalists and the modernists among China's own historians. But there was more to it than this, for, as Balazs says in Chapter 2 of this collection, "We can only understand what we already know, and what is more, we can only become really interested in something that touches us personally." This age of the collapse of established values and institutions, of feverish efforts to diagnose and prescribe for the ills of a chaotic

12. Cf. Arthur F. Wright and John W. Hall, "Historians of China and Japan," *American Historical Review, 67* (1962), 980–81.

society, of the ransacking of all traditions for possible clues to understanding and effective action—this age resembles in striking essentials the age in which he lived. And this accounts for the empathy and understanding which inform his studies of this period. While he was working on these studies in the midst of the terrors of fascism and war, scholars in the refugee universities of Southwest China turned to the study of the same period; they too were drawn to it by its obvious parallels with the age in which they lived: an age of civil war, foreign invasion, the collapse of traditional civilization.

The individual thinkers who are the subjects of several essays on the late Han period and the Age of Disunion illustrate Balazs' approach to biography as a genre of intellectual history. The three late Han thinkers discussed in Chapter 13 were chosen as illustrations of the spectrum of intellectual choice in that time of crisis. And Balazs finds them meaningful in other ways. As they reflect on what has gone wrong, they provide vital information on their times—more intimate, less formal than the official record. Again, they testify to an important transition in the history of Chinese thought: from an intellectual quest still linked to earlier tradition to the wide-open speculations of the third century.

The essay on intellectual currents in third-century China (Chapter 14) combines astute analysis with vivid evocation of the plight of a society and its elite. More than this it shows how a movement of protest devolved through time so that "What . . . had been a high state of tension which was part of a serious effort to transcend human limitations, relapsed into mere abandonment of the ordinary decencies of life. The frenzied attempt at emancipation had turned to wanton frivolity, the cry of revolt to cynical acceptance, liberty to libertinage."

Throughout his writings Balazs insisted on the intimate relation between social and intellectual history. No thinker is introduced without reference to his social origin and role or without an effort to depict the society in which he lived and thought. And in these passages, as in the studies of institutions, we see Balazs' concern with the dynamics of social and political life, with process and change. Contextual analysis of thought and concern with social dynamics are accepted modes for the study of Western history. But for Chinese history these are relatively new and of high importance. Traditional Chinese historiography, for all its richness, tended to disguise cumulative change in formulaic statements of apparently recurrent phenomena, and the static view of Chinese society perpetuated in the West by Hegel, Marx, and many others implied that China had no "proper" history. Happily the pioneering work of Balazs had parallels and sequels among historical scholars in China, Japan, Europe, and the United States, so that a genuine history of China is now beginning to emerge.

Balazs' own philosophy of history is clearly seen throughout these essays. Though he insists on the importance of economic and social institutions, he does not invest them with the powers of blind historical forces. In China, as elsewhere, he believed, the institutional order changed in response to the demands of interest groups and as men struggled to adapt what they had inherited to the realities of their own time. But the range of innovations was limited by certain historical factors peculiar to China: the relative isolation and self-sufficiency of the society, the formidable inertia of social conventions and modes of thought, the cumulative weight of historical precedent. Thus men of each generation were confronted with a range of choice— wider in time of breakdown but always circumscribed by the weight of their heritage. Out of these countless choices, made in anger, anguish, or cold calculation by men as individuals or as groups, there emerged the distinctive patterns of Chinese historical development.

In the following pages the reader will be introduced to some of the men and the forces which created a distinctive Chinese civilization. More than this he will perhaps be led along the paths of self-understanding. For to Etienne Balazs, Chinese history was not only the greatest continuous record of a civilization but something of a "mirror-image" in which Western man could learn much about himself.

Arthur F. Wright

PART I

INSTITUTIONS

SIGNIFICANT

ASPECTS OF

CHINESE SOCIETY

We do not speak of the discovery of China as we do of the discovery of America, because, although it was an event of probably equal importance, it did not happen suddenly but was a gradual process lasting several centuries.

At first there was an imaginary China, one of those fabulous lands that existed on the margins of Western consciousness, arousing curiosity as a possible field for an enterprise combining colonization and conversion to Christianity. A nascent Orientalism seized upon this new object swinging into view in order to wrest from it its secrets. Its languages, beliefs, and customs were quite naturally the first features to occupy the center of interest.

Once closer contact had been established and missionaries were stationed in the Far East, China appeared to an astonished and admiring Europe as a country imbued with the spirit of rationalism, and was idealized into the very image of enlightened despotism. It was at this point that the religions and philosophical systems of China were introduced and enlarged Western horizons.

Later, during the nineteenth century, and more or less following the lines upon which science had developed, sinologists began making lists and compiling catalogues, and annexed the new territories of history, folklore, and mythology in addition to the provinces

The material in this chapter was presented in a lecture entitled "Les Aspects significatifs de la société chinoise," given on May 2, 1952, at the Centre Culturel International de l'Abbeye de Royaumont as one of a series on Chinese civilization; it was subsequently published in *Etudes Asiatiques, 6* (1952), 77–87.

already conquered. The domains of art and archaeology were also explored by zealous field workers who located and excavated sites. Sinology, like other branches of modern science, became specialized, as the mass of material concerning the Chinese world continued to increase.

Although sinology had indubitably made progress during this long and painful voyage of discovery and had succeeded in improving its techniques, its operations were still dominated by a strictly Western point of view, and its center of interests coincided with that of the conquering powers. Such rays from the Chinese spectrum as filtered through to Western consciousness were distorted by the thick magnifying lenses of the nineteenth century. It was not until the beginning of the twentieth century, when China appeared as an active participant upon the world political scene, that the final discovery was made of an oriental society in the full ferment of change.

Both in the East and in the West, those who were aware of what was happening wondered anxiously where such a state of seething ferment would lead China. And this urgent question immediately raised another: what had been the development of China, greatest of oriental societies, at once ancient and modern, and unique from the point of view of its continuity? What laws had operated in the development of a society so different in its essentials from that of Western mankind, and in what direction were these laws tending?

Thus we see that sinology may be regarded as the collective name for a large assortment of disciplines—linguistics, ethnology, archaeology, political history, the history of art, the philosophy of religion and of science, sociology, etc.—of which China, a subcontinent with 4,000 years of history, is the common denominator; and that it was simply a natural corollary of the changing relations between the subject (the West and its science) and the object (China) that the various branches originated at different times and varied in order of importance as times changed. The subject-object relations, however, became singularly complicated, and now are reaching a point of convergence, because the object—far from being something inert or inanimate—has transformed itself with astonishing speed from object into subject. In less than no time, China changed from a medieval empire into a world power, if "power" be understood in the strict etymological sense of the word—full of potentiality, with unlimited possibilities.

While the West was now faced with the far from negligible factor of an independent China, China itself had been roused to a new self-awareness, and the Chinese were beginning to discover their own country. But the road to this discovery was indirect. In contrast to former times, when Chinese society had been turned in upon itself, those of the new generation of 1912 became so engrossed in the task of modernization, so preoccupied with imitating the technology, assimilating the ideas, and adopting the methods of the West, and so assiduous in their studies at American colleges and European universities, that they had neither the time nor the inclination to study things Chinese. What resulted from this curious detour, however, was a renaissance of Chinese sinology, which had been in a decline since the eighteenth century, but which was incomparably richer in traditions and potentialities than ours. Inspired by the intense nationalism of the new China, and urged by the necessity to grapple with the problems facing her, China's sinologists began to investigate her past and her future.

So it was that, in the period between the two world wars, when the East and the West were each beginning to wake from the self-satisfaction they had enjoyed and, having swallowed their pride, were surmounting the feeling of superiority each had had toward the other, Chinese and European scholars almost simultaneously came to discover the existence of a particular kind of society unlike any other known type, governed by different laws, following an autonomous development that had apparently been suddenly interrupted by the incursion of the West, and was now in the state of chaos that raised so large a question in the minds of contemporary spectators.

This, then, is a very brief statement of the general framework within which the problems of Chinese society must be studied. The orientation and the methods of the sociological branch of sinology have, as we have seen, been influenced both by the current political situation and by recent developments in the scientific study of man. Thus the subject I now propose to discuss in some of its aspects is an extremely complex one. Moreover, it is impossible, within the limits of an article making no pretensions to scholarly thoroughness, to deal with more than a tiny fraction of the multiple problems of Chinese society past and present; for, on the one hand, we are faced with the most formidable mass of documents, hardly yet even catalogued, concerning traditional China; while, on the other, questions relating to the new China invariably end as questions of international politics, and this very much complicates the issue. The only alternative is to select certain problems that have significance both for sinology and for twentieth-century sociology.

When taking a bird's-eye view of the vast stretch of China's history, one is struck by the persistence and stability of one enduring feature of Chinese society that might be called officialism, the most conspicuous sign of which was the uninterrupted continuity of a ruling class of scholar-officials. From the founding of the empire by Ch'in Shih-huang in the third century B.C. right up until its end in 1912, and even beyond, it was always this class of well brought up "gentlemen" who presided over China's destinies and who recorded the events of her history. There is no area of Chinese civilization, from its basic institutions to the remotest other-worldly regions of its mythology, and including its literature and art, where the influence of these scholar-officials is not immediately discernible. How should this dominant social group, peculiar to China and unknown in other societies, be defined? As an estate, or a caste, or a class?

The first thing that strikes one about this social stratum is the precarious position of its members individually, contrasted with their continuous existence as a social class. Even the highest officials were, as individuals, at the mercy of the absolute and despotic state, and were liable to disappear suddenly from view. Any one of them might be minister one day, and consigned to a dungeon the next; yet within the same state that had condemned him as an individual, the body of officials as a whole continued, undisturbed, to play its part. The twenty-four official histories, a massive monument to the reign of the bureaucracy, contain innumerable examples of capital punishment meted out to officials, or of their being "granted permission"—that is, required—to commit suicide. It may be said in passing that if the statistics of these symptomatic occurrences were to be compiled, they might well be illuminating.

In my opinion, it is justifiable to define the officials as a class if account is taken of their economic basis (salaries and ownership of land), their uniform style of life, and their traditionalist outlook. Their upbringing, monopoly of education, notions of honor, and above all their character of *literati,* which distinguished them so sharply from the illiterate masses, might weight the scales toward regarding them as a caste or as a closed intellectual aristocracy. On the other hand, the institution of literary examinations for selecting officials did introduce a limited amount of free competition into the methods by which the ruling class perpetuated itself, in spite of the fact that its supposedly democratic nature was a mere legend fostered by the officials themselves in order to conceal their monopoly. It is this factor, reminiscent of the way in which the English aristocracy maintained its position by co-opting commoners, that militates against the idea of a closed caste.

The problem of determining the structure of Chinese society is further complicated by certain features in Chinese history that partake of the nature of feudalism. I refer, of course, not to the feudalism of classical times under the Chou, previous to the emergence of a bureaucratic society, but to regressive forms of feudalism that occurred from time to time at later periods, and notably to the important role of the aristocracy during the Middle Ages, when they clung tenaciously to their latifundia and their privileges.

The ambiguities of Confucianism present an even greater difficulty. Originating in the feudal society of ancient times, Confucianism began by expressing the mentality of the feudal lords, but later it changed into a system that became the organizing power behind the scholar-officials and gave full expression to their interests, ideas, and ideals. As a result of this metamorphosis, however, certain contradictory features developed. Confucianism was used as a means of defending the interests of the gentry, and the subtlety, not to say duplicity, with which this was done has deceived many a scholar. Confucianists kept up a tenacious struggle for democracy, but for democracy within the aristocracy—an exclusive privilege for the ruling class—and were authoritarian to an extreme degree in their relations with other classes. They were opportunist, conservative, and traditionalist; these characteristics went hand in hand with certain demagogic traits, although when they spoke of the *min,* the people, what they really meant was the *po-hsing,* the "Hundred Families." It is thus easy for the unwitting to be led astray.

The Chinese Communists, as the result of a line laid down during the struggle for power within the Russian Bolshevik Party in the years between 1926 and 1936, now have a summary philosophy of history which, though useless as a means for understanding the past, is helpful for justifying their aims. According to them, the former regime in China was purely and simply a feudal one. This is a thesis which, if a certain mechanical interpretation of Marxist doctrine is accepted, provides transparent justification for both the bourgeois revolution and the agrarian reform.

I believe that a careful study of the material circumstances, the social ties, the mode of life, and the ideology of the scholar-officials would enable the following conclusion to be drawn. The social position of the literati did not depend on their upbringing, their hereditary privileges, their territorial possessions, or their personal or family wealth. On the contrary, all these various features of their social position— important as they were in maintaining it—stemmed, in the last analysis, from the function the literati performed within the society as a whole. This function was an indispensable one for the maintenance of a large-scale agrarian society composed of individual cells—peasant families, living by subsistence agriculture, and scattered over an immense territory that was physically undifferentiated—which would have disintegrated into hopeless anarchy without the presence of a solid hierarchy of administrators given discretionary powers by a central government. Every attempt to replace a system of centralized government administered by officials who could be dispatched or recalled at any moment to or from the farthest corner of the empire, by a feudal system administered locally by the landed aristocracy, always led, in China as elsewhere, to particularism. But Chinese particularism, instead of leading to the formation of separate nations as it did in the West, broke down almost immediately, not so much because of the splitting up of sovereignty as because it meant the collapse of all the institutions that were a sine qua non for public security, production, exchange, an ordered life, or, indeed, quite simply for life of any kind.

Among those institutions that could not even have come into existence, let alone be maintained, without the constant, active participation of officials in every department, I shall single out for mention only the most important. These were: the calendar, indispensable for agricultural operations; the control of rivers and of transport and irrigation canals, and the construction of dikes, necessary in the battle against the twin catastrophes of flood and drought; the stocking of reserves in the public granaries against famine (and, as we know, periodic famine was the common fate of all agricultural societies until the threshold of the twentieth century); uniform weights and measures and a uniform currency as guarantee of a regular system of exchange; the organization of defense against the perpetual attacks of the barbarian nomads; finally, the education, training, recruitment, and reproduction of elites.

It can easily be seen that all these tasks have one feature in common: while none is directly productive, each is indispensable for maintaining production, or at least contributes toward doing so. To a major extent, they obliged the administration to carry out large-scale public works and maintain command of a large labor force. Neglect of any single one of such tasks adversely affected the efficient functioning of the social system as a whole.

Another common and important feature of official duties was their political character. They did not require any detailed, specialized knowledge. What they did require was worldly wisdom and savoir faire, and a level of general education that admitted the usefulness of a certain amount of rudimentary knowledge about technical matters together with the fine art of being able to manage people; or, it might be better to say, these duties called on aptitude—acquired through experience—for planning and directing public works and being in command of the technicians, experts, and specialists. The social system did not permit its elite to narrow their personalities by specialization. To know the classics by heart and have a smattering of music, to master the rules of polite behavior and acquire a polished literary style, to be something of a calligrapher and an occasional writer of verse—these were the kinds of accomplishment considered likely to contribute more to the exercise of social and political functions than would training in some profession or study of the exact sciences; and these were indeed both the outstanding virtues and the outstanding defects of Chinese civilization when compared with the later stages of our own. Hence arose the amiable dilettantism of the *chün-tzu,* the gentleman who, in whatever situation he might find himself, had to act as the representative of a privileged governing elite.

There are two further, and somewhat unpleasant, aspects of officialism which, if less alluring to study, nevertheless have much greater bearing on our own twentieth century. They are corruption and totalitarianism.

Corruption, which is widespread in all impoverished and backward countries (or, more exactly, throughout the pre-industrial world), was endemic in a country where the servants of the state often had nothing to live on but their very meager salaries. The required attitude of obedience to superiors made it impossible for officials to demand higher salaries, and in the absence of any control over their activities from below it was inevitable that they should purloin from society what the state failed to provide. According to the usual pattern, a Chinese official entered upon his duties only after spending long years in study and passing many examinations; he then established relations with protectors, incurred debts to get himself appointed, and then proceeded to extract the amount he had spent on preparing himself for his career from the people he administered—and extracted both principal and interest. The degree of his rapacity would be dictated not only by the length of time he had had to wait for his appointment and the number of relations he had to support and of kin to satisfy or repay, but also by the precariousness of his position.

It is here that another vital institution of Chinese society played a decisive role: the institution of the extended family and the clan. Protectionism and nepotism exist in all latitudes, but nowhere have they found more fertile soil than in China. This less admirable side of officialism was encouraged and sanctioned by Confucian doctrine, which taught that the interests of the family took precedence over those of the state. Almost all the discussions between the Legalists (*fa-chia*) and the Confucianists turned upon the question: which should have priority, the family or the state?

The Confucianist emphasis on the family may make it seem contradictory to speak of the totalitarian tendencies of the Confucianist state. But the contradiction is only apparent. If by totalitarianism is meant total control by the state and its executives, the officials, then it can indeed be said that Chinese society was to a high degree totalitarian. In this as in so many other things, the Confucianists supplanted the state-minded Legalists only to carry out even more rigorously the doctrines they had preached. State control and state intervention existed here long before these activities became common technical terms. No private undertaking nor any aspect of public life could escape official regulation. In the first place there was a whole series of state monopolies—the large trading monopolies in goods for mass consumption (salt, iron, tea, wines, and spirits) and the monopoly in foreign trade—which supplied the major portion of the tax revenue. There was also the monopoly in education, jealously guarded. There was to all intents and purposes a monopoly in literature (I was on the point of saying a press monopoly), for any writings from unofficial sources that had not undergone state censorship had little hope of reaching the public. But the tentacles of the state Moloch, the omnipotence of the bureaucracy, extended far beyond that. There were regulations for dress, for the dimensions of public and private buildings, for festivals, for music, for what colors to wear; regulations for birth, and regulations for death. This welfare state superintended, to the minutest detail, every step its subjects took from the cradle to the grave. It was a regime of red tape and petty fuss—yards and yards of tape and never-ending fuss.

Chinese ingenuity and inventiveness, which have provided so many of the amenities of life, such as silk, tea, porcelain, paper, and printing, would no doubt have continued to enrich China and would probably have brought it to the threshold of the industrial age, if they had not been stifled by state control. It was the state that killed technological invention in China. Not only in the sense that it crushed *ab ovo* anything that went against or gave the appearance of going against its own interests, but also because of the customary attitudes so firmly implanted for reasons of state. An atmosphere of routine, traditionalism, and immobility, in which any innovation or initiative not demanded and sanctioned in advance is regarded with suspicion, hardly conduces to the spirit of free research.

It might be thought that collective responsibility, another characteristic feature of imperial China, would be a natural corollary of its family system. But we know this is not the case, because we have seen with horror how in a recent totalitarian system innocent people were made responsible for real or imaginary crimes committed by relatives, and no such type of family as the Chinese extended family existed there. In China it appears to have been the more ferocious upholders of the idea of state control who introduced the theory and practice of intimidation through collective responsibility, against the wishes of the Confucianists. It remains true, however, that after the Chinese state had become completely Confucianized, it continued to use this terrible weapon against potential internal enemies.

These, then, are one or two important aspects of Chinese society, consideration of which may help us to understand China's history. They have at the same time a very great theoretical interest for those who are concerned with the structure of modern society. It is no doubt obvious that in speaking about the social and economic problems of a no longer existing Confucianist state run by scholar-officials, I have unavoidably touched on many a question concerning a totalitarian and bureaucratic society that had not yet come into existence, or is only now coming into existence, in China and elsewhere.

It is not my intention to discuss here the future of China beyond making a few concluding remarks about it. I think that everyone, whether friend or foe of the new regime, will agree that industrialization is the key to China's problems, including elimination of poverty. This is a tremendous, long-term undertaking. Indeed, to transform a backward country the size of China—an ancient agricultural society without specialists or technicians, without a proletariat of any sizable dimensions, without capital, and with a bourgeoisie which, to put it plainly, consists of the remnants of a class destined to disappear —into a fully industrialized one is in itself a superhuman task. But in addition, the project is burdened from the start by the dead weight inherited from centuries of bureaucracy, and one may well ask whether this particular conjunction of circumstances (which incidentally links China with Russia, through its Asiatic and bureaucratic features, much more closely than any number of oaths of friendship and pacts of alliance can) is going to augment or diminish the chances of success. Who is going to win the race? Industry and its new masters, the bureaucracy of the Communist Party, or the peasant and the old form of bureaucracy now fallen into disrepute? Will the old congenital sores of officialism, corruption, underhand dealings, unscrupulous ambition, lack of responsibility remain open? One is left wondering, and even if the matter concerned China alone, it is not likely that the answers would be provided in a hurry. But the fate of China is now indissolubly linked with the fate of the whole of modern society, which is everywhere undergoing the same leveling process and becoming more and more uniform, and in which there are strong tendencies toward bureaucratic control. It is the ultimate development of the whole of modern society—at present a secret known only to the gods—that will supply the final answer.

CHINA AS A

PERMANENTLY

BUREAUCRATIC

SOCIETY

The image the West has had of China has changed from time to time, and no doubt will change again. Of course an image to some extent reflects the viewpoint of the observer, thus distorting the reality that lies behind it. First impressions, however, are usually correct, and this holds true when two civilizations first come into contact just as much as when two people meet for the first time. Upon familiarity, individual features will become more sharply defined, or some may become blurred, but the general impression of the first encounter will be found to be valid.

The first image of China formed in the West, if we discount the rationalist wisdom with which the eighteenth-century "philosophers" clothed it, was that of a mandarinate. A strange society it seemed—bizarre, even, for it lacked so many of the constituent elements of Western society at that time, such as the Church and the nobility—yet a society in which, because of the preponderant role of its "philosophers," everything was well ordered and the wheels of an omnipotent state turned without a hitch. The impressions of the first observers, to whom the rule of the all-powerful scholar-officials seemed

This was a lecture written in 1957 entitled "La Pérennité de la société bureaucratique en Chine," published in *International Symposium on History of Eastern and Western Cultural Contacts, Collection of Papers Presented,* compiled by the Japanese National Commission for UNESCO (UNESCO, 1959), pp. 31–39.

the distinctive feature of the world—a world sui generis—that had newly been discovered, were fully in accord with reality.

Since the time of the first encounter, study of the scholar-officials has gone on uninterruptedly. Sometimes it has been undertaken with the conscious intention of investigating the essential features of the mandarinate, how it came into being, its history, and the conditions under which it operated; more often, even when sinologists thought they were confining their researches to Chinese language, literature, philosophy, or art, they were in fact studying the distinctive products of this one particular social stratum.

We can understand only what we already know, and, what is more, we can become genuinely interested only in something that touches us personally. It is therefore hardly surprising that Edouard Chavannes, when he was translating the works of Ssu-ma Ch'ien in those carefree days around 1900, failed to be moved by the cry of distress in that letter—constituting also Ssu-ma Ch'ien's last will and testament[1]—which denounced the autocratic state for the humiliations inflicted upon its subjects, and discussed with great lucidity the problem whether to commit suicide under a despotism. If Chavannes had translated this letter half a century later, its message would almost certainly have been full of meaning for the great sinologist. The fact is that we have only recently become aware of certain aspects of China that seem to be permanent features.

When I speak of "permanent features," I do not have in mind the idea of an "Eternal China," which is simply an empty cliché. To what, then, do I refer? It seems to me that there are certain aspects of the social structure of China that are permanent—namely, its bureaucratic features. These we are only now beginning to understand because we ourselves are experiencing similar tendencies common to all societies of the twentieth century, whether the pre-industrial, underdeveloped societies of Asia, or the industrialized, highly developed societies of the West. This may bring us to a better understanding of the past history of China, and that in turn may throw light upon those deep-seated and alarming tendencies—totalitarian, state-centered, bureaucratic—that are to be discerned as we move toward a unified world, everywhere pulsating with the same rhythm.

---

1. Letter from Ssu-ma Ch'ien to Jen An, 91 B.C., *Han-shu* 62, *Wen-hsüan* 41. The translation by Chavannes is in *Les Mémoires historiques* (Paris, 1895), *1*, ccxxvi-ccxxxviii.

THE KEY TO CHINESE HISTORY

The ideas of Hegel concerning the nature of Asiatic societies have often been dismissed on the ground that he lacked a knowledge of the facts. It is indeed an easy matter to refute the Hegelian conception of a China stagnating in immobility, for with each advance in knowledge it can be seen more and more clearly that China's history was full of upheavals, abrupt transitions, and gradual changes. Yet Hegel was right, to the extent that he sensed the unchanging character of Chinese social structure, and in this he is singularly in accord with the opinion of almost all historians of China, no matter what nation or ideological camp they may belong to. The often pointless debates on the periodization of Chinese history that began in the thirties, and will no doubt last for a long time in the future, always come up against certain phenomena of an undeniably enduring nature.

You may paste on labels (Antiquity, Early or Late Middle Ages, Modern Times); you may cut it up into longer or shorter slices; but, whatever you do, you cannot conjure away the sheer length of time the Chinese Empire lasted, founded in 221 B.C. and still surviving at the beginning of the twentieth century, or deny the permanence of the imperial institutions and the perenniality of certain phenomena such as Confucianism, which endured in spite of successive metamorphoses. Explanations may differ, interpretations contradict each other, but the underlying reality persists, a majestic mountain of solid, incontrovertible fact.

Now, it seems to me that the only valid method for letting light into this solid mass of historical fact is to seek out the causes of continuity—that is, try to discover the specific and significant features of Chinese social structure. I shall have to confine myself to discussing the social structure of imperial China, for it would take me far beyond the limits of the present essay to make comparisons with earlier periods, however interesting and instructive that might be. And I can only point out the more striking of its distinctive features, since anything approaching a complete description of the social structure of imperial China would require not an essay but several large tomes.

What, then, were its most striking features?

1. In the first place, China was a large *agrarian* society, highly developed but using traditional techniques, and established on a subcontinent that lacks any marked geographical articulation. Its cells,

scattered over an immense territory whose main arteries were a system of waterways, existed in an economic autarchy that made each of them an individual unit, and isolated each unit from every other. These cells were the peasant families that composed the overwhelming majority of the population. They were self-sufficient; but without the system of economic exchanges and the organizational framework imposed from above, they would have disintegrated irremediably into their component particles, into an anarchy that would have made impossible not only the distribution, but also the production of goods, and indeed the maintenance of life itself. It was, in other words, a pre-industrial, nonmaritime society, based on a peasant subsistence economy.

2. This society was *bureaucratic* because the social pyramid—which rested on a broad peasant base, with intermediate strata consisting of a merchant class and an artisan class, both of them numerically small, lacking in autonomy, of inferior status, and regarded with scant respect—was capped and characterized by its apex: the mandarinate.

3. The class of *scholar-officials* (or mandarins), numerically infinitesimal but omnipotent by reason of their strength, influence, position, and prestige, held all the power and owned the largest amount of land. This class possessed every privilege, above all the privilege of reproducing itself, because of its monopoly of education. But the incomparable prestige enjoyed by the intelligentsia had nothing to do with such a risky and possibly ephemeral thing as the ownership of land; nor was it conferred by heredity, which after all can be interrupted; nor was it due solely to its exclusive enjoyment of the benefits of education. This unproductive elite drew its strength from the function it performed—the socially necessary, indeed indispensable, function of coordinating and supervising the productive labor of others so as to make the whole social organism work. All mediating and administrative functions were carried out by the scholar-officials. They prepared the calendar, they organized transport and exchange, they supervised the construction of roads, canals, dikes, and dams; they were in charge of all public works, especially those aimed at forestalling droughts and floods; they built up reserves against famine, and encouraged every kind of irrigation project. Their social role was at one and the same time that of architect, engineer, teacher, administrator, and ruler. Yet

these "managers" before their time were firmly against any form of specialization. There was only one profession they recognized: that of governing. A famous passage from Mencius on the difference between those who think and those who toil perfectly expresses the scholar-officials' outlook: "Great men have their proper business, and little men have their proper business . . . Some labor with their minds, and some labor with their strength. Those who labor with their minds govern others; those who labor with their strength are governed by others. Those who are governed by others support them; those who govern others are supported by them." [2]

4. Being specialists in the handling of men and experts in the political art of governing, *the scholar-officials were the embodiment of the state,* which was created in their image—a hierarchical, authoritarian state, paternalistic yet tyrannical; a tentacular welfare state; a totalitarian Moloch of a state. The word "totalitarian" has a modern ring to it, but it serves very well to describe the scholar-officials' state if it is understood to mean that *the state has complete control over all activities* of social life, absolute domination at all levels. The state in China was a managerial, an interventionist state—hence the enduring appeal of Taoism, which was opposed to state intervention. Nothing escaped official regimentation. Trade, mining, building, ritual, music, schools, in fact the whole of public life and a great deal of private life as well, were subjected to it.

5. There are still other reasons for speaking of a totalitarian state. In the first place, there was a *secret-police atmosphere* of mutual suspicion, in which everyone kept watch on everyone else. Then there was the *arbitrary character of justice.* In the eyes of the authorities, every accused person was assumed to be guilty. Terror was instilled by the principle of *collective responsibility* (which, contrary to what one might suppose, had no connection with the Confucianist ideal of the family), making every subject shake in his shoes, and the scholar-officials most of all, for, although they ruled the state, they were also its servants. I should like to add that this last point is only apparently contradictory. The truth is that in all totalitarian societies it is a fundamental principle that public interest comes before private interests, and that reasons of state take priority over the rights of the individual

2. *Mencius* III A, 4; trans. James Legge, *Chinese Classics, 2,* 249–50.

human being. The inevitable corollary is that an official in his capacity as a representative of the state is sacrosanct, but as an individual he is nothing.

A final totalitarian characteristic was the state's tendency to clamp down immediately on any form of private enterprise (and this in the long run kills not only initiative but even the slightest attempts at innovation), or, if it did not succeed in putting a stop to it in time, to take over and nationalize it. Did it not frequently happen during the course of Chinese history that the scholar-officials, although hostile to all inventions, nevertheless gathered in the fruits of other people's ingenuity? I need mention only three examples of inventions that met this fate: paper, invented by a eunuch; printing, used by the Buddhists as a medium for religious propaganda; and the bill of exchange, an expedient of private businessmen.

In view of its contemporary relevancy, one additional feature of the bureaucratic state may be worth mentioning here: the panicky fear of assuming responsibility. To avoid getting into trouble was the Chinese bureaucrat's main concern, and he always managed to saddle his responsibilities on to some subordinate who could serve as a scapegoat.

6. The scholar-officials and their state found in the Confucianist doctrine an ideology that suited them perfectly. In ancient times, Confucianism had expressed the ideals of those former members of the feudal aristocracy who had formed a new social stratum of revolutionary intelligentsia, but in Han times (206 B.C.–A.D. 220), shortly after the foundation of the empire, it became a state doctrine. The virtues preached by Confucianism were exactly suited to the new hierarchical state: respect, humility, docility, obedience, submission, and subordination to elders and betters. In comparison with the usefulness of virtues such as these, ancestor worship and the cult of the family were no more than additional, though welcome, features. Moreover, the new elite found it convenient to adopt the Confucian nonreligious, rationalist outlook. Mysticism was usually a cloak for subversive tendencies, and the scholar-officials, anxious above all to maintain the position they had won, felt that it was something to be guarded against. Prudence dictated that they should remain soberly realistic and down to earth. Prudence also dictated that the new Confucianism should be conformist and traditionalist in character: strict adherence to ortho-

dox doctrines was the surest defense against the pressures of other social groups. Thus the contradiction between the rationalism of early Confucianism and the traditionalism of its later development created a tension within the mandarinate which can be explained by the play of interests—of vital interests—within the society as a whole. The conflict of interests also explains the contradiction between, on the one hand, the claims to be a democracy (claims real enough as far as internal relations within the group of scholar-officials were concerned), and, on the other, the actual existence of an oligarchy—the contradiction, that is, between the two poles of Confucianist political doctrine.

I do not wish, however, to go into the whole question of Confucianism, which is far too complex a matter to deal with in passing. The only point I want to make is that the continuity of Confucianism depended entirely upon the continued existence of the scholar-officials' centralized, hierarchical, and bureaucratic state. Whenever this state was at bay, whenever the scholar-officials had to let other actors take the center of the stage (never for long), the Confucianists went into retirement and kept quiet, taking cover in order to prepare a triumphant return.

These, then, seem to me the features of Chinese social structure that help to explain the persistence of bureaucratic government in China.[3] Before attempting to formulate an explanation, however, I must comment on explanations previously offered.

First, a question of terminology. Recently the word "gentry" has acquired some notoriety in the West because of efforts by some sinologists[4] to translate the Chinese expression *shen-shih*—their efforts, in other words, to find a name for the ruling class of scholar-officials. If it were simply a matter of a quarrel over words, nothing could be said against "gentry." But this term, borrowed from English usage, by emphasizing ownership of land is unfaithful to the Chinese concept.

3. The same ideas are also discussed in Chapter 1, "Significant Aspects of Chinese Society," and in Chapter 11, "Tradition and Revolution in China."
4. For instance, W. Eberhard, *Conquerors and Rulers. Social Forces in Mediaeval China* (Leiden, 1952); Chang Chung-li, *The Chinese Gentry* (Seattle, 1955).

Another theory[5] that has been much discussed is the notion of China as a 'hydraulic' society. This theory is too narrow; it takes into account only one element in a complex whole, and from the many functions fulfilled by the mandarinate selects one only: that concerned with hydraulic constructions. Now, vital as the hydraulic activities undoubtedly were, the political and administrative functions of the bureaucracy were certainly very much more important.

Finally, the question arises whether it is justifiable to dress up the mandarinate with the adjective "feudal." This is a question which of course goes well beyond terminology. The Chinese Communists, having abandoned Marx' original scheme (which divided the development of society into four successive stages: slave society in classical antiquity, Asiatic society in Asia, feudal society in the Middle Ages, and capitalist society in modern times), adopted in its place a scheme borrowed from "vulgar Marxism," and have got into the habit of giving the name "feudal" to everything that happened between a postulated slave society (the dating of which varies widely) and the year of grace 1949. While refraining from going into the reasons for this curious use of the term, let me simply say that it gives rise to unnecessary and often childish contradictions. For instance, many of the problems discussed in recent historical studies would be solved immediately if the "feudalists" mentioned were to be divided into scholar-officials (that is, the ruling bureaucratic class) and large landowners who are properly so called. In saying this, I suggest not that there was nothing feudal about China's bureaucratic society, but simply that the difficult task of finding out which elements were feudal is obviously going to be hopelessly confused by using a language that calls all cats gray.

Returning to the question of continuity, let us attempt a summary answer to the problem, for to understand in detail why bureaucratic society lasted so long in China would require deep and prolonged study. There can surely be no other ruling class to compare with the mandarinate for capacity to survive, wealth of experience, and success in the art of governing. It is true that as rulers they cost the Chinese people dear. The strait jacket into which the scholar-officials forced the amorphous body of China was agonizingly uncomfortable, and inflicted innumerable frustrations and sufferings. Yet this costly con-

5. Expounded in numerous articles by Karl A. Wittfogel. See his latest book, *Oriental Despotism: A Comparative Study of Total Power* (New Haven, 1957).

traption served a necessary purpose. It was the price paid for the homogeneity, long duration, and vitality of Chinese civilization. As many an episode in Chinese history has shown, if it had not been for the scholar-officials, acting as benign shepherds and keeping the feudalists in order (the real ones this time) while maintaining an iron control on the unity of the empire, particularism would have won the day, and, with the break-up of sovereignty, Chinese civilization would have collapsed altogether. The fact that the mandarins' motives were not disinterested made no difference to the final outcome. Besides, in a peasant China it was a rule without exception that the alternative to the reign of the bureaucracy was anarchy.

CHINA AS THE MIRROR IMAGE OF MODERN WESTERN CIVILIZATION

The history of Chinese bureaucratic society is instructive enough in itself to repay investigation. For the comparative sociologist it has in addition an outstanding virtue: it can be used as a mirror image in reverse of everything that is unique in the history of the West. What I mean by this is that the history of modern social development in the West (1500–1914), when reflected in the mirror of Chinese history, is seen to be the very reverse of what happened in China. The fact that there are certain symmetrical features that are absent in the one and present in the other should enable us to deepen our understanding of these features and of the whole of which they form a part.

In surveying this vast field, I can of course do no more than point to several signposts and indicate a few paths that lead toward the exploration of a whole stupendous process. Most people would agree in defining the modern Western world, once it had reached full maturity in the nineteenth century, as the world of competitive capitalism,[6] and would regard it in general as an industrialized society having liberal and democratic leanings and having some features that derive from the Mediterranean city-states and others from the period of enlightened despotism in Europe. The essential thing about its social structure is that it is based on free labor and on a technology that results from a science of nature using mechanical, mathematical, and experimental methods. Further, the civilization it has produced can be described as rationalistic, individualistic, and nationalistic.

6. I have taken this expression from G. Gurvitch, *Déterminismes sociaux et liberté humaine* (Paris, 1955).

Here again I have simply singled out what seem to me to be the most important features. If, however, they are accepted as the starting point of our inquiry, then a glance at the social structure of bureaucratic China will be enough to bring to notice a curious reciprocity. Everything convex on one side is concave on the other. One is almost tempted to speak of a European *Yang* and a corresponding Chinese *Yin*.

It was, in fact, impossible for such a thing as a nation, or nationalism, to exist in an empire that looked upon itself as the universe, the *t'ien-hsia,* conceived as composed of concentric circles becoming more and more barbarous the further they lay from the Chinese core. Aside from sporadic heretics among the Taoists and a few eccentric rebels, there was no individualism either. And except for the rationalist ventures of Confucianism, which were somewhat limited and in any case soon stifled by its obligatory traditionalism, one can scarcely speak of the kind of rationalism known in the West, with its use of logic, reasoning power, and rhetoric.

It is unnecessary to dwell on the absence of the natural sciences in China. Lacking systematic hypotheses expressed in mathematical terms and verified experimentally, Chinese science never got beyond the protoscientific stage, despite the fact that this initial stage was full of promise and that there was plenty of scientific aptitude.[7] This is not the place to go into a detailed analysis of the causes inhibiting the birth of science in China. Most probably the main inhibiting cause was the intellectual climate of Confucianist orthodoxy, not at all favorable for any form of trial or experiment, for innovations of any kind, or for the free play of the mind. The bureaucracy was perfectly satisfied with traditional techniques. Since these satisfied its practical needs, there was nothing to stimulate any attempt to go beyond the concrete and the immediate.

As for labor, there was no supply of free labor except for state enterprises. The peasant labor force was a carefully guarded preserve which private enterprise was categorically forbidden to exploit. It is probably not an exaggeration to say that the Chinese peasant preferred being fleeced by the state than by a manorial lord or an individual contractor,

7. See J. Needham, *Science and Civilisation in China,* Vol. 2: *History of Scientific Thought* (Cambridge, 1956); and "Mathematics and Science in China and the West," *Science and Society,* 20 (1956), 320–43.

finding state exploitation less hard to bear than exploitation by private individuals. But in any case he could choose only the lesser of the two evils. The "protection" of the mandarinate was a heavy burden, but there was no social group strong enough to protect him against the mandarinate. This is the exact opposite of what happened in Europe. There, the serf was able to take refuge in free towns under the protection of the autonomous bourgeoisie. This is where the heart of the matter lies: Chinese towns, far from being the bulwark of freedom, were the seats of the mandarinate, the centers of state administration.

Bearing in mind all the other areas where social development has taken a different course from that of Western society, we have only to compare the latter with China's bureaucratic society to appreciate fully the "miracle" that occurred in Europe during the sixteenth and seventeenth centuries. The concatenation of circumstances that brought capitalism to birth there and thus set in motion the industrialization of the entire world has all the appearance—when seen in this light— of being a freak of fortune, one of history's privileged occasions, in this case granted solely to that tiny promontory of Asia, Europe. It is tragic that Europe is only coming to take justifiable pride in this achievement at a time when her predominance is becoming a thing of the past.

A question that merits thorough investigation is why the buds of capitalism, which most certainly did exist in China in the form of mercantile capitalism, never came into flower. We are still a long way from being able to provide the answer. It is perhaps permissible, however, to anticipate the findings by making some conjectures. The scholar-officials' state was so strong that the merchant class never dared to fight it openly in order to extract from it liberties, laws, and autonomy for themselves. Chinese businessmen almost always preferred to reach a compromise rather than fight, to imitate rather than branch out on their own, to invest money safely in land and carry on the permitted form of usury rather than risk putting their money into industrial enterprises. Their abiding ideal was to become assimilated, to be part of the state by becoming—or seeing their children or grandchildren become—scholar-officials themselves.

But the mirror I have spoken of must first of all be polished if we are to see through to the image reflected there. Chinese historiography is the most massive monument ever raised to glorify a particular social class. History was written by scholar-officials for scholar-officials; accordingly all other social groups are passed over in silence or relegated to a purely secondary role. What is needed is to make their voices heard through the few surviving documents deriving from other than official sources, so that by restoring the dialogue between the official and unofficial groups, the arbitrarily falsified image of the Chinese people as a whole may be corrected.

TWENTIETH-CENTURY SOCIETY LEARNS
A LESSON FROM THE MANDARINATE

There is almost complete parallelism between the period of enlightened despotism in Europe, when the state intervened as arbiter between the rising bourgeoisie and the feudal nobility, and the period of China's history beginning with the Sung (960–1279). China lacked only one important feature of the European scene: the beginnings of mechanization.

We are better able to appreciate this parallel development today than we would have been at an earlier time, for the world events that have recently occurred have attuned our ear to any note of absolutism, state intervention, state control, or authoritarian methods.

Today we are witnessing a convergence in development all over the world such as has never been seen before. The same tendencies are at work alike in economically underdeveloped countries (all of which—whether primitive or highly civilized—have undergone some form of colonization by the West) and in the highly developed Western countries that have done the colonizing. These tendencies might well be called "totalitarian," and could be regarded as signposts on the road to bureaucratic, technocratic state control.

The extraordinary thing is that in this process of development, which was set in motion by World War I and the Russian Revolution of 1917 and accelerated by World War II, the final destination seems to be everywhere the same, even though the social and economic stages forming the various points of departure differed widely. In every country, whether underdeveloped or superindustrialized, it is always organized state capitalism that triumphs. This makes all societies alike, because it gives rise to the same tendencies. The group takes precedence over the individual, and the supreme power of the state is uncontested. Organization wins over competition, and everyone prefers to give up his freedom and submit. It would appear that efficiency is valued more highly than individual rights and the rule of law. Finally, the axiom that ends justify means is universally accepted. These are the well known features of the twentieth century.

The foregoing statements are not set forth from a presumptuous desire to supply an explanation of universal validity for everything. My purpose, much more modest, is to touch lightly upon the question of the two Chinas, the old and the new—on what links the one with the other and what links both to the determining factors of our times. Here, without any doubt, we are dealing with one of the most fascinating of all "culture contacts," and one which is of incalculable importance.

Russia, an underdeveloped country—which under its former government had features recalling the uneven development of the colonies as well as features similar to those found in Asiatic countries (and which is, moreover, indeed a part of Asia, its Mongol conquerors having left indelible traces upon it)—is now supposed to be taking a leap into the unknown of socialism. In actual fact, she is doing all she can to become industrialized and to catch up with the West. It would be impossible to make such a superhuman effort without the driving power of a strictly organized ruling stratum in an all-powerful state. This new bureaucracy copies unaware, or rather re-creates, many of the patterns of thought and organization belonging to the old Chinese scholar-officials, beginning with intolerance and the single-party system, continuing through monopoly of public opinion, education, and foreign trade, and ending with collective responsibility, shirking of responsibility by key officials in the hierarchy, worship of discipline, the *pao-pien* method (painting the memory of the dead either black or white), permission to commit suicide as a special measure of grace, and so on.

Meanwhile, in the West, for quite different reasons and with the greatest reluctance on the part of all concerned, state control has been introduced more and more. In order that capitalism might be saved, laissez-faire and free enterprise have gone by the board and centralized organization has begun to take their place—first introduced to carry on the war (National Socialism having already established totalitarian methods in Germany) in order to survive at all, and later retained in order to live in peace without the encumbrance of outmoded institutions. Now is the time of the managers, of the technocrats, and of planning. Planning has definitely won the day over the open-market economy—planning with all its accompanying phenomena, so numerous and so well known that it would be tedious to list them.

And modern China? How could it be expected to have escaped from its past, or from following the example of its great neighbor, or from going in the same direction as the hated yet admired West? Above all, how could it have evaded the inescapable necessity to become industrialized, to become modernized, even if this meant having to skip several stages in order to catch up with the West? To the unbiased observer such questions supply their own answers, for the answers are dictated by the inherent necessity of the situation, a far more ruthless master than the most dictatorial of governments.

It does not require very much skill at reading between the lines to discern from some of the speeches by government ministers the omnipresence, to this day, of the old bureaucratic spirit in China.[8] The official diatribes against the scourges of bureaucracy make this only too plain: fraud, corruption, "feudal" mentality, opportunism, slavery to routine, pedantry, formalism—and still the list is far from complete. Bureaucracy is certainly rife, in all its forms.

To conclude these brief remarks on modern China, let me say only that nothing can stop her from pursuing her path toward becoming a great industrial nation. That the price is exorbitant goes without saying. But the West, which has plenty of spare capital that could easily be used to help defray the cost, continues to sulk, and China must

8. I should like to recall here the striking passage in the address given by the President of the Chinese People's Republic at Yenan on May 2, 1942. See Mao Tse-tung, *Hsüan-chi* (1956), *3*, 853. I quote from the English translation in C. Brandt, B. Schwartz, and J. K. Fairbank, *A Documentary History of Chinese Communism* (Cambridge, Mass., 1952), p. 410: "In this respect I can say a word about my own experience in the transformation of my feelings. I started out as a student, and in school developed the *habits of a student*. It did not seem proper for me to do even a little bit of hard work such as carrying my own baggage, in front of a whole crowd of students who were unable to shoulder a load or pick up a heavy weight. *At that time I felt that the only clean people in the world were the intellectuals, and the workers, peasants, and soldiers were all comparatively dirty.* I could wear the clothes of other intellectuals because I thought they were clean, but I did not want to wear the clothes of the workers, peasants, or soldiers because I felt they were dirty" (My italics).

farà di se—must go ahead and industrialize on her own, independently of, and in spite of, the West.

It would be rash to make any further prognostications. My point is that, in spite of all the changes that have taken place in the world, the bureaucratic society of an empire that lasted for two thousand years is still with us as an extremely active force.

CHINESE

FEUDALISM

The basic view held by Joseph R. Levenson that imperial China (200 B.C.–A.D. 1900) was not a feudal but a bureaucratic society—a view with consequences that go well beyond the field of Chinese studies, being incompatible with the official doctrine adopted by the Chinese Communist Party—is one that I have been propounding for years. Without going into great detail, I should like to discuss here some points in Levenson's argument.

It is certainly incorrect to consider, as does Rushton Coulborn,[1] that lack of specialization ("slight degree of separation of leadership functions") is an essential characteristic of feudalism. Functional specialization is part and parcel of the division of labor and remains more or less embryonic until the appearance of industrialized societies. In other words, it is not only feudalism that is typified by division of labor in which specialization of functions is little developed. This characteristic is shared by other, nonfeudal forms of social organization.

It is necessary to insist on this point. Coulborn put forward two defining characteristics of feudalism: government in private hands and lack of specialization. Levenson rejects the first of these as being inapplicable; accordingly, with one of the defining factors being absent, he very correctly repudiates, along with Derk Bodde, the idea that

1. Rushton Coulborn, ed., *Feudalism in History* (Princeton, 1956). See the editor's introduction.

The remarks in this chapter are critical comments written in 1956 on J. R. Levenson's review of Rushton Coulborn, ed., *Feudalism in History* (Princeton, 1956). Levenson's review appeared in *Far Eastern Quarterly, 15* (1956), 369–72 and these comments in *Journal of Asian Studies, 16* (1957), 329–32.

imperial China was feudal. After rejecting the first of Coulborn's criteria, however, Levenson admits the existence of the second! But if this second criterion, lack of specialization, is also excluded, then the thesis that China during the greater part of her history was not a feudal society is to that extent strengthened.

It can, and indeed must, be excluded—first, because it is not an essential characteristic, not a specific aspect of feudal society, as I have just shown; and secondly, because the question of the specialization of functions has a complexity of its own in China. When the division of labor had already reached a fairly advanced stage, Confucianism aimed at—and in fact achieved—its own peculiar form of specialization of functions: all social functions were to be kept separate from the political function of the ruling class, the "leadership" of the scholar-officials. This was the only function that was recognized as a distinct profession, and it remained a closed monopoly. The theory and practice of the Confucianist system might be summed up in a quip: to be a specialist in government (a scholar-official) is incompatible with any other form of specialization.

The dynamic view of feudalism adopted by Levenson—where did feudalism lead? Did it contain the seeds of capitalism within it?—is excellent. A dialectical, creative method is the only justifiable one.[2]

Levenson's reasoning seems at first sight to be perfectly logical: since the so-called feudalism of ancient China (the pre-Ch'in period) gave rise to a bureaucratic society, equidistant from both feudalism and capitalism, the feudalism of ancient times (the Chou dynasty) becomes ipso facto suspect, dubious, to be handled with care.

2. The life of a human being can be judged only after it is over. This is an existentialist idea that I think is also applicable to societies and social classes. The French Revolution has become something quite different since 1917, and the significance of the October Revolution is constantly changing (Stalin, the Chinese Revolution, etc.). There have been many different expressions of this idea. For instance:

> Time past and time future
> What might have been and what has been
> Point to one end, which is always present.
>
> *   *   *
>
> Or say that the end precedes the beginning,
> And the end and the beginning were always there
> Before the beginning and after the end.
> —T. S. Eliot, *Burnt Norton*

There is, however, a flaw in this formally impeccable logic. In the first place, to assume from what has happened in the West that there will be a succession of inevitable and unvarying stages of social development is both a theoretical blind alley and an error—the error of reverting (in the domain of historiography) to the old imperialist outlook of the white man. This error on the part of Mr. Levenson, who argues very well against ontological analogies, is no doubt an unconscious one.

But there is more. To begin with, it seems to me undeniable that there were strong tendencies toward capitalism at the end of the Chou period (the period of the Warring Kingdoms). The tendencies toward capitalism from some time in the eighth century (which present-day Chinese historians delicately term *meng-ya,* "buds"), and still more under the Sung, seem to me to be clearer still. Then why did China never reach the capitalist stage? The answers to the questions so pertinently formulated by Mr. Levenson[3] are extremely difficult and would require hundreds of factual studies. Before making some suggestions in what is necessarily a premature attempt to provide these answers, some preliminary remarks are called for.

Absolutism as it existed in Western Europe (where it occupied the center of the stage before a fully developed bourgeoisie emerged) has so many points of resemblance to the imperial regime in China that a priori the argument concerning a nonfeudal ancient period, posited because feudalism did not lead directly to capitalism, loses much of its force.

It is necessary to make a clear distinction between "capitalist" elements in a feudal society and those in a bureaucratic society, between the "buds" that formed in the entrails of Chou society and those borne within the imperial society.[4]

3. "What are the forces inhibiting Chinese capitalism even while an *ostensibly* feudal, hence potentially capitalist society evolves into something anti-feudal . . . Why does a *hypothetical* feudalism yield to a bureaucratic society, which is not only anti-feudal but anti-capitalist as well? . . . because, perhaps, in the Chinese environment down to modern times, centrally directed bureaucratic action, anti-feudal by nature, may have been a *sine qua non* of a viable social order . . . Recurrent bureaucratic exploitation . . . of an anti-feudal state power seems— *without* capitalism and yet with economic advantages—to have superseded a feudal type of exploitation of land withdrawn from the reach of the state" (the first two italics are mine). Levenson review, p. 571.

4. This is not the place to discuss the various periods into which one could or should divide this whole epoch of 2,000 years.

Would it not be more logical, and at the same time more in conformity with the facts, to say[5] that the authentic feudalism of Chou was superseded by bureaucratic state centralism, without any intervening stage; and that this development, while untypical and abnormal for the West, is precisely what is typical and normal for China? There would then be no need to deny the feudal character of Chou *post festum* or, rather, *post mortem*. It is obvious to anyone with any knowledge, however slight, of the history of different societies and different civilizations that feudalism—Chinese or Western, or African or Japanese or Russian—is not constructed from blueprints, is not a standardized product manufactured by some universal brain which is either divine or credited with the attributes of divinity.

Very little is known even now about the history of China. The veil that has been drawn by Confucian historiography over the many and often ferocious struggles between the opposing social forces still hides significant detailed facts from us. The veil must be lifted.

If one thinks for a moment of the prolonged death agony of feudalism in Europe, of its tenacious hold even in our own times, one comes to a better understanding of the persistence of feudal elements in a noncapitalist society such as China.

When I speak here of capitalism, or of capitalist tendencies or elements, I refer always to mercantile or moneylenders' capitalism, whether private or state, never to industrial capitalism. What ultimately prevented the blossoming of capitalist buds in China seems to me to be the fact that China was undifferentiated geographically, and lacked a system of separate nation-states (counterproof: the Mediterranean and the medieval West).[6] Lack of the necessary geopolitical preconditions resulted in the birth, growth, and perpetuation of a centralized state—bureaucratic, absolute, and omnipotent, and embodied in a ruling class of scholar-officials. If it had not been for this uncomfortable but useful corset, this cruel but necessary strait jacket, the world would not have witnessed the spectacle of a civilization characterized by such astonishing vitality that it was able to endure for

5. ". . . the undeniable qualitative change between pre-Ch'in and post-Ch'in society can be seen as transition from an *incompletely* feudal to an anti-feudal society; the inception of the latter, since it is also anti-capitalist—a permanent depressive of capitalism, in fact—comprises the *incompleteness* of the former" (my italics). Levenson review, p. 571

6. One might add to these the period of the Warring Kingdoms, precisely because it was a pluralist universe.

many centuries and remain homogeneous and uniform in spite of its diversity.

Many questions are posed by the long reign of a dominant class that endured intact throughout the centuries, continuously improving its methods and surviving long periods of adversity; but these very factors also supply the key to a number of problems. For instance, the rationalist-traditionalist dualism found in the scholar-official class can be explained by the fact that the role of this class never changed. Confucianism, originally rationalist and nonreligious, became and remained traditionalist and conservative, for there was no need for the scholar-officials to develop its original antifeudal traits beyond the point required for maintaining their uncontested sway. Nothing is more foreign to the Confucian spirit than the idea of progress.

It is also the long reign of the ruling class that explains both the prestige it enjoyed and its relationship to other classes. In particular, its relations with the merchant class were determined by the equilibrium between them, continuously maintained in the interests of the scholar-officials and the state in spite of the many factors tending to upset the equilibrium. To put it more bluntly, every time the merchant class succeeded in attaining some degree of liberty, or arrogating to itself some right, or securing an advantage, the state intervened, curtailed the liberty, and arbitrarily took over, wiping out the advantages gained. The merchant class, for its part—and here, I think, we reach the crux of the matter—always chose to haggle rather than fight, preferring individual baksheesh to corporate "liberties," temporary accommodations to permanent charters. Whenever a new invention (printing, bills of exchange, paper money, water mills) made its appearance in circles which the scholar-officials regarded as hostile, they sooner or later seized it in order to profit from it at the expense of the inventors, who were dismissed from the scene. As a result of this recurring process the scholar-officials and the merchants formed two hostile but interdependent classes. There was an interpenetration, a symbiosis, between them: the scholar-official became "bourgeoisified," while the merchant's ambition turned to becoming a scholar-official and investing his profits in land. Their common ground was that peculiarly Chinese phenomenon, corruption, and their normal reciprocal relationship might be described as one of bully-squeeze. All relations between them were of a practical, ad hoc nature, and there was never any question of making a reasoned assessment of the social implications involved.

Another permanent depressive of capitalism was the nonexistence of free labor. The scholar-officials, in constant fear of a possible coalition between bourgeoisie and peasants, made a point of withdrawing peasant labor from any kind of capitalist exploitation and reserved to themselves the exclusive right to exploit this labor, their own form of exploitation being paternalistic, more or less easy-going, and (because indirect) more or less disguised. We must not forget that after Han times the ruling class fought a stubborn battle on two fronts: against the feudal lords descended from Hsiang Yü, and against the peasants, the sons of Ch'en Sheng.[7]

7. That there have been many deserters to the other side from the ranks of the peasants during the course of Chinese history—the founder of the Han dynasty for one—makes no difference.

THE BIRTH

OF CAPITALISM

IN CHINA

During his first campaign for the correction of unorthodox tendencies in the Communist Party, Mao Tse-tung, in a famous speech delivered on February 1, 1942, made the following statement: "One hundred years have elapsed since the Opium War, yet in regard to the development of Chinese capitalism, no theoretical work which is truly scientific and in accord with the realities of Chinese economic development has been produced."[1] Since then, little more has been done. Why? Before answering the question let me first state the problem.

It is now common parlance to speak of the "underdeveloped" countries, but it is not always realized that the expression beclouds a remarkable fact—namely, that the world is divided into a small number of Western countries at an advanced stage of industrialization on the one hand, and on the other, the vast majority of countries—mostly in Asia, Africa, and South America—in varying stages of industrialization but none with a standard of living comparable with that of the old industrialized countries of Europe and the United States; the latter, in contrast, might be called "overdeveloped." This overdevelopment is due to the driving power and rapid expansion of capitalism. In the process of expansion, the pre-industrial countries were exploited as

1. Brandt, Schwartz, and Fairbank, *A Documentary History of Chinese Communism,* p. 378.

This was originally a lecture given in English at the Universities of Oxford and Cambridge in March 1960. It was subsequently published in *Journal of Economic and Social History of the Orient, 3* (1960), 196–216. The text here has been slightly altered.

colonies for providing raw materials and manpower to ensure the smooth working of the capitalist system. There was, however, a wide variation in the economic and cultural levels of the countries thus exploited. It is scarcely necessary to insist on the differences in time and space between, say, primitive African tribal groups and complex societies like the Ottoman empire or the powerful and intricately organized Chinese state of the past. This immediately raises the question: why was it that no form of capitalism comparable with that of the West ever arose in countries at such a high level of civilization as these? Or did it? Of course I do not refer here to capitalist elements introduced from outside, or to capitalist features developed in imitation of the Western pattern—which, by the way, when introduced, tend after due fermentation to dislocate and eventually destroy the recipient civilization.

Now, curiously enough, the only person to consider this question at all seriously with regard to China has been the German sociologist, Max Weber. Perhaps even he did not fully appreciate its implications. In all parts of the world, with the exception of Western Europe (which Paul Valéry called the tiny "promontory of Asia"), there is an absence of any native form of capitalism, and apparently no autonomous development in that direction; and the discovery of this absence makes us suddenly realize the miracle of what happened here. The possibility of using the pre-industrial societies, whether civilized or not, as a mirror in which to see our own development enables us to arrive at a more just assessment of it, and is, I think, one of the main advantages to be derived from studying them.

Coming back to China, let me formulate the question as follows. Why was it that, in spite of very favorable conditions—for China was technologically and scientifically ahead of the West until the time of the Renaissance—Chinese civilization never gave rise to capitalism? Were there ever the beginnings of capitalistic development—an embryonic capitalism that got strangled in the womb? Or did even such beginnings never occur? If they did, what prevented them from developing? Why did the buds never blossom? What are the main reasons for the failure? I will later try to give a few tentative answers.

But first let me mention the difficulties that one encounters in approaching the problem. There is no need to speak of Western sinology. Fully occupied with philological hair-splitting, the sinologists never found the interest or the time to investigate such frivolous things as the economic foundations and the social structure of a great society.

What did the Chinese themselves do in this field? We have observed the findings of Mao. What has been the response of his countrymen to his appeal to study Chinese capitalism? And what has his own reaction been?

With regard to the last point, let us take as an example one of Mao's most astonishing slogans. In his report "On the Present Situation and Our Tasks," of December 25, 1947, he tried to define the particular form of capitalism found in China, and coined the monstrous term "comprador-feudal state-monopoly-bureacratic capitalism." Of course, this was a slogan; but it is also a more or less adequate description if we translate it into the terms of Mao's interpretation of reality. The first part of the label, "comprador-feudal," is simply an abusive way of referring to the Chinese commercial and industrial bourgeoisie of the treaty ports, who were in close contact with foreign powers, and to the large landowners. At the tail end of the term, "state-monopoly capitalism" merely means that in Kuomintang China the famous families of Chiang Kai-shek, T. V. Soong, and H. H. K'ung monopolized the economic life of the whole country. This section of the bourgeoisie Mao calls "bureaucratic."

I have analyzed this curious slogan not with any desire to throw ridicule on its author but in order to convey the immense difficulties scholarly research encounters when attempting to deal with a country dedicated to a great revolutionary task and in a state of upheaval. I could mention a number of shackles that hinder serious research on the genesis of capitalism in China.

In the first place, there is "feudalism" (in quotation marks). As is well known, Marx worked out a general evolutionary theory of human development, comprising four stages or rising steps: the communism of primitive tribal communities; the slavery of the ancient world; the feudalism of the Middle Ages; and the capitalism of modern times that will be supplanted in the end by socialism or full-fledged communism. Marx did not, however, remain content with this Hegelian and unilinear scheme; he wanted to enlarge it when he came to study Russian, Chinese, and particularly Indian society. He therefore tentatively added another stage, which he called "Asiatic society," and for the time being left it alongside the other stages, not yet having decided where it belonged in the progressive evolutionary series. This very significant point is not generally known, and in the catechism of vulgar Marxism is simply passed over.

The Chinese communists of the thirties did not, however, ignore it during their strenuous discussions about China's past, present, and future. Several of them tried to get hold of the original Marxian analysis in order to work out the specific form of evolution peculiar to China and thus foresee the lines on which it would probably develop. They were, however, soon silenced by the overwhelming events that were taking place on the political scene.

The great Chinese National Revolution of 1926–27, which was led by the Chinese bourgeoisie, presented the handful of Chinese communists and, even more, their Russian teachers with a terrible dilemma. Should they join forces with the Kuomintang, the Nationalist Party of the Chinese bourgeoisie, or, foreseeing the inevitable estrangement, should they preserve their full independence and freedom of movement?

At this very moment the Russian Communist Party was torn with internal disputes, and the Bolsheviks, already split on the question of China, were furiously and desperately taking sides. Trotsky and his followers declared that the Chinese communists must be unremitting in their fight against the Kuomintang, the proletarian revolution being the order of the day. Stalin and the majority decided to support the Kuomintang, holding that China's present stage was that of the bourgeois revolution. I cannot, of course—nor do I want to—recapitulate here the history of the last thirty years. For our purpose it will be sufficient to recall the days of April 1927, when Generalissimo Chiang Kai-shek slaughtered the flower of the Chinese communists. This in no way prevented the Stalinist fraction, which soon became omnipotent, from propping up their tactical blunder by theoretical reflections. According to the above-mentioned Marxist schema, the proletarian revolution could only occur subsequent to the rule of the bourgeoisie. It followed logically that if support had been given to the bourgeois Kuomintang, it was only because the inexorable calendar of History had indicated that this was the season of the revolution of the bourgeois or capitalist class, which in turn meant—and here, of all these twists and turns, is the crux of the matter—that China as it was then was not at the capitalist stage but at the feudal stage and, furthermore, that all foregoing periods cannot have been anything else but feudal.

You must excuse this quibble. It is essential to understand the mentality behind it—a mentality eager to establish not what actually happened in history but what ought to have happened—if the rest of the circumstances are to become comprehensible.

Now that the feudalism of China's past has been officially adopted as state doctrine, it is nearly impossible for Chinese historians to express any difference of opinion. It *is* possible, however, and happens time and again, for a historian to give a conscientious and accurate description of a period or a social stratum which have nothing feudal about them at all, but in order to get his paper published he is obliged, a priori or a posteriori, to paste the label "feudal" on them. It is not too difficult to do this, because the word, now devoid of special meaning, is used simply in the sense of "reactionary," and designates everything pertaining to landlordism, in the way that *hobereau* is used in French, or *Junker* in German, or, if I am right, "squirearchy" in English.

I don't need to expatiate on the baneful results of this attitude. Instead of yielding the careful analysis and recognition of differences demanded by historical research, it allows everything to get thrown together into the melting-pot. To give one example only: although it is an undeniable fact that there existed opposition, competition, and an implacable hatred between the scholar-officials and those docile instruments of absolutism the eunuchs, both are declared to be the representatives of feudalism.

The second difficulty is a direct outcome of the foregoing. The official Party doctrine being that China was a "semifeudal semicolonial" country *until* the communist take-over in 1949, or at least until the Opium War in 1842, it is almost impossible to present a different interpretation of China's recent past, or, if the attempt is made, it is only with a good deal of uneasiness and hesitation.

The third obstacle standing in the way of a study of capitalism is the dead weight of obligatory quotations from the bible. It is an inescapable duty to quote a few verses from the Old or the New Testament—I mean, Marx and Lenin, or Stalin and Mao. The quotations are used either to embellish one's own ideas or, more important, to hide them by paying lip service to the authorities. In either case, one is covered. This effort to play safe by buttressing even the most innocuous opinions by a quotation at present clogs much communist historical writing.

The last difficulty that I must mention, and that brings us to the proper subject of this paper, is a serious one. It is the paucity of relevant documents. Very few nonofficial documents have survived, and particularly few containing clues to the development of the despised trading class. But this may be because, since neither Chinese nor Western historians were formerly interested in such documents, nobody has searched for them. It is known that papers belonging to business firms, which would have provided invaluable source material, were sometimes used for wrapping parcels, and there are many other instances of waste and irreparable loss of similar materials. Nevertheless, a serious and systematic search for documents, such as is nowadays carried out for archaeological evidence, would be certain to bring in a rich crop of hitherto unknown sources. As it is, the existing sources would provide work enough to go on with if only scholars would decide to rescue them from the dust of libraries instead of embarking on yet another translation of the *Tao-te-ching* or an equally revelatory treatise on yoga.

Certain fallacies persist: for example, that there is no true bourgeoisie in China, ergo it never existed; or, since there is no place for it in the schematic model of development, it cannot exist. If we drop such preconceived ideas as these, along with the notion of the necessarily unilinear development of mankind, we can perhaps supply an answer to the question: why did Chinese society, highly civilized as it was, not give rise to capitalism; or if it did, why was it a form of capitalism different from ours? It must be understood, of course, that I am speaking of a pre-industrial society, which is only now carrying through a belated industrial revolution. In other words, I exclude from the start all those alien elements of industrial capitalism that were introduced into China during the past century, from the opening up of China in the 1850s until 1949.

There is, or should be, a consensus of opinion today about the structure of Chinese society before the Western impact, or at least about its main features. A huge agrarian country, the vast majority of its inhabitants were peasants. There was a comparatively small middle class of handicraftsmen and merchants. And finally, at the top of the structure was a thin layer of scholar-officials, the ruling class. These famous literati, often called gentry, small in number but of immense power, dominated Chinese society for more than 2,000 years. I don't like and don't recommend the term "gentry," because in this society more landed property was acquired through office than office was acquired through ownership of landed property. Of course, being a landowner gave one a better chance of obtaining the education necessary for office. But the position of the landed aristocracy was shaken by the introduction of a civil service and of the literary examination system from the eighth century A.D. onward.

Several factors inherent in Chinese society make its structure difficult to grasp. I refer, for instance, to the ambiguities—more than seven types—of the devices used by the ruling class to strengthen their position. For one thing, there is the immense monument it erected to its own glory—the *Official Histories*—concerned almost entirely with the doings of the scholar-officials. Theirs is a closed bureaucratic universe, and only occasionally do we meet on its margins intruders from the outside world: peasants, who appear merely as taxpayers or as villains, i.e. rebels; merchants, who also appear as taxpayers, or as instigators of corruption. As for craftsmen, they hardly appear at all. No representative of these classes takes on the character of a living person; they are mere accessories, not subjects in their own right but simply the objects of the bureaucrats' actions.

Another example is the ambiguity of the social hierarchy. A permanently vigilant demagogy, handled with a consummate skill worthy of modern political propaganda, would make us believe that the peasant was the crown of the universe and that everybody was anxious for his well-being. There was, we are to understand, no possible comparison between the nobility of agriculture—the "fundamental occupation" as it was called—and other occupations, all of which were secondary, especially that of the merchants, whose baseness the Confucians never ceased to trumpet. In actual fact, an understanding existed between the scholar-officials and the merchants that operated against the interests of the peasantry, and it was far easier for a merchant to climb the social ladder than it was for a farmer. In the Former Han period, there was a proverb that said:

> For the poor to seek riches
> Farming is not so satisfactory as crafts;

> Crafts are not as good as trading.
> To prick embroidery does not pay
> As much as leaning upon a market-door.[2]

Nevertheless, wealth was not in itself enough for the attainment of social prestige. The gentleman had wealth *and* education. It was, perhaps, easier for the wealthy to become educated, but it was quite impossible for the illiterate to obtain a post.

A passage from the eighteenth-century novel, the *Unofficial History of the Literati (Ju-lin wai-shih)*, illustrates another ambiguity, the dissonance between the officials' creed and their practices:

> While in office [the hero, Tu Shao-ch'ing] showed no respect for his superiors but simply tried to please the people, talking nonsense about "fostering filial piety and brotherly love, and encouraging agriculture." Such phrases are mere figures of speech to be used in compositions, yet he took them seriously, with the result that his superiors disliked him and removed him from his post![3]

The relations between the officials and the merchant class were stamped by the fact that the officials, in their capacity as the ruling class—endowed with learning that enabled them to supervise and coordinate the activities of an agrarian society, and thus to acquire their dominant position in the state—enjoyed an all-pervading power and prestige. In these relations, as seen from above, every means of keeping the merchant class down and holding it in subjection seemed permissible. Compromises, exceptions, favors, pardons—all were allowed so long as they were retracted at the earliest opportunity. Claims, titles, privileges, immunities, deeds, charters were never granted. Any sign of initiative in the other camp was usually strangled at birth, or if it had reached a stage when it could no longer be suppressed, the state laid hands on it, took it under control, and appropriated the resultant profits. As seen from below, there was, in these relations, no legal way of obtaining an immunity, a franchise, since the state and its representatives, the officials, were almighty. There remained only an indirect way of obtaining one's due: bribery.

The outstanding feature in these relations is the absence of pluck,

2. *Han-shu* 91.7a, trans. N. L. Swann, *Food and Money in Ancient China* (Princeton, 1950), p. 434.
3. Trans. Foreign Languages Press (Peking, 1957), *The Scholars*, p. 461.

the complete lack of a fighting spirit, on the part of the middle class. On the one hand, they felt impotent in the face of a competitor who seemed to hold all the advantages. On the other, they had no real desire to be different, to oppose their own way of life to that of the ruling class—and this inhibited them even more. Their ambition was limited: to find a position, if only a modest one, inside the ruling class, reflecting the social prestige attached to officialdom. Their consuming desire was that they, or their children, should become scholar-officials.

This is one of the secret springs accounting for China's particular course of development. The other is corruption. Corruption was, in fact, the main point of contact between the opposing classes. The merchants could not have operated their policy of bribery if it had not been for the practices of embezzlement and "squeeze" on the part of the officials. This kind of division of labor, while it may have been advantageous for a few individuals, not only was eventually to spell ruin for officialdom, but also was lethal so far as improvement of the status of the bourgeoisie is concerned. It prevented the middle classes from consolidating and extending momentary advantages, and prevented the bourgeoisie from achieving consciousness as a separate, autonomous body with its own interests.

Let me illustrate what has so far been said with a few examples chosen at random.

Private initiative was responsible for the invention of the first instruments of credit. In the eighth century A.D., under the T'ang dynasty, when commercial activities were expanding rapidly, merchants found that large-scale transfer of cash was cumbersome, laborious, and perilous. They invented "flying money," by means of which merchants, on depositing cash at certain specified offices, received a written receipt guaranteeing reimbursement in other provinces. In 811 the government prohibited the use of flying money by private citizens and adopted the system for its own credit transfers. Merchants were allowed to deposit cash at government finance offices in the capital against payments to be received in the provinces. A 10 per cent fee was charged on the drafts.

During roughly the same period, the Buddhists invented printing for the purpose of religious propaganda. The state took over this invention and used it for the contrary purpose of diffusing the Con-

fucian doctrine, and then proceeded to persecute the Buddhist church
—not, it is true, because of this, but for several other reasons.

The first protobanks to issue promissory notes, which soon became
a kind of paper currency, were founded by rich merchants in Szechwan, which was one of the trading centers during the eleventh century. To begin with, the government recognized sixteen of the larger
merchants, and granted them a monopoly in the issue of these "exchange media" (*chiao-tzu*), which brought in a fee of 3 per cent. But
a few years later, in A.D. 1023, a government monopoly replaced the
private monopoly.[4]

Another example is afforded by the practice of lending money. In
the Chinese economy, usury played perhaps an even greater role than
it did in Europe during the Middle Ages. The crucial point, however,
is that lending at exorbitant interest was not only not prohibited by
law, but actually practiced by the state. During early T'ang times, the
highest legally permitted rates of interest were 6 per cent per month
on private loans, and 7 per cent on government funds. During the
Sung dynasty, the corresponding ceiling rates were 4 and 5 per cent.[5]

In the Sung period merchants' guilds were obliged to supply government needs on demand. This obligation was the cause for many griev-
ances, because the price paid by the government was lower than the
market price, and the merchant whose turn it was to supply the goods
had himself to pay the transport costs. At the petition of the butchers'
guild in the capital, the government granted, in A.D. 1073, a kind of
"privilege", according to which members of the corporations were to
pay a monthly fee for exemption from this obligation and the government was to pay the market price for the goods. Twelve years later,
however, the state returned to the former system. One of the reasons
for this setback is quite typical. The guilds forced petty merchants to
join the corporation if they had not yet done so in order that they
would share the burden of paying the exemption fee.[6]

Yet another example, which is an excellent illustration of the different pattern of urban development in China and in the West, is

4. L. S. Yang, *Money and Credit in China* (Cambridge, Mass., 1952), pp. 51–53.
5. Yang, p. 95.
6. S. Katō, "On the Hang or the Associations of Merchants in China," *Memoirs of the Tōyō Bunkō, 8* (Tokyo, 1936), 62.

provided by the ownership of house property in the cities. In the big cities that grew up during Sung times, many houses were built for letting purposes. Most of the houses, shops, and building lots were government owned, and a special state agency was established for their administration, rent being collected on a daily basis from the poor people in the cities lest the arrears should be too great.[7]

It is not fortuitous that these examples I have chosen should all come from late T'ang or Sung times, for this was the period during which urban development went hand in hand with intense commercial activity. We are therefore compelled to look for the germs of capitalism as early as the latter half of the eighth century. But in doing so, we must never forget the essential difference between Chinese and Western towns—of which my last example is a case in point. The difference is this: while the Western town was the seed-bed and later the bulwark of the bourgeoisie, the Chinese town was primarily the seat of government, the residence of officials who were permanently hostile to the bourgeoisie, and thus always under the domination of the state.

Nor is it a matter of chance that the first great thrust of the Chinese bourgeoisie happened during a period—late T'ang and more especially Sung times—when national sovereignty was divided. It is my firm belief that whenever national sovereignty was divided, and the power of the state and the ruling scholar-officials was consequently weakened, the middle class flourished as a result. Other instances apart from the Sung period are provided by the lively, brilliant epoch of the Warring States in ancient times and, during the Middle Ages, the period of the Three Kingdoms and of the division of China between the northern barbarian and the southern national dynasties. But even in times which favored the merchants, the state and the state monopolies were a heavy drag on commercial activities.

This can be illustrated in greater detail by mining and the salt industry, which afford typical examples of how the workings of early capitalism in China were hampered by bureaucratic regulations. Both were outstandingly thriving enterprises, in which the largest fortunes were acquired. Yet both, together with the tea trade, foreign trade, and military supplies, were more or less equally prosperous whether they operated under state license, state control, or state monopoly.

Mining had always been under state control, particularly the copper

7. S. Katō, *Shina keizaishi kōshō* (Tokyo, 1953), 2, 239–46.

and silver mines, which provided metal for the mints, and the iron workings, which provided the raw material for tools and weapons. From Sung times onward, the use of coal became more and more widespread, replacing charcoal in foundries and for cooking. We have detailed descriptions of mines dating from around A.D. 1600, from which we learn that the galleries went to a depth of 100 feet, and that equipment included bamboo pipes for drainage, pumping fresh air into the tunnels, and evacuating the gases.

Since theoretically all the soil belonged to the state, state ownership of metal ores was an established principle. But this did not hinder private enterprise. At the beginning of the Ming dynasty (1368–1644), the state produced for its own needs. There was no market, and the mines were closed down if metal reserves were considered to be sufficient. The state-owned mines employed large numbers of miners and foundry workers who were exempt from corvée and military service but had to pay the ordinary tax. Usually they provided the tools and the fuel. The labor force was assessed not on an individual basis but per household, these households or families being regarded as tax units, corresponding to the peasant households. In the iron works of Tsunhua near Peking, founded by the famous Yung-lo Emperor (1403–24), at the beginning of the fifteenth century there were about 3,000 workers, including professional metal workers, artisans on duty, civil and military unskilled helpers, and convicts. The output of this particular iron works was about 500,000 catties (or pounds), and the production figure for all iron works combined was somewhere between 10 and 20 million catties (that is, between 6,000 and 12,000 tons). Miners and smelters worked only during the six winter months, when there was no agricultural work to be done. The workers received as wages one pint (about 0.028 bushels) of grain a day.

But during the late sixteenth century a great change took place. Taxes on mines ceased to be a previously fixed amount and became a percentage of actual output. This stimulated the growth of private enterprise and brought about the decline of state-owned mines. There were now prosperous entrepreneurs, and among the workmen there were foremen and specialized professional miners, both of whom were paid according to output, the foremen receiving in addition a refund for moneys spent on tools, fuel, and wages. The profit on production was shared out in the following proportions: state, 30 per cent; entrepreneurial expenses, 50 per cent; wages, 20 per cent. Despite the burden of tax and the occasional application of severe laws—for instance, that prohibiting the opening of mines—and other inhibiting factors such as seasonal production to fit the requirements of agriculture, there was a steady growth of private enterprise and of production for profit.

Before leaving the mining industry of the Ming period, I should like to quote a characteristic statement. During the last ten years of the sixteenth century (to be exact, from 1596 to 1605), there was the great scandal of the silver rush. For fiscal reasons, the state tried to open silver mines everywhere, and whenever a mine was found to be lacking in ore, the eunuchs, who were the driving force behind the whole project, attempted to make up for the deficit by harsh exactions. At last, when the scandal could be hushed up no longer, the repentant Wan-li Emperor declared: "It is no longer permitted to open private mines without authorization; the important thing is not to disturb the bowels of the earth." [8]

A word should be said about the development of copper mining in Yunnan during the eighteenth century. Opened under the Mongols, the copper mines of this southernmost province developed steadily under the Ming dynasty. Up until A.D. 1706 the state collected a tax of 20 per cent on the amount of copper produced, which in that particular year was 81,000 ounces—about twenty times the amount in 1685. After that a state monopoly was established. The government now not only collected a 20-per-cent tax in kind, but also had the right of pre-emption—of buying the rest of the output at a very low price. To deliver copper to anyone other than the authorities was regarded as smuggling and meant confiscation and fines. But the new regulation, so unfavorable to private enterprise, increased smuggling to such an extent that the government found it wiser to give in and permit the free sale of the copper that remained after duty was paid. Production figures went up immediately: in 1724, one million catties were produced; in 1726, two million; in 1727, over three million.

The prospect of higher profits stimulated the government to tighten its grip, and, with a better price as the only concession, a return was made to the former practice: tax and purchase of the remaining out-

8. *Shen-tsung shih-lu* 416. On mines during the Ming period, see Pai Shou-i, "Ming-tai k'uang-yeh ti fa-chan," in the symposium *Chung-kuo tzu-pen chu-i meng-ya wen-t'i t'ao-lun chi* (Peking, 1957), 2, 947–93.

put. At the end of the eighteenth century new concessions were made: purchase at higher prices and permission to sell ten per cent of the remaining output on the free market. Between 1740 and 1810 the output capacity of about fifty mines reached the figure of 6,000 to 9,000 tons (10 to 15 million catties), produced by 200,000 to 300,000 miners.

Now let me say a word about the organization of production. A yardmaster (or master of the mine) appointed by the government, with several clerks and policemen under him, supervised the running of the mine, the payment of tax, and the sale of copper. He was assisted by seven foremen, who were sometimes elected by their team and then officially recognized, but were more often appointed by the government. Each foreman was in charge of a particular sphere of activities, these being settlement of disputes, payment of wages and other disbursements (cashier), and responsibility for furnaces, food supply, galleries, pit props, and coal supply.

The mines were divided into great yards and little galleries, the latter often being sublet to other entrepreneurs, and exploited either by individuals or by partnership associations. Work continued night and day, several teams to each gallery. The teams included both miners and maintenance men, who saw to propping up the galleries, proper functioning of the ventilation system, and operation of the drainage pumps. There were in all from 100 to 200 men according to the size of the mine. The work of the smelters was even more complicated. For instance, it took six men to operate the great 12-foot-long bellows, each working a two-hour turn every twelve hours.

In administering the mines, the government used a combined system of wage advances and tax deduction. The monthly advance for wages was recovered the following month by a levy of a corresponding amount of copper deducted from the total output along with the amount deducted for payment of tax in kind. In return for the advances on wages, the producers had to pay:

(a) the tax, or excise duty, in kind (as already mentioned)

(b) a certain quantity of copper (the amount regulated by the government) in exchange for the right to sell freely the rest of the output, after deductions

(c) the so-called "copper restituted to the public," a contribution to outlay and expenses

(d) the "copper for fostering probity" (*yang-lien t'ung*), a grant given to managers to forestall attempts at extortions

Finally, they had to sell the rest of the output at government-fixed prices.

Once the government had received its share and had bought up the quantity of copper it required, it had no further interest in the production or the profit margin of the entrepreneurs. But till then supervision was arbitrary and tyrannical. In order to prevent smuggling, the furnaces were kept under strict control, and the copper was immediately checked, weighed, and taxed as it came out of the furnace. According to a contemporary account, the tax varied arbitrarily between 9 and 20 per cent. In addition, there were the exactions, the inevitable "squeeze," extorted by corrupt officials. The whole administration was more concerned with policing activities than with promoting production. The response on the workers' side was to organize in secret societies.

The contractors were rich merchants from the neighboring provinces of Kiangsu, Hupei, Szechwan, and Kuangtung. They provided the capital and hired the manager, the technicians (for dealing with props, ventilation, pumping, etc.), the foremen, and the workers. The latter were recruited from among the poor people of the same provinces, and they usually sought work in the mines when the harvest was over, but came swarming in crowds at any season as soon as word went round that a new and prosperous mine had been opened.

There were two forms of remuneration for the workers: monthly wages, not related to output and profits, and the share system, known as "rice and shares" (*mi-fen*), or "association of brothers" (*ch'in-shen ti-hsiung*). Under this partnership system the workers received their food and 30 per cent of the profit; 10 per cent of the profit went to the manager, the technicians, and the foremen; the share of the entrepreneur—the lion's share—was 60 per cent.[9]

I should like to lay special emphasis on this system, because a similar system was a feature of early Western capitalism, especially in the silver mines from the fourteenth century. Found mostly in German

9. On the mines of Yunnan, see Wang Ming-lun, "Ya-p'ien chan-cheng ch'ien Yün-nan t'ung-k'uang-yeh ti tzu-pen chu-i meng-ya," in the symposium cited in note 8 above, *2*, 673–84.

silver mines, it is known by the German name *Verlag*. Another point that deserves attention is that both partners in the entrepreneurial system of the Yunnan copper mines, entrepreneurs and wage workers alike, came from other provinces and so were in fact strangers. This was a noteworthy feature, involving among other things a certain lack of submissiveness.

The salt monopoly had always been a major source of revenue for the Chinese state. Taxes on consumer goods are attested as early as the sixth century B.C. From T'ang times on, the *gabelle* produced a large proportion of the state revenue. In order to enforce the monopoly against smugglers and make the salt industry a going concern, the government had recourse to merchants to distribute salt, as this was too cumbersome an undertaking for the state agencies to carry out, particularly with a growing increase in population.

Under the last dynasty, the salt tax amounted yearly to about five million taels. Originally half the amount of the salt tax—and after the middle of the eighteenth century 40 per cent of it—was collected in the largest and richest of the eleven salt administration areas of middle and southeast China, called Liang-Huai. Thanks to the existence of a large number of documents, it is possible to calculate that the Liang-Huai traders—those "unchallenged merchant princes of China"—distributed annually to 75 million people (a quarter of the total population in the eighteenth century) more than 600 million pounds of salt, with an average annual profit of about seven million taels. Let us see how this trade worked and what became of the money earned by the merchants.

The salt masters were originally small independent manufacturers who had a small but quick return and no risk; but during the eighteenth century they came more and more under the sway of the wholesale dealers. By 1800, only half of them remained owners of salterns, and even when they were the legal owners of their small manufacturing works, they were in fact wage earners under the control of the capitalists. The wholesale dealers at first only bought salt from the owner-manufacturers and sold it to the salt distributors, but later they became large-scale producers. As such, they ran a considerable risk because of the perishable nature of salt. Salt was stored for a year before being sold to the transport merchants. The factory merchants bought up the property of bankrupt salt masters, or shared profits with them as joint owners. These factory merchants owed their position to government recognition. Only thirty of them were recognized, and, in a jump from the "Verlag" system to full-fledged capitalism, they were able to keep tight control not only over the manufacturers, but also over the small-scale merchants, who were often their agents. The producers made an annual profit of about one-and-a-half to two million taels, of which they pocketed 60 per cent, leaving the remaining 40 per cent to be divided half-and-half between the depot merchants and the salt makers.

Profits were even higher on the distribution side of the trade. The transport merchants made about five million taels annually. Since Sung times a grain-salt exchange system had operated. The merchants transported grain to the frontier for military supplies, and received in exchange salt tickets, issued by the government, which authorized the receipt of government-monopoly salt in the interior. During late Ming times (sixteenth and seventeenth centuries), salt tickets could be bought for cash, and the frontier merchants became salt merchants of the interior. The established practice, typical of the whole organization, which remained in operation until the middle of the nineteenth century, was as follows. The inalienable right to sell salt was farmed out to rich merchants who could pay the gabelle in advance; the names of these licensed monopoly merchants were entered in an official register, called the shipment register (*kang-ts'e*), because the annual quota of salt distributed in the Liang-Huai area was divided into so many shipments.

The organization of these transport merchants, of whom there were only 230 in Liang-Huai, is a revelation for anyone interested in Chinese capitalism. There were, in fact, only thirty head merchants, half of them owners of the monopoly license, the other half only leaseholders. They were responsible for arrears in tax payment and for the conduct of the whole merchant body, that is, for the 200 retailers—"small" men compared with the head merchants, but mostly men of substantial means, usually required to trade under the name of one of the head merchants. They were milked by the head merchants by two main devices: the high rate of interest on loaned capital, and the practice of shifting the burden of "squeeze" to the entire group of transport merchants; meanwhile, the head merchants appropriated a large share of the "treasury fee" (*hsia*). The treasury fee was money for expenses incurred in entertaining officials and for contributions to local administration; it was paid out of the common treasury of the entire merchant body, but handled exclusively by a few merchant treasurers. This practice was of course encouraged by high officials in the salt administration, who shared the fat bonus with these few merchants. There was a powerful clique of four or five merchant chiefs selected by the salt administration, but this arrangement became a public scandal and had to be abolished in 1724. Even so, the hierarchy, with all its tensions of give and take, stands out clearly enough: high officials → local administration → merchant chiefs → head merchants → small merchants. And below them, of course, were the consumers—the peasants who bore the burden of the tax.

We come now at long last to the crucial question of accumulation. What did the salt merchants do with the enormous profits gained during the years of high prosperity, profits estimated at 250 million taels for the second half of the eighteenth century? Let us first answer another question: where did the merchants come from and how did they live?

Most of the Liang-Huai merchants were either emigrants from Shansi who had formerly been frontier merchants, or men from Hui-chou in Anhui province who became famous as the Hsin-an merchants, so called after the ancient name of their home town. By late Ming times both groups were notorious. For those who recall the connection established by Max Weber between the austere Puritan tradition of thrift and early capitalism, the following passage from a description of China about A.D. 1600 will have a familiar ring:

> The rich men of the empire in the regions south of the Yangtze are from Hsin-an [ancient name of Hui-chou], in the regions north of that river, from Shansi. The great merchants of Hui-chou have made fisheries and salt their occupation and have amassed fortunes amounting to one million taels of silver. Others with a fortune of two or three hundred thousand can only rank as middle merchants. The Shansi merchants are engaged in salt, silk, reselling of grain. Their wealth even exceeds that of the former. This is because the Hui-chou merchants are extravagant, but those of *Shansi are frugal*. In fact, *people of Hui-chou are also*

> *extremely miserly as to food and clothing,* . . . but with regard
> to concubines, prostitutes and lawsuits, they squander gold like
> dust.[10]

The descendants of these hard-working and frugal men, in the
second or third generation after the original fortune had been made,
acquired very different habits. They became status seekers, spending
fabulous sums in an endless quest for social prestige. Their response
to the ruling-class principle of "keeping tradesmen in their place" was
to compensate for lack of social prestige by ostentatious living. They
indulged in eccentricities and expensive hobbies, "dogs, horses, music,
and women"; they owned beautiful pleasure gardens; they became
bibliophiles, collectors, and art connoisseurs; they patronized and sub-
sidized scholars on a lavish scale and held veritable literary salons.
Dozens of famous literati—poets like Yüan Mei (1716–98), philosophers like Tai Chen (1724–77), historians like Ch'ien Ta-hsin (1728–
1804)—were their guests and protégés. And it is certainly a fact that,
even allowing for the not entirely voluntary contribution of 41 million
taels to the imperial treasury (for the emperor's personal expenses)
during the second half of the eighteenth century, their mode of life,
clan solidarity, and expenses for education diverted most of the accumulated capital to noneconomic uses.

Another impediment to the development of capitalism was the traditionally preferred investment in land. Although the rent from land
probably amounted to no more than 30 to 40 per cent of the return
from businesses such as pawnbroking, moneylending, and shopkeep-
ing, we find that the laws of the Peking club of the townsmen from
Hui-chou—the famous Hsin-an merchants—decreed that any unused
public funds of the club "should be invested only in the purchase of
real estate for receipt of rent, and should not be lent for interest, *in
order to avoid risks.*" "Small risk and high prestige were two major
factors which had made investment in land attractive." [11]

The history of the development of Chinese capitalism has an inter-

10. *Wu-tsa-tsu* 4.25b, trans. and quoted by Ho Ping-ti in his excellent article,
on which I have leaned heavily here, "The Salt Merchants of Yang-chou: A
Study of Commercial Capitalism in Eighteenth Century China," *Harvard Journal
of Asiatic Studies, 17* (1954), 130–68; see pp. 143–44. Cf. Saeki Tomi, *Shindai
ensei no kenkyū* (Kyoto, 1956).

11. Yang, *Money and Credit in China*, pp. 102–03.

mittent character and is full of leaps and bounds, regressions and relapses. I should like to give one last example to illustrate this discontinuity. With the decline of the salt trade, the capital of the salt merchants was transferred to the more profitable business of pawnbroking. The chain of pawnshops founded as a state institution at the beginning of the eighteenth century was taken over by them, and the capital invested was called public funds "entrusted to merchants to produce interest." [12]

The following points may serve as a summary of the arguments presented above.

First: I can give no exact date for the birth of capitalism in China. All I know is that the tendency will be to set this date further and further back, from the nineteenth to the eighteenth to the seventeenth century and so on, finally arriving at the Sung dynasty (tenth to thirteenth centuries), which in my opinion marks the beginning of modern times in China. Still, the discontinuity just mentioned distorts the steady, simple, ascending line so much favored by school textbooks.

Second: with regard to industrial capitalism, we must never forget that the purpose of machines is to economize labor or time. In China there was never any dearth of labor; on the contrary, China always had plenty of it. The superabundance of cheap labor certainly hampered the search for time-saving devices. Nevertheless, what was chiefly lacking in China for the further development of capitalism was not mechanical skill or scientific aptitude, nor a sufficient accumulation of wealth, but scope for individual enterprise. There was no individual freedom and no security for private enterprise, no legal foundation for rights other than those of the state, no alternative investment other than landed property, no guarantee against being penalized by arbitrary exactions from officials or against intervention by the state. But perhaps the supreme inhibiting factor was the overwhelming prestige of the state bureaucracy, which maimed from the start any attempt of the bourgeoisie to be different, to become aware of themselves as a class and fight for an autonomous position in society. Free enterprise, ready and proud to take risks, is therefore quite exceptional and abnormal in Chinese economic history.

12. Cf. Abe Takeo, "Pawnbroking in the Ch'ing Period," in *Haneda Tōyōshi ronsō* (Kyoto, 1950), pp. 1–36. The total number of pawnshops went up from 7,685 in 1685 to 23,139 in 1812.

Third: if capitalism is interpreted as meaning only competitive capitalism, or free enterprise (which has nearly disappeared in our world), then there never has been capitalism in China. But if state capitalism is admitted as forming an integral and important part of the phenomenon we call capitalism, then it appears to us in China as a hoary old man who has left to his sturdy and reckless great grandson a stock of highly valuable experiences.

And just because we live in the epoch of state capitalism, both in the old capitalist countries of the West and in the new "People's Democracies" of the East, the matter is one of great relevance to us today.

FAIRS

IN CHINA

It might be useful to preface this chapter with a few introductory remarks about the difficulties that are encountered when the comparative
study of institutions is carried into the Chinese field. These difficulties
are of two kinds. The first follows upon the fact that Western sinologists have demonstrated an almost total lack of interest in the social
and economic aspects of China; strangely enough, until quite recently
they have devoted their studies almost exclusively to the language, religion, philosophy, and literature of China. As for history, instead of
concentrating upon the rhythms and trends of China's internal development, they have directed their researches to peripheral matters,
and have been greatly occupied with the more picturesque and alluring
facets of external relations. Possibly the fact that they themselves were
foreigners explains why they have been so captivated by relations between the Chinese and the barbarians. From the Chinese viewpoint,
the need to adapt to modern times, with which the country was
abruptly faced over a century ago, so dominated China's intellectual
as well as material development that Chinese scholars were often
forced to abandon the study of their own country's affairs in order to
devote all their energies to assimilating the ideas, technology, and institutions of the new style of conqueror from the West. It is only during the last thirty years, and only after having undergone the discipline
of modern European ways of thought and methods of investigation,
that they have become conscious of facing the Herculean task of taking
stock of the history of an oriental society three or four thousand years
old.

This article originally appeared under the title "Les Foires en Chine," *Recueils
de la Société Jean Bodin*, 5 (1953), 77–88.

In undertaking this task, the Chinese have the advantage over their Western colleagues from the linguistic point of view, but both come up against the same obstacles. This brings us to the second kind of difficulty pertaining to the study of Chinese institutions, a much more serious one than the first because it arises from the very nature of the society that is the object of study. I refer to the distinctive feature of Chinese society that we have mentioned before—the existence of a class of scholar-officials. From the foundation of the empire toward the end of the third century B.C., this class remained the embodiment of the bureaucratic state; it not only dominated every aspect of social life, but left its imprint on the entire cultural heritage, and particularly on all historical writings. China's written history, one of the most voluminous produced by any nation in any language, is an official history. It was written by scholar-officials, who were experienced in all government and administrative matters, but who maintained a guarded, even hostile, attitude toward private institutions. Hence Chinese historical writings scarcely mention the ruled-over classes—the peasants, the artisans, and the merchants—except insofar as their relations with the state were concerned, and even then no more than the bare minimum deemed worthy of note by the literati in their capacity as officials of the fiscal administration. Trade was traditionally regarded as an occupation that went against the public interest, and the commercial profession was considered dishonorable, superfluous, and even positively harmful, because it was held responsible for immoral luxury, parasitism, and usury. Needless to say, a society as highly civilized as China's could not have done without trade and handicrafts, least of all the bureaucrats at the top, whose way of life entirely depended on them. Trade, and usury too, was often carried on with the connivance of officials, who strove not only to gain control over it but to snatch the profits as well; yet it was never mentioned except in terms of condemnation. Thus it is only indirectly—by what can be gleaned from moralistic writings, from discussions between officials and merchants on commercial competition, from administrative measures, or from the chance mention of the role of a trader in the career of an official personage—that we are able to obtain any information about commercial activities. Hardly any private documents exist, and there are no charters of any kind—an indication of how completely the commercial bourgeoisie and the artisans failed to wrest any privileges from the despotic state, or to gain that autonomy that was so decisive a factor in the very different course of development in the West.

Nevertheless, fragmentary though our knowledge of Chinese institutions is, we cannot for this reason neglect the study of their development. On the contrary, we must compensate for the lack of documents by making the fullest possible use of those that are available.

Did fairs exist in China? It is not easy to answer this question. The language has no special term to distinguish fairs from markets.[1] The commentary of one of the most ancient of the classical books, the *Book of Changes* (*I-ching*)—ascribed to Confucius—attributes the establishment of fairs to Shen Nung, the "Divine Farmer," who was one of the legendary emperors. "He caused markets to be held at midday, thus bringing together all the people, and assembling in one place all their wares. They made their exchanges, and retired, every one having got what he wanted." [2] My only reason for quoting this vague statement is that it is the sole reference cited by a modern Chinese dictionary to indicate the existence in ancient times of "temporary markets at fixed times and places." For reasons I shall come back to presently, it seems to me probable that it was during the Middle Ages— that is to say, during a period when the empire was divided and China was ruled by dynasties of varied racial origins—that we shall find institutions bearing the nearest resemblance to the medieval fairs of the

1. The main terms are *shih* "market," *chi* "gathering," *ch'iu* (originally "mound") "market," "fair," *hui* "meeting," and their combinations (*shih-chi, chi-shih*, etc.). The term that seems to correspond best with our word "fair" is *hui*, particularly in the compound *miao-hui*, used of "meetings" or "gatherings" held in front of temples on fixed dates—usually a festival—once or twice a year. Another term for annual markets was *nien-shih*, which is translated word for word by the German *Jahrmärkte*, used in the same way. Under the Ch'ing dynasty, 1644–1911, they were called *hui-ch'ang* or *lang-hui*, an example being the "market for new silk" at Nan-hsün-chen (borders of Chekiang and Kiangsu provinces). The institution of temple fairs goes back to T'ang times (about the middle of the ninth century). See T'ao Hsi-sheng and Chü Ch'ing-yüan, *T'ang-tai ching-chi shih* (Shanghai, 1936), pp. 89 ff.; Katō Shigeshi, "Tō-Sō jidai no ichi" (an article in Japanese on T'ang and Sung markets which appeared in the *Mélanges Fukuda* (Tokyo, 1933), reprinted in the posthumous collection of his works, *Studies in Chinese Economic History* (Tokyo, 1952), *1*, 347–79, particularly pp. 369–74. Cf. Sogabe Shizuo, "On the Market-Towns in Ancient China" (in Japanese), *Tōhō gaku, 3* (1952), 40–43.

2. *I-ching*, Hsi-tz'u II, 2, 4, trans. James Legge, *Texts of Confucianism*, Part 2 (Oxford, 1882), p. 383.

West. The "Economic Treatise" of the official history of the Sui, which
is the best source of information about the institutions of the Middle
Ages, gives the following picture of trade under the Eastern Chin
(317–419):

> For every purchase of slaves, of horses or oxen, of fields or houses,
> there was a written contract; a due of 400 cash was paid on every
> 10,000 cash, 300 on the part of the buyer and 100 on the part of
> the seller, and this due went to the Treasury. When there was no
> contract [that is, in transactions of lesser value] there was still a
> payment of 4 per cent. . . . Thus there were people who com-
> peted with each other in carrying on trade and who did no agri-
> cultural work; this is why they had to contribute an equivalent
> amount of tax, the intention being that they should be given a
> severe warning. That may have been the pretext, but a considerable
> profit was made from these transactions. Furthermore, at each of
> the fords to the west and east of the capital [Nanking], a Master
> of the Ford was established, together with a police station and
> five sailors, in order to control contraband goods and smugglers.
> Goods such as reeds, charcoal, fish, and firewood, on passing
> through the ford had to have a due of 10 per cent paid on them,
> which went to the Treasury. . . . To the north of the river Huai
> there were more than 100 big markets and more than 10 small
> ones; in all the big markets, officials were posted and the taxes
> were heavy. At that time, people suffered severely under them.[3]

This information is obviously too inadequate to allow us to decide
whether these "big markets" were fairs, or whether, on the contrary,
they had a purely local character. Fortunately we can supplement the
official source by a private document, written in 547. This is a description of the Buddhist monasteries of Loyang, the capital of the barbarian dynasty known as the Northern Wei (386–534), which gives us
more exact details.[4] The Great Market of Loyang, eight leagues in
circumference, was on the outskirts of the capital, and round it were
grouped, in a species of closed communes called *li* (literally, hamlets,
villages), quarters containing merchants and artisans. Within the market each guild or trade had its own quarters, its street being lined with

3. *Sui-shu* 24.9a (compiled around A.D. 629–644.
4. *Lo-yang ch'ieh-lan chi* (*Ssu-pu ts'ung-k'an* edition) 4.8a–10b.

the warehouses, shops, and booths of one corporation. The two quarters to the east of the market, known as "Commercial Relations" and "Circulation of Goods," were where the big traders were housed. The quarters to the south held the places of amusement and the taverns, inns, and brothels. The west side was the domain of alcoholic beverages, where the distillers' cellars and the shops for selling spirits were situated. The poetic names "Maternal Love and Filial Piety" and "Final Resignation" concealed the rather more prosaic occupations of the quarters where the coffin makers and undertakers were established. Finally, the two wealthy quarters called "The Gold Shops" and "Weighing of Values" were probably where the goldsmiths, jewelers, and moneychangers were grouped. So far, this is clearly nothing more than a regular market for supplying the capital and its surroundings. But if we continue our perusal of the document (which describes, and naïvely deplores, the accumulation of wealth in these quarters, the intense activity there, the display of luxury goods by the big traders, their magnificent houses, etc.), we come to a passage that seems to refer to real fairs. In another part of the city, on either side of the Imperial Way—hence *extra muros*—stood the four "Mansions of the Barbarians," embassies of a sort, with their four corresponding villages, called *li* (*vicus*), which I mentioned earlier, where the nationals of each country lived. These *li*, reminiscent of the *Vicus Allemanorum* at Provins or the *Vicus Angliae* at Lagny, bore names of a somewhat symbolic nature, such as "The Return to Legitimate Power" or "The Return to Virtue," which imply that, though the T'o-pa Wei may have regarded their neighbors as barbarians, the inhabitants themselves were in fact either people from the south or envoys of border tribes, all of whom regarded themselves as Chinese. The author of the document holds that at least 10,000 families inhabited these quarters; he states that "innumerable" foreigners, barbarian merchants, and visitors from all countries came to live in China, and that a special market was at their disposal, to the south of the river Lo, called "Market of the Currents of the Four Cardinal Points"—in other words, an international market or fair. This market of foreign merchants, who were no doubt grouped by nationality, was apparently in no way inferior to the Great Market.

According to another unofficial source, some six centuries later the Buddhist temple Hsiang-kuo-ssu, situated within the walls of Kaifeng, the Sung capital, opened its gates five times a month to merchants who

were grouped according to trades within its vast arcades. This covered
market was called "The Exchange of Ten Thousand Families."[5]

When the empire was reunified under the great T'ang dynasty (618–
906), the characteristic feature of the economy was the control exercised by the state. The greatest problem was how to provision the
court, the capital with its many officials, and the surrounding countryside, which lacked the requisite supplies. This problem was solved by
means of a carefully worked out bureaucratic organization based on
a mixed economy in which the private sector was always to some extent under state control, or at least in which the production of iron
and the sale of salt were state monopolies. The staple goods—cereals
and cloth—reached the capital through a complicated network of stages
of transfer, the key to which was held by the public authorities, since
river transport, canals, and granaries were state enterprises. Every prefecture and subprefecture with a population of over 3,000 families
(about 15,000 persons) had the right to establish a regular market
supervised by a market manager. In large towns such as Ch'ang-an
and Loyang, where there were several markets, each manager had an
assistant, a secretary, and several scribes and supervisors. Every shop
had to have a sign. The markets were made up of numerous quarters
each of which contained the shops and warehouses of merchants in
the same trade or the booths of artisans engaged in the same craft.
These quarters had formerly been called "stalls," "rows," or "lines,"
but since the seventh century had come to be known under the name
of "streets" (*hang*), and contained the germ of the guild organization.
Trade was so prosperous that the authorities were gradually obliged to
tolerate the independent quarters established by merchants beyond the
bounds of the market. The merchants in these quarters continued to
be members of the same trade organizations they had belonged to
before moving, and by the beginning of the eighth century the expression *hang* had begun to acquire its later meaning of guild or corporation. To judge by the role played by these corporations, their rise
seems to have been favored both by the state and by trade. While the
merchants believed they could safeguard their professional interests
better by organizing themselves in corporations, the public authorities
for their part found that this helped them to get their demands more

easily accepted, so that through the instrumentality of those occupying positions of responsibility they were able to maintain control over the entire corporation, and thus to gain command, through the corporations, over the whole body of merchants. There was close cooperation between the public authorities and the big wholesalers who, under a licensing system, were granted the right to operate one or another of the state monopolies. This explains the preponderance of such wholesalers within the guild organization. Some of the guilds thus came to acquire special privileges, and there was a certain monopolistic flavor about the corporations as a whole. The commercial tax of 3.3 per cent was comparatively light, but trade suffered under the much heavier burden of all kinds of irregular taxes and special duties, forced loans, the tax on capital, the turnover tax, right-of-way dues, and exactions of every variety. The burden became unbearable at those times when the Treasury was hard put to it to find funds for military expenditure, and sought desperately for new sources to tap. The "contributions on behalf of the army" were often the equivalent of a requisition, or consisted purely and simply in confiscation of a fifth or even a quarter of the merchants' capital. In addition to these extraordinary but to some degree legal contributions demanded by the state, there were the innumerable exactions, commissions, and gratuities which were perpetually extracted by officials and by state employees of lower rank, and which were by definition uncontrollable and entirely arbitrary.

All the accounts of T'ang economic life concern an age that saw the rise of internal and external trade, yet none of them contains a word about fairs.[6] This may be explained simply by the scarcity of information. I think however that the real reason lies elsewhere. Is it likely that a centralized state, served by a vast bureaucratic organization controlling almost every movement of people and things, would regard with favor—or even tolerate at all—a periodic assembly of merchants and of merchandise, when it had any number of coercive means at its disposal for subjecting both to its own interests? Is the state not bound to have been distrustful of, if not hostile toward, the least sign of

6. Cf. R. Des Rotours, *Traité des fonctionnaires* (Leiden, 1947–48), pp. 434–40 and 717; S. Katō, "On the Hang or the Associations of Merchants in China" (in English), *Memoirs of the Tōyō Bunkō, 8* (Tokyo, 1936), 45–83; E. Balazs, "Beiträge zur Wirtschaftsgeschichte der T'ang-Zeit," *Mitteilungen des Seminars für Orientalische Sprachen, 34–36* (1931–33), and "Les Institutions de la Chine jusqu'en 1400," *Histoire générale Glotz, 10,* Part II (in press).

independence or free enterprise?[7] We are much more likely to find that fairs took place during those periods when several states were disputing for dominance over China, whether in the time of the Warring States (fifth to third centuries b.c.) or during the Middle Ages (third to sixth centuries a.d.) or in Sung times (960–1279), when North China was conquered by the successive barbarian dynasties of the Ch'i-tan (the Liao dynasty, 907–1125), the Ju-chen (the Chin dynasty, 1115–1234), and the Mongols (the Yüan dynasty, 1280–1367). Even so, in Sung times the institution of the "mutual market" held on the frontier between the rival empires, which cannot have been anything but a kind of fair, suffered from the restrictions inherent in the state monopoly of external trade.

The horse fairs provide sufficient indication of how such restrictions operated. Since China was poor in stock farming, horses required for the army had to be bought outside the country, the usual suppliers being the nomad herdsmen of the northwest borderlands, Tibetans, Tanguts, and Uighurs. The horse trade had its center in the southeast of what is now the province of Kansu. The usual method adopted by the state was the purchase of "contract horses," which were sent in convoys, provisioned at the state's expense, from the frontier to the capital, Kaifeng, where special officials then dispatched the horses to the various provincial armies. The arrangement was that the state paid the barbarians 1,000 cash in advance for each horse, the remaining payment being made after it reached the capital. Another method consisted in the direct and outright purchase of horses of either Chinese or barbarian provenance at places specially assigned along the frontier.

7. Characteristic in this respect are the severe restrictions on dealings with the Northern barbarians at the "mutual markets" contained in a T'ang decree; see N. Niida, *Tō-ryō shū-i* (Tokyo, 1933), p. 715; cf. T'ao and Chü, *T'ang-tai ching-chi shih*, p. 93, and Katō, "Tō-Sō jidai no ichi," p. 356. In Szechwan, one of the most advanced and most autonomous provinces of China, several annual fairs were held from T'ang times onward, for medicaments (herbs), and for "silkworms"—i.e. a spring agricultural fair. But these fairs, which grew up in connection with festivals held at Buddhist and Taoist temples, were soon viewed with suspicion by the government authorities. Katō ("Tō-Sō jidai no ichi," p. 373) reports that in 1010 an official wanted to prohibit the fair for medicaments. Under the Sung, a tax was levied on one of the Szechwan fairs by the local authorities; another, held at the sacred mountain, the Heng-shan in Honan, which in the official mind had become too large in scale, was provided with a police station; see the travel diaries of Fan Ch'eng-ta (1126–93), his *Wu-ch'uan-lu* (1177), and his *Ts'an-luan-lu* (1172).

The horses were then either dispatched in convoy to the capital or sent direct to the armies. The state had pre-emptive rights: it was forbidden for private individuals to buy Tibetan horses before the government authorities had made their choice. However, the private sector could not allow such profitable business to escape, and the traders in the neighboring province of Szechuan did brisk business in horse-dealing.[8]

Foreign trade—a field in which it was essential for the state to intervene, since the trade in arms and the flight of cash closely affected national defense—was another highly profitable source of revenue. Overseas trade under the Sung, continuously increasing in both volume and extent, reached from Japan through South Asia (Indochina, Malaysia, India) to the Near East and Africa. The ships of the Arab merchants, formerly the most numerous and the most active, had met with formidable competition from the Chinese junks, and were soon outdone by them. The goods exported and imported remained the same as under the T'ang: from the Chinese end, textiles, porcelain, tea, cash, precious metals, lead, tin; from the foreign end, incense, perfumes, spices, pearls, ivory, coral, amber, shells, agates, crystal, and others. The most conspicuous signs of trade expansion were the four commissariats set up at Chüanchow in Fukien, Ningpo, and Hangchow in Chekiang, and Kiaochow in what is now Shantung, in addition to the earlier "commissariat for the merchant navy" at Canton, established under the T'ang. The commissioners were at once customs inspectors, godown managers, police inspectors for aliens, and, above all else (in theory at least), executives of state control over maritime trade. In practice, their various roles made them extremely powerful people, and it no doubt depended on their character and upbringing, and on the watchfulness of the central government, whether they jealously guarded the rather nebulous state monopoly of maritime trade, or were more inclined to favor private interests and, first of all, their own interests. The Chinese official had better grounds than Louis XIV for saying, "l'Etat c'est moi," and the elasticity of the regulations allowed plenty of play to his cunning. The commissioners had public funds at their disposal for the purchase of foreign goods, the capital being provided by the "Trade Monopoly Court" that had been established at Kaifeng in 976. It was at Kaifeng that the goods bought by

8. *Sung-shih* (Official History of the Sung) 198.2b–4a.

the commissioners were assembled for sale to the public at a high price. The state reserved for itself the right of pre-emption, and deducted in advance a portion of the goods in kind as a form of customs duty. What remained could not enter into free circulation until customs duty proper and monopoly tax had been paid. It would appear that these various deductions amounted to between 10 and 40 per cent. Foreign or Chinese merchants could then freely dispose of the remaining goods, if they were in possession of the due form of certificate issued by the commissioners of the maritime trade ports.[9]

It goes without saying that in the military areas in the north and northwest, which were under constant threat of attack, trade was much more rigorously controlled than on the seacoast, where there was no fear of invasion. The frontier was sometimes open and sometimes closed, depending upon the relations obtaining at the time between the Sung and their powerful neighbors. From 1067 onward all foreign trade was in the hands of the Triple Commissariat (which combined the services of the Ministry for Home Affairs, the Treasury, and the office of the Commissioner for the Salt and Iron Monopoly). That the state never succeeded in sealing off the frontier completely is proved by the many decrees renewing prohibitions against private trade. Nevertheless the regulations undoubtedly served to prevent the free expansion of trade.

My contribution to the study of fairs is regrettably very meager. When research has been done on the local gazetteers, of which there is a very large number (over 5,000 in the Library of Congress in Washington),[10] there should be much more material than is at present available on the subject of fairs. Meanwhile, if it is permissible to draw conclusions from the material so far examined, I suggest the following explanation for the apparent absence of fairs in China, or for the embryonic or even abortive nature of the nearest approach to fairs. It was in the medieval cities of Northern Italy that fairs blossomed into life, and these cities enjoyed the autonomy of the city-state. Such autonomy is a direct antithesis of the bureaucratic regime of centralized autoc-

9. On foreign trade, see *Sung-shih* 186.8a–11a, and J. Kuwabara, "On P'u Shou-keng" etc., *Memoirs of the Tōyō Bunkō*, 2 (1928), 1–79, and 7 (1935), 1–104.

10. It is on the basis of 225 local monographs that Katō Shigeshi established the number, frequency, and character of local markets under the Manchu dynasty in his article "The Periodical Market of Villages under the Ch'ing Dynasty" (in Japanese) in *Tōyō Gakuhō, 23* (1936), 153–204.

racies in Oriental societies. If the connection between fairs and autonomous cities is valid, then *ex hypothesi* the institution of fairs could clearly never have developed in China on the same scale as in medieval Europe. By way of verifying this hypothesis, it might be useful to examine the role of fairs in the Byzantine Empire and in ancient Egypt, where social organization was nearest to that of China.

CHINESE

TOWNS

To speak of towns is to speak of the bourgeoisie—such was the underlying assumption of those studies of urban development undertaken from the nineteenth century onward, in which a clear distinction was made between town and country because of differences in mode of life, social structure, and means of subsistence. It was the presence of a specifically urban class, which may loosely be termed the bourgeoisie, that was taken as the defining characteristic of the town, whether the town in question was the *polis* of classical antiquity, the medieval city with its artisans and merchants, or the modern industrial town. The interest in problems concerning the nature, origin, and development of towns was in itself largely due to historical developments resulting from the rise of the bourgeoisie.

But in China there were towns that had no urban class comparable to the Western bourgeoisie. Merely to make this statement at once reveals the kind of interest that comparative study of Chinese towns may have to offer. It also explains why, although a whole library of books has been written about all the varied aspects of Western towns, there is almost no literature on Chinese towns.

In this essay, I shall limit myself to discussing the kind of town described by the above statement, and shall leave out of consideration the modern Chinese town with its municipal institutions, administration, and other features that have been either directly imported from the West or modeled strictly on the Western pattern. However in-

This article originally appeared under the title "Les Villes Chinoises. Histoire des Institutions Administratives et Judiciaires," *Recueils de la Société Jean Bodin,* 6 (1954), 225–39.

structive it might be to do so, I will refrain from discussing the question how Western-style urban centers having more than one ethnic group lose their specifically Western character to a remarkable degree when merely forming small enclaves within the general framework of an oriental society.

In ancient China, the peasants had to stay in their hamlets, while the feudal lords and their followers lived within the shelter of city ramparts (*ch'eng*). The difference between the manorial cities (*i*) and cities that were the capitals of principalities (*tu*) cannot have been very great. "The seignorial residence, built upon a height and flanked by towers, looked like a fortified village, with suburbs where markets were held clustering around its base." [1] The only thing that distinguished the capital cities from these towns was the ancestral temple of the resident prince. [2] The square, walled towns that were built during the feudal period in defense against waves of barbarian invasions were sparsely inhabited.

> These cities of refuge were of a combined *agricultural* and *military* nature, being *permanent camps* built to house the warriors and, when necessary, to shelter the entire population of agricultural workers. They were surrounded by a double rampart, but the cultivated fields extended into the town, which had to be self-sufficient in times of siege . . . Just as there were merchants' quarters clustered round the walls of the seignorial citadel, so suburbs for merchants and artisans developed at the points where the roads emerged through the gates of the square towns of the plains. Thus the *agricultural-cum-military towns* were also market centers. [3]

Mencius (second half of the fourth century B.C.) speaks of a medium-sized town the interior ramparts of which were three *li* in circumference and the exterior ramparts seven *li* in circumference, that is to say, about 4,900 and 11,400 feet respectively. [4] Yet the Eastern Chou capital, to the north of the river Lo, which was in theory the most

1. Marcel Granet, *La Civilization Chinoise* (Paris, 1929), p. 284.
2. *Tso-chuan*, Duke Chuang, year 28.
3. Granet, *La Civilization Chinoise*, p. 286 (my italics).
4. *Meng-tzu* II B, 1.

important city of the empire and bore the revealing name Lo-*i* ("the *citadel* of the Lo"), was only 172,000 feet square, that is, less than 13,000 feet in circumference. The conclusion drawn by Henri Maspero, the historian who knew most about ancient China, was that "toward the end of the Chou dynasty, the number of towns with double ramparts seems to have increased, but they remained very small in size." [5]

All the Chinese terms for "town" that I have mentioned [6] go back to the feudal period, and it seems to me not without interest that they contain the same basic ideas as come to mind when we think of the rise of the town under Western feudalism, or rather, when we recall the main arguments used in the elaboration of theories on the origin of towns (walls, fortifications, markets).

More significant, however, is the rural origin of the town wards dating from the early days of the empire—probably the first towns really to merit the name. In the Han period (206 B.C.–A.D. 220), the wards of the capital Ch'ang-an—there are said to have been 160 of them—were called *li* and written with the same Chinese character that today designates both the Chinese league (equivalent of about 1,650 feet) and a village or hamlet. We shall see presently what purpose lay behind the division of the towns into wards; for the moment, it is enough to draw attention to the undoubtedly rural or agricultural character of these "streets" or urban "districts," which explains why they were called *li*.

Throughout the Middle Ages towns were laid out as follows. They were surrounded by a moat and a rampart, the length of which varied between 4,900 and 20,000 feet, and they were squared off into wards which, instead of being called *li*, were now more usually called *fang*. These rectangular wards were surrounded by walls, and the only means of communication between them was through gates giving on to the main streets. Within the wards there were alleyways. The important feature of these towns was that the wards were closed off at night, and a report made by the police inspectors of Ch'ang-an in the year 831 tells us that it was forbidden, except for officials above the

5. Henri Maspero, *La Chine antique* (Paris, 1927), p. 25; cf. p. 148.
6. These are: *ch'eng,* rampart, wall, town; *tu,* capital (the character contains the radical meaning "walled town"); *i,* walled city, fortified citadel, seignorial town, and, under the Han, the administrative center of a subprefecture. Cf. Swann, *Food and Money in Ancient China,* p. 125. To these should be added *shih,* market.

third grade (there were nine grades), to have a gate giving directly on to the street.[7] Having been kept closed all night, the ward gates were opened at dawn, at a signal which, until 636, was given by the shouts of the military patrol echoing from street to street, and later by drums placed in the street. In the treatise on officials in the *New History of T'ang* the paragraph on the police of the capital gives the following account:

> At sunset, the drums were beaten eight hundred times and the gates were closed. From the second night watch, mounted soldiers employed by the officers in charge of policing the streets made the rounds and shouted out the watches, while the military patrols made their rounds in silence. At the fifth watch, the drums within the Palace were beaten, and then the drums in all the streets were beaten so as to let the noise be heard everywhere; then all the gates of the wards and markets were opened.[8]

The old dictionaries say that the rectangular wards were called *fang* because their walls, like dikes, protected (*fang,* a homonym) the people enclosed within them. But the police report quoted above reveals the true sociological etymology of the word when it speaks of maintaining public order, and of how easily criminals would escape if everyone could open or shut his own house door as he wished before the official drum had sounded. This preamble makes quite clear what most preoccupied the officials who governed the towns, and their main preoccupation becomes even clearer when we come to consider the center of the town. That was where the seat of the authorities lay, separated from the rest of the town, in the two capitals and the big prefectural towns, by a second wall. In the capitals, the forbidden city enclosed the imperial palaces, the important buildings, the ministries, and all the various offices. Gates linked this strictly guarded inner city with the outer city where the townspeople dwelt. The T'ang Code, which provides the fullest documentation of medieval legislation, still lists a punishment of 70 blows of the rod for any ordinary mortal—that is, any civilian inhabitant of the town—who was found guilty of trespassing on the ramparts, the enclosures surrounding office buildings, or even the walls of wards and markets.[9] The markets were near

7. *T'ang hui-yao* 71 (Collection of Important Documents of T'ang, A.D. 961).
8. R. Des Rotours, *Traité des fonctionnaires,* pp. 536–37.
9. *T'ang-lü shu-i* 8, Article 6.

the inner city, occupying an area equivalent to two wards. The shops and stalls either were placed against the walls surrounding the inner city, or formed streets where the members of each corporation, trade, or guild were grouped together. The activities of the merchants were closely supervised, and all transactions, prices, and equipment strictly regulated.

Summary though this description of the Chinese town may be, perhaps it gives sufficient indication why there was a drift from the towns to the villages during medieval times, in direct contrast to the growth of towns during the Middle Ages in the West. In China, the town was dominated by officials who represented the imperial government, particularly insofar as judicial and fiscal matters were concerned, and since (unlike our towns) it did not embody the idea of emancipation and of liberty, neither did it act as a magnet to the people of the countryside. On the contrary, all those who rebelled against the oppressive powers of the official hierarchy took refuge in the villages so as to escape from the clutches of bureaucracy.[10] The villages had always enjoyed some degree of autonomy, with a council consisting of representatives chosen from among the village notables, usually by free election, and they retained enough of this primitive form of self-government to compare favorably with the towns. Moreover, they were far enough away from the seat of authority to be protected from the arbitrary exactions of officials in the imperial administration. This is a line of inquiry that is only just beginning to be pursued in the few attempts so far made to study Chinese towns, but it was brilliantly anticipated by Max Weber in his famous essays on the sociology of religions. It was he who invented the striking formula: "town" equals the seat of the mandarins and no self-government; "village" equals self-government and no mandarins.[11]

Growing commercial activities and the expansion of continental and maritime trade under the T'ang (618–906) brought about an increase in the urban population, and it was clearly going to be difficult for the government—despite its autocratic and bureaucratic powers—to

10. See Miyakawa Hisayuki, "Villages in the Period of the Six Dynasties" (in Japanese), *Asiatic Studies in Honor of Tōru Haneda* (Kyoto, 1950), pp. 875–913.

11. Max Weber, "Die Wirtschaftsethik der Weltreligionen. I. Konfuzianismus und Taoismus," *Gesammelte Aufsätze zur Religionssoziologie* (Tübingen, 1922), *I*, 381: " 'Stadt' gleich Mandarinensitz ohne Selbstverwaltung—'Dorf' gleich Ortschaft mit Selbstverwaltung ohne Mandarinen."

maintain the artificial system of dividing up the townspeople into rectangular wards, and to continue regulating every detail in the life of a large community. From the second half of the eighth century the rigid rules governing the layout of towns broke down, and the custom of shutting off the wards was abandoned. From the novels of T'ang times it can be seen that the ward system itself was by then already in decline, and it had altogether ceased to exist by the second half of the eleventh century, toward the end of Northern Sung (960–1126). The surviving local gazetteers of this period provide us with evidence that in many towns the inhabitants had overflowed the cramped confines of the walled checkerboard, and had established themselves *extra muros* in suburbs known as "wings" (*hsiang*). A concomitant phenomenon was the disappearance of permanent enclosed markets; instead, shops, warehouses, and booths had been set up, first in the districts near the market, and later dispersed throughout the town. The existence of a nocturnal market in the capital from the eighth century on provides subsidiary proof that the wards, even if they had not yet entirely disappeared, were at any rate no longer under strict rules of nocturnal closing.[12]

Lively descriptions survive of the two largest towns of the Sung period. It is both interesting and revealing to note that it is precisely works such as these that, in contradistinction to the main and extremely voluminous body of Sung literature, were written not by scholar-officials but by private individuals with no official function who remained unknown or anonymous. This is not fortuitous. The professional honor of a scholar or an official—in short, of a gentleman—would never have permitted him to take an interest in such frivolities, and the authors could only have come from bourgeois, plebeian, nonofficial circles. Their social origin is in fact clearly revealed by the obvious affection and even pride with which they describe every detail of the streets, shops, traveling shows, pleasure grounds, inns, and taverns.

When we read the description of the splendors of Kaifeng (the Northern Sung capital) in the early twelfth century, and of Hangchow

12. See Katō Shigeshi, "On the Development and Prosperity of Cities and City Life during the Sung Period" (in Japanese), reprinted from *Mélanges Kuwabara* (Kyoto, 1931) in his *Studies in Chinese Economic History, 1,* 299–346. It is, as far as I know, the only serious study of the Chinese town that has so far appeared.

(the capital of Southern Sung) in the middle of the thirteenth,[13] we realize that these must undoubtedly have been very large towns indeed. As both were imperial cities, their inner ramparts enclosed the court with all its palaces as well as the many ministries, offices, storehouses, granaries, arsenals, and other public and private buildings connected with the government and the central administration. Although in theory all government officials had their needs supplied by the grain and cloth that flowed into the capital as tax payments in kind, those who received high and medium salaries must among them have had enough money left over to support large numbers of merchants, artisans, and laborers. The outer city and the suburbs housed the warehouses and workshops of the guilds and corporations of grain merchants, butchers, fishmongers, tailors, hatters, candlemakers, goldsmiths, saddlers, hardware merchants, barbers, and so on. They also contained inns with several stories, taverns, teahouses, and pleasure grounds (*watzu*), all of which were full of people practicing low-class professions —actors, singers, prostitutes, fortune-tellers, professional storytellers, jugglers, and the like.[14] A world of upstarts such as these had no business in a society supposedly organized according to the Confucian hierarchical pattern. Yet there it was, as large as life; and it was this new urban stratum that gave birth to the novel and the drama. The sociologist will realize immediately that here is the beginning of something quite new: the rise of a new social class in the interstices of the traditional social structure.

It is rather difficult to arrive at any very exact idea of the size of such towns as these, since writers were never able to envisage them

13. *Tung-ching meng-hua lu* (Memories of the Splendors of the Eastern Capital), a description of Kaifeng, in 10 chapters, by an author called Meng Yüan-lao (ca. 1150); *Tu-ch'eng chi-sheng* (Famous Sites of the Capital City), by an anonymous author who describes himself as "an old man who waits patiently," a description in 14 paragraphs of Hangchow (1235), dealing with markets, guilds and corporations, taverns, restaurants, teahouses, trade agencies, amusement quarters, the festival of the god of the soil, parks and gardens, boats, shops and warehouses, residential districts, unemployed persons, and temples and altars; *Mengliang lu* (Account of the Remembered Splendors of the Former Capital), a detailed description of Hangchow in 20 chapters by Wu Tzu-mu, a native of the town (preface dated 1274). On all three works, see the Imperial Catalogue, *Ssu-k'u t'i-yao* 70 (Commercial Press edition, 2, 1523 and 1527).

14. Katō, "On the Development and Prosperity of Cities and City Life during the Sung Period," pp. 334 ff. Cf. the same author's "On the Hang or the Associations of Merchants in China," 45–83.

as other than a combination of separate administrative districts. They must sometimes have extended over quite a wide area, for we occasionally find figures giving a total circumference of from twelve to as much as nineteen miles.[15] But, as I mentioned earlier, the territorial extent of a town gives little indication of how urban it was, for gardens and even fields were often to be found *intra muros*. The size of the population seems to me a more reliable criterion, but here again we come up against the difficulty of the division into administrative districts. Hangchow in the middle of the thirteenth century had a population of 500,000 at the very least.[16] Confirmation of the approximate accuracy of this figure is provided by reports in the chronicles of the number of houses destroyed by fire in 1201 and 1208: 52,000 houses in the first fire, and in the second, about ten government buildings and —*expressis verbis*—58,092 private houses! [17]

But we have something better than figures: we have the account of an eyewitness who was a citizen of Venice. The astonishment expressed by that typical specimen of the newly formed Western bourgeoisie is more eloquent than the most accurate of statistics. Here is how Marco Polo saw Hangchow, that eastern Venice, known at the time as *hsing-tsai* (transcribed by Marco Polo as Quinsai), the "temporary residence" of the Sung:

> The city is so great that it hath an hundred miles of compass. And there are in it twelve thousand bridges of stone,[18] for the most part so lofty that a great fleet could pass beneath them. And let no man marvel that there are so many bridges, for you see the whole city stands as it were in the water and surrounded by water . . . there were in this city twelve guilds of the different crafts, and each guild had 12,000 houses in the occupation of its workmen. . . . *The number and the wealth of the merchants, and the amount*

15. Katō, *Studies in Chinese Economic History*, pp. 301 ff. Cf. Des Rotours, *Traité des fonctionnaires*, Appendix II (maps of the capital).

16. The two subprefectures of Ch'ien-t'ang and Jen-ho, which together formed the town of Hangchow, had a population of 432,046 at the time of the census of 1273 (and of 145,808 around 1170, 320,489 around 1250) according to the *Mengliang lu* (*Chih-pu-tsu* edition) 18.2b. Cf. A. C. Moule, "Marco Polo's Description of Quinsai," *T'oung Pao* (Leiden, 1937), *33*, 105–28.

17. Cf. L. Wieger, *Textes historiques* (Hsien-hsien, 1922), 2, 1639 and 1643.

18. There were in fact 347 bridges; cf. Moule, "Marco Polo's Description of Quinsai," p. 118.

of goods that passed through their hands, was so enormous that no man could form a just estimate thereof. . . . Moreover it was an ordinance laid down by the King that every man should follow his father's business and no other, no matter if he possessed 100,-000 bezants. . . . All the streets of the city are paved with stone . . . And the Ocean Sea comes within 25 miles of the city at a place called Ganfu [Kan-p'u, the port of Hangchow], where there is a town and an excellent haven, with a vast amount of shipping which is engaged in the traffic to and from India and other foreign parts, exporting and importing many kinds of wares, by which the city benefits.

Of the city of Soochow he says:

They possess silk in great quantities, from which they make gold brocade and other stuffs, and *they live by their manufactures and trade.* The city is passing great, and has a circuit of some 60 miles; it hath merchants of great wealth and an incalculable number of people. Indeed, if the men of this city and of the rest of Manzi [*Man-tzu:* a derogatory term used by the Mongols for the southern Chinese, subjects of the Sung] had but the spirit of soldiers they would conquer the world; but they are no soldiers at all, only *accomplished traders and most skilful craftsmen.* There are also in this city many philosophers [literati] and leeches [doctors].

Finally let us hear what Marco Polo, the secret agent of Khubilai Khan, has to say about Peking, the capital of the Genghis Khan branch of the Mongols:

Moreover I tell you that in this city of Cambaluc [Khan-balik, the city of the Khan] there is so great a number of houses and of people, between inside the town and outside; for you may know that there are as many suburbs as gates . . . that there is no man could tell the number. For there are many more people in those suburbs than in the town. And in these suburbs stay and lodge the merchants and the travelling foreigners, of whom there are many from all parts to bring things as presents to the lord and to sell to the court . . . Moreover I tell you that there are as beautiful houses and as beautiful palaces in the suburbs as in the town, except those of the great lord. [And on prostitution:] . . . inside the town dare live no sinful woman . . . they all live outside in the suburbs. And you may know that there are so great a multitude of them for the foreigners that no man could believe it, for I tell you that they are quite twenty thousand who all serve men for money, and they all find a living. . . . Then you can see if there is great abundance of people in Cambaluc since the worldly women there are as many as I have told. And you may know that dearer things and of greater value and more strange come into this town . . . than into any city of the world, and greater quantity of all things. . . . And this happens because everyone from everywhere brings there for the lord who lives there and for his court and for the city which is so great and for the ladies and for the barons and the knights of whom there are so many and for the great abundance of the multitude of the people of the armies of the lord, which stay around as well . . . so that so much of everything comes there that it is without end.[19]

Marco Polo's ingenuous tone, his very exaggerations, are clear enough indication of how large these Chinese towns must have been in Sung and Mongol times. Several points for comment arise. The first thing to strike one is how thoroughly urban in character these towns were, the majority of their inhabitants apparently merchants and "men of all crafts." Secondly, one must remember the peculiar character of the Mongol period, which differed from periods of Chinese rule in this respect: for political reasons, the Mongol world conquerors entered into partnership with the commercial bourgeoisie in order to exploit their conquered territory. The Mongol emperors, themselves incapable (because they were insufficiently educated) of governing a highly developed agrarian society, and harboring justifiable doubts as to the loyalty of the indigenous ruling class of scholar-officials, instinctively chose a new method of ruling. They entrusted the high administrative posts and the lucrative task of farming the taxes to Muslim financiers, who were all foreigners, usually of Central Asian origin (from Bukhara, Samarkand, etc.), and placed privileged

19. *The Book of Ser Marco Polo,* translated and edited by Sir Henry Yule (3d ed. revised by Henri Cordier, London, 1926), *1,* 412 ff. (Peking), *2,* 181 (Suchow) and 185 ff. (Hangchow); A. C. Moule and Paul Pelliot, eds., *The Description of the World* (London, 1938), *1,* 235–37, 324–25, 326 ff. Cf. G. Pauthier, ed., *Le Livre de Marco Polo* (Paris, 1865), *1,* 313 ff.; *2,* 489 and 493.

citizens of other conquered countries in positions of control over the indispensable Chinese administrative personnel. The policy of racial discrimination was shrewdly applied. The more civilized peoples of North China, such as the Ch'i-tan and the Ju-chen, as well as Tibetan monks, Nestorian artisans, Uighur technologists, Transoxanians, Arabs, and Turco-Iranians, were all used against the indigenous Chinese of the South. But the key figures in the application of this policy were the merchants from Central Asia, astute and sharp-witted business-men who were clever as liaison officers and quite unscrupulous in financial transactions. The most important among them, and the most hated by the Chinese people, were the Muslim usurers. They enjoyed special privileges and formed banking societies or guilds of mutual aid, known as *ortaq,* for financing the caravan trade; also, they were notorious for their money-lending transactions at exorbitant rates of interest, in which they enjoyed the active participation of the Mongol aristocracy, the principal guarantors.[20]

A final remark concerning the special nature of this period before I draw some general conclusions. It is, I think, incontestable that the outstanding features of Mongol times—the expansion of trade, the rise of a distinct merchant class, and, in general, the development of the urban population at the expense of the rural population—had been stimulated by the wars and by the breakup of the empire into con-tending national states that had occurred during the three centuries before the Mongol conquest. The Sung imperial government had been faced with the urgent need to maintain national defenses against the rival states of the Ch'i-tan, the Hsi-hsia, and the Ju-chen, and had constantly turned for help to the big merchants, many of whom, after serving as licensed suppliers to the army, had become financiers and farmers-general. We must not forget, however, that the dominant feature of the merchant class was that it never attained any kind of autonomy, not even in the peculiarly favorable circumstances for pro-

20. See Meng Ssu-ming, *Social Classes in China under the Yüan Dynasty* (in Chinese), Yen-ching Monographs, 16 (Peking, 1938). On the *ortaq* societies (in Chinese, *wo-t'o*), see Weng Tu-chien, "A Study of Wo-t'o," *Yenching Journal of Chinese Studies, 29* (Peking, 1941), 201–18, and Murakami Masatsugu, "Ch'üan-fu-ssu and Wo-t'o under the Yüan Dynasty" (in Japanese), *Tōhō Gakuhō, 13* (1942), 143–96. Cf. R. Grousset, *Histoire de la Chine* (Paris, 1942), pp. 288 ff.

moting their interests that obtained under the Mongols. Such privileges as the big traders gained were never the result of a fierce struggle, but were sparingly granted by the state. The procedure for making claims of any kind remained for the merchant or the artisan what it was for the rest of the *misera plebs:* the petition, the timid request humbly addressed to the authorities—the scholar-officials—who were the representatives of the all-powerful state.

To illustrate the position of the merchants, I will give two examples of typical procedures. Whereas in the West, as everyone knows, it was the urban patrician class that sold or let sites, premises, workshops, and other commercial or industrial establishments to the artisans and merchants,[21] in China it was the state that was the ground landlord, the state and the officials that built and let shops, warehouses, and other commercial buildings.[22] Again: the state did occasionally borrow money from the big traders when it was in difficulties, on terms favorable to the private sector of the economy; but the borrowing was more often than not in the nature of a forced loan, imposed from above.

The guilds and corporations were obliged to supply the government with a required amount of their products at lower than market prices, and with transport costs paid. The abuses this practice had given rise to can easily be imagined, and in 1073 a number of the Kaifeng corporation of butchers requested permission to cancel the onerous obligation to provide such supplies, and to pay instead a regular tax, levied on all the corporations, which became known as "money for exemption from corporation obligations" (*mien hang-i ch'ien*). This was to be a voluntary arrangement, entered into on condition, of course, that merchandise should then be sold to the government at current market prices. The request was granted; but about ten years later the former practice was reverted to, simply by virtue of a decision of the government authorities,[23] on the ground that the arrangement had no legal basis—which, being interpreted, meant that the arrangement was no more than a temporary and retractable favor, a kindness freely extended but not to be counted upon, as easy to withhold as to grant, according to the whim of those in power.

21. Cf. W. Sombart, *Der moderne Kapitalismus* (Munich, 1922), *1*, 645.
22. Katō, *Studies in Chinese Economic History*, p. 342.
23. Katō, "On the Hang or the Associations of Merchants in China," p. 62.

In concluding this very superficial survey, I must insist, as Max Weber did forty years ago,[24] on the negative factors accounting for the arrested development of towns and of an urban class in the East and particularly in China. These are, in the first place, the absence of charters, of legalized status, of a system of jurisprudence, and, above all, of a code of civil law. Next, there was the lack of civic liberty, of secure privileges, and of autonomy in the administration of towns, so that the towns—unlike those of the West—did not become a magnet for the countryside. The town was therefore unable to fill the role of social catalyst. Unlike our towns, it could not become the center of attraction because its life remained dominated, as indeed the entire social organism was dominated, by the omnipresent and omnipotent state—that is, the uncontested, absolute, and despotic power of a class of scholar-officials who could not tolerate any form of private enterprise, or who seized any private undertaking that had by chance succeeded in flourishing, in order to stifle it.

24. Weber, "Die Wirtschaftsethik der Weltreligionen. 1. Konfuzianismus und Taoismus," 290 ff., 374, 380 ff.

MARCO POLO

IN THE CAPITAL

OF CHINA

There are certain significant moments in world history when two civilizations are in collision. They contend with each other, admire each other, and sometimes even interpenetrate. The greater the difference between the two civilizations, and the less they know of each other, the more violent will be the shock—both materially and spiritually—and the more fruitful the results of the collision.

In some of these encounters, in which the two adversaries consist of entire peoples or continents, both sides are more or less aware of what is happening, as in the modern world with its fierce struggle between East and West which has been raging for half a century before our very eyes, involving every one of us.

But there have been other culture contacts that never cease to astonish us, in which only a few individuals, or a few small groups, have discovered each other. I am thinking, for instance, of the encounter between the ideas of enlightened absolutism of Voltaire's time on the one hand, and on the other the enlightened despotism of K'ang-hsi and Ch'ien-lung, the great Manchu emperors for whom learned Jesuits acted in the capacity of technical advisers, while at the same time serving as interpreters to a restricted but cultured public avid for their "edifying letters." And there has been yet again another kind of encounter, perhaps the most extraordinary of all, in which a whole new world reveals itself to the astonished eyes of one man alone, who to

This article, written in 1954, originally appeared under the title "Marco Polo dans la Capitale de la Chine," *Oriente Poliano* (Rome, 1957), pp. 133–54.

his credulous contemporaries imparts his unbelievable discovery, the details of which remain nevertheless imperfectly understood in spite of the profound influence exerted by his revelations. I need hardly explain that the example I have in mind is the astonishing Odyssey to the world-empire of the Mongols undertaken at the end of the thirteenth century by that son of the rising bourgeoisie of the West, Marco Polo, whose seventh centenary is this year being celebrated in Italy and, indeed, in the whole civilized world.

Others more qualified to do so may speak about Marco Polo himself, about his journeys, and about the *Divisament dou Monde,* the account he dictated when in prison in Genoa to Rustichello da Pisa— an inexhaustible subject concerning which learned scholars are still making discoveries. My own topic is more restricted: it will be exclusively concerned with China—or rather, with the greatest town in China at that time, a town Marco Polo visited, marveled at, and described in a lively chapter as fresh and pungent today as when his companion noted it down for posterity.[1]

China, which was the young Venetian's main field of operations, had only just become reunified under the rule of the Mongols. The nomad conquerors ruled through intermediaries, for they were not themselves sufficiently educated to govern a highly developed agrarian society, and harbored a well founded suspicion of the former ruling class of the fallen Sung dynasty—the Chinese scholar-officials. The Mongol emperors, such as the great Khubilai Khan who took Marco Polo into his service, instinctively chose new methods of government. These consisted, as we noted in the previous chapter, of employing privileged foreigners to supervise and control the Chinese administrators. Thus side by side with Marco Polo, who was confidential adviser to the great Khan, we find Tibetan monks, Nestorian artisans, Uighur technological experts, Transoxanians, Turco-Iranians, Arabs, and merchants from Central Asia, all of them glib and intelligent as liaison officers, astute as men of business, and devoid of scruple in financial transactions. The Muslim usurers, who enjoyed special privileges at the court in Peking, played a dominant role in trade, which—although

---

1. *The Book of Ser Marco Polo,* translated and edited by Sir Henry Yule, 2, pp. 185 ff.; A. C. Moule and Paul Pelliot, eds., *The Description of the World, 1,* 326 ff., and 2, xlvi; G. Pauthier, ed., *Le Livre de Marco Polo, 2,* 493 ff.; L. F. Benedetto, *Marco Polo. Il Milione* (Florence, 1928), pp. 143 ff.

intercontinental—was nevertheless firmly based in China, the most important source of revenue for the Mongol conquerors.

The China of the Sung period (960–1279) was the most advanced country in the world at that time: a highly civilized society in process of emerging from the Middle Ages; an agrarian society composed of peasants and officials, but already developing a new urban class as a result of the intensifying commercial activities and the rise of continental and maritime trade; having dozens of efficiently administered towns that were expanding rapidly and could compare with the greatest cities in medieval Europe, often indeed surpassing them in luxury and refinement.

An astonished witness of the teeming life of these Chinese towns was Marco Polo himself. But he was not the only one. His superlative account can be set against, and completed from, contemporary Chinese sources.

Descriptions have survived of several of the large towns of the time, and these works not only enable us to appreciate with admiration what an incomparable observer Marco Polo was, but supply a background to his wanderings, though perhaps leaving room for regret that the Chinese observers did not have the wide-open eyes and the unbiased view of the Western traveler. Nevertheless, one thing about these works—a fact worth mentioning, because it is revealing—is that unlike most of the voluminous literature of Sung times, which was almost entirely written by the mandarins or scholar-officials, they were written by private individuals with no official function, who remained unknown or anonymous. Nor is that a matter of chance. The obvious affection, the pride even, with which they speak of the everyday aspects of their wonderful town, their detailed descriptions of such special features as traveling fairs, streets, and shops, the commercial activities and the pleasures of the inhabitants, demonstrate the unusual social background of these men—unusual, that is to say, for educated Chinese. There is no doubt that these writers must have belonged to non-official circles, more or less bourgeois or plebeian in character; for the professional honor of a scholar or a high official—in short, of a gentleman—would never have allowed him to take an interest in such frivolities.

It is hardly surprising, then, that these works remained scorned and disregarded in China, and little known in the West; their neglect is still less surprising if we remember that they are written in the spoken language of the time, with frequent slang expressions and colloquialisms that are hard to understand. I will mention here only the titles of a few books about Hangchow, the capital of Southern Sung.

The *Tu-ch'eng chi-sheng,* "Famous Sites of the Capital City," gives in fourteen paragraphs a complete description of Hangchow, from the various places of worship, gardens, districts, and streets, to the shops, taverns, and restaurants. This short work is anonymous, the author describing himself as "the old man who endures patiently," [2] and its date is 1235, that is, before Marco Polo's arrival in China, or indeed before his arrival in the world at all.

Another and more important work, written about the year 1300, bears the peculiarly Chinese title of *Wu-lin chiu-shih,* that is to say, "Anecdotes about Wu-lin," another name for Hangchow taken from a hill in the neighborhood. Its author was Chou Mi (1232–99), a well known writer and Chinese patriot who rebelled against the rule of the Mongols. This older contemporary of Marco Polo lived in Hangchow—and may have met him in passing in Kuei-hsin street where he lived—so that everything he says in the ten chapters of his book is the authentic account of an old inhabitant of the town, an eyewitness well acquainted with its life and institutions. It is characteristic that Chou Mi signed the preface to his book with a nom de plume meaning "hermit." [3]

The author of the third and most important work is Wu Tzu-mu, a writer about whom we have no information whatsoever. The title of his detailed and picturesque description of Hangchow is revealing: *Meng-liang lu,* which might be translated as "The Dream of Happiness" but which literally means "Account of the Gruel Dream," an allusion to a story in which a poor peasant dreams of a life of marvelous luxury during the short time it takes the keeper of the poverty-

2. *Nai-te-weng.* On this work(*Wu-lin chang-ku ts'ung-pien* edition), extracts of which are contained in the *Shuo-fu,* see the Imperial Catalogue, *Ssu-k'u t'i-yao* 70 (Commercial Press edition 2, 1527), and A. C. Moule, "The Wonder of the Capital," *The New China Review,* 3 (1921), 12–17 and 356–57.

3. *Ssu-shui ch'ien-fu,* "the hermit of Ssu-shui." Chou Mi is better known as the author of the historical jottings entitled *Kuei-hsin tsa-chih* (Miscellany of Kuei-hsin Street) and of the *Ch'i-tung yeh-yü* (Remarks of a Rustic from Shantung). On the *Wu-lin chiu-shih* (*Chih-pu-tsu chai ts'ung-shu* edition), see *Ssu-k'u* 70, 2, 1528.

stricken inn to heat up his supper, a bowl of gruel. The real meaning, therefore, of *Meng-liang lu* is "dreaming of splendors in the midst of deprivation"—namely, the splendors of the former capital of Sung. The preface is dated September 16, 1274, the very year in which Marco Polo is thought to have arrived in China. This book in twenty chapters is our most important source of information about Hangchow at the end of the thirteenth century.[4] I will shortly quote a few passages from it.

In addition to these titles one might mention travel diaries, poems, memoirs, and, above all, the three great monographs about Hangchow dated 1169, 1250, and 1268, the last a monumental description of Hangchow in 100 chapters.[5]

I cannot avoid saying a few words about Hangchow's previous history, from the time of its foundation as a walled city around 600. It had been a sleepy provincial town, and neither its warm, damp climate that Northerners find insupportable, nor its geographical position in the southeast corner of the empire, made it seem a likely future metropolis. But it lay at the terminus of the Imperial Canal, the great artery to the North, and not too far from Canton, the flourishing international port in the South, and it was favorably situated on the seacoast halfway between the Yangtze basin and the south coast; as a result, Hangchow soon became the pivot of river and maritime trade. In addition, the fertility of Chekiang (the province in which Hang-

4. The *Meng-liang lu* (Mll), quoted here according to the *Ts'ung-shu chi-ch'eng* edition (Shanghai, 1939), Nos. 3219–3221 (this punctuated edition is the best to date), treats of the following topics: seasonal festivals (chapters 1–6); topography of Hangchow (7); official buildings (8); ministries and other offices (9); offices, stores, army, police, firemen, postal service (10); surroundings, the port, dikes and sluices (11); the West Lake and navigation (12); markets, guilds, trade, and finance (13); gods, cults, and temples (14); schools, monasteries, pagodas, celebrated sites (15); restaurants, inns, etc. (16); famous people native to Hangchow (17); population, products, taxes, charity (18); gardens, pleasure grounds, clubs, unemployed, beggars (19); marriage, prostitution, pastimes, theater, professional storytellers (20). Cf. *Ssu-k'u* 70, 2, 1527.

5. These are the *Ch'ien-tao Lin-an chih* (Description of Lin-an in the Period 1165–73), by Chou Ts'ung, governor of the town, of which only three chapters survive (cf. *Ssu-k'u* 68, 2, 1462); the *Ch'un-yu Lin-an chih* (Description of Lin-an in the Period 1241–52), by Shih O (cf. *Ssu-k'u wei-shu shu-mu t'i-yao*, 4.4a–b), of which only chapters 5–10 survive; and the *Hsien-ch'un Lin-an chih* (Description of Lin-an in the Period 1265–74), by Ch'ien Yüeh-yu, military governor of the town from 1270 to 1274 (cf. *Ssu-k'u* 68, 2, 1469).

chow is situated) and the ease of communications in this region must have been of great importance when the center of population and wealth began to shift at the end of T'ang times, and still more under the Sung, from the northwest to the southeast.

Thus, about 1000, Hangchow became one of the centers of the famous "Commissariat for the merchant navy," which supervised the coastal trade. Growing steadily in volume, overseas trade now extended far and wide, ranging from Japan through Indo-China, Malaysia, and India to the Near East and Africa. Chinese junks, in competition with the ships of Arab merchants, sailed all the seas. The most important Chinese exports were textiles, porcelain, tea, copper cash, and precious metals, while the principal imports were incense, perfumes, spices, pearls, ivory, coral, amber, agates, and crystals. The commissioners, very powerful people, were at the same time warehouse managers, customs inspectors, and police inspectors for foreigners. At their disposal, they had public moneys that had been set aside for the purchase of foreign goods if the demand for them at court should exceed the 10 to 40 per cent of the merchandise subtracted as a tax in kind on imported goods.[6]

The accumulation of wealth was reflected in the continuous growth of the population. The number of inhabitants of Hangchow increased from 80,000 families in T'ang times to 200,000 families toward the end of the eleventh century. By the end of the thirteenth century, when Marco Polo visited the town, Hangchow must have had a million or even a million and a half inhabitants. It is true that the official census figure is under half a million, but this is only for the city proper. I shall come back to this question.[7]

It was, however, only after a national disaster had taken place that Hangchow really began to flourish. In 1126, after a desperate if con-

6. On the "Commissariat for the merchant navy" see *Sung-shih* (*T'u-shu chih'eng* edition of 1888) 167.8b and 186.11b; *Sung hui-yao, chih-ḳuan* section, 44; and "Sung-tai t'i-chü shih-po ssu ts'ai-liao" in *Bulletin of the National Library of Peiping*, 5 (1931), 5, 27–48; Li Hsin-ch'uan (1161–1243), *Chien-yen i-lai ch'ao-yeh tsa-chi* (History of the Institutions of the Southern Sung) (*Ts'ung-shu chih'eng* edition), A 15, 217. Cf. J. Kuwabara, "On P'u Shou-keng," *Memoirs of the Tōyō Bunḳō*, 2 (Tokyo, 1928), 1–79, and 7 (1935), 1–104.

7. Cf. Katō Shigeshi, *Studies in Chinese Economic History* (Tokyo, 1953), 2, 404–20.

fused struggle, the Ju-chen barbarians captured Kaifeng, the Sung
capital, and led away into the steppe two noteworthy prisoners: the
Son of Heaven in person, and Hui-tsung, the abdicated emperor—
that august dilettante, a dabbler in painting and calligraphy, who was
the incarnation of the decadent refinement, the inertia, and the policy
of peace at any price that had characterized the beginning of the
twelfth century. An upsurge of national energies at the last moment
had not been able to organize a strong enough resistance against the
invaders. There was panic, followed by the fall of the capital and of
the dynasty, the flight of a divided court, and a general disordered
exodus to the South.

China now had to seek a new center from which to reorganize, and
find a new capital, before she could entertain thoughts of reconquest.
After two years' hesitation between Wu-ch'ang, Ch'ang-sha, and Nanking, a decision was finally made, under pressure from the barbarian
horsemen who were about to cross the Yangtze. The choice fell on
Chekiang, as the province least exposed to attack, and perhaps also
for a sentimental reason: the mother of Kao-tsung, founder of the
Southern Sung dynasty, was a native of Chekiang. So the court was
established at Hangchow, as well as could be managed, and quarters
were prepared for the ministries and for the officials, some of whom
had to find lodgings in the town.[8] But in order to eliminate any
shadow of doubt as to the intentions of the dynasty and demonstrate
its firm decision to reconquer the occupied parts of China, the town
was never known as anything but the "temporary residence" (*hsing-
tsai*). This was the name by which Marco Polo knew the town,
transcribing it as Quinsai. Let us note in passing the anomaly that
although the town had several other names besides this one, the
one name it was never known by at that time is the modern name—
Hangchow—which I have been using. The reason lies in the Chinese
system of administration. The city itself consisted of two subprefectures, Jen-ho hsien and Ch'ien-t'ang hsien (the latter taking its name
from the river Che, also called the Ch'ien-t'ang), and these, along
with several other subprefectures, composed the prefecture of Hang-

8. Hsü I-t'ang, "Nan-Sung Hang-chou chih tu-shih ti fa-chan" (The Development of Hangchow as a Metropolis during the South Sung Dynasty), *Bulletin
of Chinese Studies, 4* (1944), 231–87.

chou (hence the modern name for the town). This, in turn, was the seat of the higher prefecture of Lin-an.

Thus Hangchow was not only the residence of the emperor and his court, but also, from the point of view of civil administration, at one and the same time a prefecture embracing several subprefectures, the seat of a higher prefecture, the capital of a province, and the capital of the empire. A further important feature should be mentioned: the Imperial Guard was garrisoned there.

The military character of the old Chinese towns (which, as we have seen, were in the nature of fortresses, each surrounded by a rampart and divided within into a checkerboard of square districts partitioned off from each other and with a strict watch kept over them) had for several centuries been gradually changing in the face of the natural and irrepressible expansion of urban life. In time, residential areas became established beyond the outer of the two walls—there being, in Hangchow as in the other big towns, an inner and an outer wall— so that the markets and the merchants and other inhabitants of these suburbs could escape from the clutches of the bureaucratic autocracy with all its regulations. But such limited freedom was not comparable to the liberties and self-government of Western towns. The Chinese town was never anything but the seat and the undisputed domain of the mandarinate.[9]

A typical instance of this is the refusal, on the part of the authorities, to accede to a request made by the civil governor of Hangchow in 1156 to permit the districts *intra muros* to have the same form of civil jurisdiction as that already enjoyed by the districts *extra muros*. The very name given to the latter is significant: they were known as *hsiang* —literally meaning "wings," but also referring to garrisons for provincial troops. Within the walls, the town was divided into eight districts, not counting the forbidden, or imperial, city that was comprised of the imperial palaces and the most important of the buildings housing the central government and administration, a whole series of ministries, secretariats, and offices. Outside the walls, there were two districts covering a very wide area, including the famous Hsi-hu or West Lake, which enabled Marco Polo to say that there was a lake thirty leagues long within the town. The modified form of jurisdiction, established in 1141, which was exercised by the officials admin-

9. See Chapter 6 above, "Chinese Towns."

istering these two districts was limited to ordinary criminal offenses punishable by less than sixty strokes of the rod.[10]

The area covered by Hangchow was very large, the outer wall measuring 70 Chinese leagues or about 23 miles in circumference. The town had 18 gates, several of these being water gates through which waterways ran. Indeed, Hangchow was crisscrossed by canals, reminding Marco Polo of his native Venice. Most of the new buildings, palaces, offices, and granaries were placed beside a canal to facilitate communications, and this explains the large number of bridges. The 12,000 stone bridges mentioned by Marco Polo were perhaps not so much a naïve exaggeration on his part as a round figure indicating a large number (he also speaks of 12,000 trades), similar to the Chinese use of "ten thousand," meaning "many."

However that may be, hydraulic undertakings were an important part of Hangchow life, and several well known names in Chinese literature are connected with them, such as Po Chü-i (772–846), who initiated irrigation projects when he was prefect of the town, and the writer-poet-aesthete Su Tung-p'o (1036–1101), who had wells dug, the lake improved, and the rivers and canals cleaned out. The chief concern was to ensure a supply of drinking water from the West Lake, which was situated on a higher level than the town. From the beginning of the Sung period, the ministry in charge of water works paid special attention to the water supply; the lake was cleared by a special detachment of troops appointed for this purpose, the wells were repaired and cleaned out, and the water courses were cleaned and enlarged.[11]

Water met another need in the life of Hangchow, not directly utilitarian, but nonetheless important: it was used as a means for fighting fires. The town was frequently ravaged by fires during the hot season, and the danger was increased by the wooden construction of all the houses. The chronicles report about twenty big fires in the "temporary residence," five of which were of disastrous proportions. In 1201, 52,000 houses were destroyed in the blaze, and shortly afterward a second huge fire destroyed about a dozen government buildings and 58,000 private houses—which provides confirmation of the large number of

---

10. Hsü I-t'ang, pp. 267–69; cf. Li Hsin-ch'uan, *Chien-yen i-lai hsi-nien yao-lu* (Chronicle of the Years 1127–62) (*Ts'ung-shu chi-ch'eng* edition), 175.2891.

11. Cf. *Sung-shih* 97, and Hsü I-t'ang, pp. 270–73.

inhabitants. The constant danger of fires had various repercussions. In the economic sphere, for instance, it resulted in exemption from the commercial tax on wood for building purposes; in the sphere of religion, it led to a superstitious obsession about fire and a widespread cult of water deities, particularly of the Dragon King (*lung-wang*).[12]

Another aspect of the unceasing fear of fire was the excellent organization of fire-fighting forces in Hangchow. There were fourteen fire brigades within the walls and nine without. These stations, of which the *Meng-liang lu* gives a lively description,[13] sent out patrols to keep watch over the wealthy districts and to give the alarm in cases of theft, fire, or other emergencies. At the most vulnerable places in the town, where the streets were narrow and every inch of space was occupied, so that traffic was congested, there were watch towers that gave warning at the slightest suspicion of smoke, by means of flags or, at night, lanterns. The soldier-firemen were well equipped. They had ropes and ladders, buckets and hatchets, scythes, lanterns, signal flags, and even protective clothing, all paid for by the state.

It was also as a protection against fire, as well as theft, that merchandise was stored in warehouses. If the account in the *Meng-liang lu* is to be believed, there were several dozen warehouses of this kind, each containing thousands of rooms, built beside a small lake and entirely surrounded by water, for the express purpose of storing the merchandise and equipment belonging to wealthy storekeepers in Hangchow and merchants from abroad. The writer remarks that this was a very convenient and advantageous arrangement, and indeed it must have been, for the owners who let space in these warehouses to the merchants maintained guard patrols around the buildings to keep watch over the goods deposited there.[14]

Houses and land in Hangchow, as in other towns, belonged to both public and private owners. And since rents were always rising, the government from time to time decreed remissions of rent—either exemptions or temporary reductions—for political or religious reasons, acts of mercy designed to pacify public opinion.[15] There was a government office that dealt with the renting of houses and land belong-

12. Hsü I-t'ang, pp. 261–65.

13. *Mll* 10.87–88; cf. A. C. Moule, "Marco Polo's Description of Quinsai," 106–28. The relevant passage is translated on pp. 122–23.

14. *Mll* 19.179.

15. Cf. Katō, *Studies in Chinese Economic History*, pp. 239–46.

ing to the state. The fact that remission of rent was counted by the day makes it permissible to suppose that the poor of Hangchow—laborers, artisans, peddlers, etc.—paid their rent on a daily basis. And I can well believe that the state, and private landlords as well, might have found it wise to ensure that the rent was collected on a daily basis. Here is what the *Meng-liang lu* says about it: "The office for letting shops and multi-storied houses is to the north of the Liu-fu bridge. The state authorities have installed employees there to control the letting of these houses, according to the number of people dwelling in them, and to collect and control the rents paid by the tenant families and the annual payment of rents for land not built on." [16]

Another passage is devoted to acts of mercy:

On occasions of prayers offered by the Court and the Ministries for fine weather or for rain, or when they pray for snow or for good omens; or on the occasion of the birth of a prince and the birthdays of Their Majesties; or at times of excessive rain or snow or unreasonable frosts, when the people are in want; or again on the occasion of the grand ceremonies [of the sacrifice to Heaven] and of the Sacred Palace as well as of ceremonies of congratulation, at all these times an imperial announcement is promulgated giving notification of the gift of 200,000 strings of cash in paper money to the army and to the people. It is a fact that the prefecture of Hang is the place where the emperor resides, and this is the sole reason for these favors. At the same time, since many dwellings and sites belonging either to the State or to private owners are let out to tenants who pay rent or ground rent, graded into large, medium, and small rents, on the occasion of the above-mentioned prayers and ceremonies, the appropriate official bureaus put up notices about the remission of rents and ground rents, for a duration of three to seven days on large rents, five to ten days on medium rents, seven to fifteen days on small rents. If the rents of the dwelling houses have not yet been reduced according to the various scales specified, on the occasion of the grand ceremonies and of acts of mercy [amnesties, etc.], a rent of 1,000 cash is reduced by 300 cash, that is to say [adds the author, so as

16. *Mll* 10.84.

to leave no possible doubt about it], State and private owners only collect 700 cash.[17]

I have quoted this passage because it gives clear indication of the growth of town life in Hangchow—one might almost say, of the tendency toward tenements and barracks—while at the same time it illustrates the fundamental difference between the Western town and the Chinese town: in the latter, it was not the patricians or the bourgeoisie that were the main proprietors of real estate, but the bureaucratic state.

But enough of sociology! Let us rather proceed on a conducted tour of the town, whose narrow streets, sometimes paved, and always smelly, may be full of the stale odors of cooking but are overflowing with life, noise, and incessant activity. There are shops and booths in every nook and cranny. The trades and guilds, once confined to their own quarters, or each having its special street (whence the name *hang*), have spread all over the town, as have the markets. There are two dozen trades, ranging from weavers and tailors, through masons and carpenters, potters and brickmakers, to gilders, lacquer workers, and makers of oil and candles.[18]

Merchants are even more numerous, for Hangchow is first and foremost a commercial city. Hard pressed by the government—they have to pay all sorts of taxes and tolls whose arbitrary nature was more burdensome than the actual amounts paid—and looked down on by the officials, the merchants manage nevertheless to arrange things for themselves, do good business, and get rich. For this vast conglomeration of people cannot get along without them, and even the officials are obliged to make use of their services if they want to keep up a suitable style of life by exchanging their salaries, paid in grain and money, for various consumer goods and for the luxuries and comforts of life.

The townspeople consumed large amounts of food. According to a proverb quoted by the author of the *Wu-lin chiu-shih,* the people of Hangchow daily used 30 ells (or 300 feet) of wood for pestles to

17. *Mll* 18.171.
18. The *Hsien-ch'un Lin-an chih,* Ch. 19, lists 17 guilds (*hang* or *t'uan*); *Mll* 13.112 lists two dozen, and 22 trades (*tso*). Cf. *Wu-lin chiu-shih* 6.14a–17a, and Hsü I-t'ang, pp. 250 ff.

pound the required amount of grain.[19] The various writers mentioned above reckoned that the daily consumption of cereals was between 2,000 and 4,000 piculs, that is, 140 to 280 tons a day. But it would be best if we put ourselves in the hands of an expert guide and, if you would care to, take a walk with him in "the belly of Hangchow." I am sure that if Wu Tzu-mu had known Zola this is the title he would have given to the sixteenth chapter of his book.

Let us first of all go to the rice market. "In Hangchow," says the *Meng-liang lu,*

the houses are crowded close together and the number of inhabitants, within and without the walls, is certainly more than some 100,000 families, which is more than a million individuals. Apart from the amount consumed by the government offices and palaces, the families of officials, the households of wealthy families, and also the salaried employees of all the administrative departments (who receive some of their salary in kind), the daily consumption of the ordinary people within and without the walls is certainly not less than 1,000 to 2,000 piculs. They all have to get it from the shops. Thus our prefecture depends on a supply of rice from other parts of the country, which comes to the market from Su-chow, Hu-chou, Ch'ang-chou, Hsiu-chou, the Huai River region, and Canton. The Hu-chou market, the Rice-market Bridge, and the Black Bridge are where the rice guilds are situated, and there all the merchants from other parts sell their grain. There are numerous varieties of rice, such as early rice, late rice, new-milled rice, winter-husked rice, first quality white rice, medium quality white rice, lotus-pink rice, yellow-eared rice, rice on the stalk, ordinary rice, glutinous rice, ordinary yellow rice, short-stalked rice, pink rice, yellow rice, and old rice.

I have included this list of the various kinds of rice, not because of any intrinsic interest it may have, but because it is a good example of the many other catalogues, even longer than this one, typifying the ingenuous pride of the author in his command of the subject and,

19. See *Wu-lin chiu-shih* 6.16b; cf. Ch'üan Han-cheng, "Nan-Sung Hang-chou ti hsiao-fei yü wai-ti shang-p'in chih shu-ju" (The Consumption and Importation of Commodities to the Southern Sung Capital Lin-an), *Academia Sinica Bulletin,* 7 (1936), 91–116, esp. p. 98.

even more, his pride in the sheer existence of so many products. The new awareness on the part of the merchant class of the nature of their society—a feature indicative of the historical trend, and common to both China and the great independent cities of the Italian peninsula —expresses itself in these interminable catalogues, in which the writers do their best to make an exhaustive inventory of everything, and so give a complete picture of all the elements, without exception, composing their universe. The *Meng-liang lu* continues:

> Let us now speak of the shops within and without the walls. Every shopowner depends entirely on the head of the guild for fixing the market price of rice. The rice is sent direct to each shop and put on sale there. The shopkeeper arranges a fixed day for paying for his supply of rice, whereas the small agents at the rice market go in person to each store to make delivery to their clients . . . The town of Hang always likes rice-barges to be coming in pell-mell from all parts and finds it very convenient that they should arrive all day long without pause. Besides there are, of course, people there for unloading the sacks, and the porters and coolies have their chiefs who are in command over them. Each boat has its boatman, who receives the cargo. Although the transport arrangements at the rice market are complicated, there are never any disputes or altercations. In this way the shopkeepers spare their energies and the rice is brought directly to the shops.[20]

It might almost be said that as far as its techniques and credit arrangements are concerned, this organization of wholesalers and retailers, even if rudimentary, is approaching that of a modern town.

The butchers and pork butchers were every bit as well organized as the rice merchants. Several assistants stood in the street outside their stalls, flourishing their knives and ready to cut off, in the twinkling of an eye, the piece of meat chosen by a customer. About a hundred animals, brought in early in the morning, were slaughtered daily, and the pork butchers had already sold about a dozen whole pigs by midday. They were also regular suppliers to inns and restaurants.[21]

Although it would be impossible to enumerate all the contents of

20. *Mll* 16.146–47.
21. *Mll* 16.147–48.

such a rich text as the *Meng-liang lu,* I should like at least to quote the paragraph about the fish markets, primarily because fish—apart from rice—was the main item of diet in the South, but also because this passage has more general interest:

> The population of Hangchow is very dense both inside and out-side the walls, and the town stretches over a wide area. In no matter what district, in the streets, on the bridges, at the gates, and in every odd corner, there are everywhere to be found bar-rows, shops, and emporiums where business is done. The reason for this is that people are in daily need of the necessities of life, such as firewood, rice, oil, salt, soya sauce, vinegar, and tea, and to a certain extent even of luxury articles, while rice and soup are absolute essentials, for even the poorest cannot do without them. To tell the truth, the inhabitants of Hangchow are spoiled and difficult to please.
>
> Let us take fish, for example. This merchandise comes from the commanderies of Wen, T'ai, and Ssu-ming [i.e. Ning-p'o; all three are in Chekiang]. On the south side of the town, near the sluice-gate against the impure water [of the river Che], the guilds of the merchants from other parts of the country assemble. That is where both fresh and salt fish are collected together, and where the market is held for the fishmongers from inside and outside the town, not less than 100 to 200 in number. I list here all the various items sold by the fishmongers . . . The fishmongers also sell salt provisions, silver-fish, crabs, dried fish from the Huai, small crabs, salted duck, fried duck, fried mullet, frozen fish, frozen dried fish, fried bream, loach fried in batter, fried eel, boiled fish, and white shrimps fried. In addition, these goods are sold by hawkers in the streets, to satisfy the needs of customers in the little lanes and alleyways, which is very convenient.[22]

With your appetite thus whetted, I now invite you to follow our guide into some of the innumerable restaurants, taverns, inns, drink shops, teahouses, and bars of the town. Let us first take a look at the teahouses (*ch'a-fang* or *ch'a-ssu*):

> The restaurants of the capital city of Kaifeng were in the habit of hanging up famous pictures so as to catch the attention of

22. *Mll* 16.148.

passers-by and attract customers. Nowadays, the tea-houses in the town of Hang do the same: they make arrangements of the flowers of the four seasons, hang up paintings by celebrated artists, decorate the walls of the establishment, and all the year round sell unusual teas and curious soups. During the winter months, they sell in addition a very fine powdered tea, pancakes, onion tea, and sometimes soup of salted beans. During the hot season they add as extras plum-flower wine with a mousse of snow, a beverage for contracting the gall-bladder, and herbs against the heat, etc. . . . . At present, the tea-houses lay out a display of flowers, in which are arranged curious pines, strange cypresses, and other plants. The walls of the room are decorated, and business is done to the click of clappers and the sound of singing. Only porcelain cups are used, and things are served on lacquer trays, there being neither cups nor other utensils made of silver. At the nocturnal market, in the main street, there are peddlers, and hawkers with barrows, who serve passers-by with infusions of tea and with soups.

As a rule, the tea-houses (*ch'a-lou*) are a rendezvous for young men of wealthy families, and for officials from various offices coming off duty, etc., who practice on musical instruments and sing all sorts of airs and refrains. These establishments are called "those with the hanging signs." The reason why people like going to tea-houses has nothing to do with drinking tea or soups; but since the tea serves as an excuse, a lot of money is made out of it. There are also tea-houses which are special meeting places for domestic servants, and others where laborers and artisans belonging to all the various crafts meet.

The list continues with noisy places where "a decent man does not set foot"; establishments, such as Mother Wang's, where marionette shows are given; and teahouses where people of good position meet. There are also beggars who go from door to door selling tea, great favorites with the gossips because they bring the tittle-tattle of the neighborhood. Finally, "Buddhist, Taoist, and other monks who want to take part in [the funeral rites of] praise for the dead first go round with tea from door to door because they think that will be a way of making themselves noticed." [23]

23. *MII* 16.139.

The restaurants and taverns of Hangchow were both varied and highly specialized. A prospective customer was faced with a difficult choice among elegant restaurants, restaurants for noodles and ravioli, vegetarian restaurants, patisseries, inns and bars, pubs and bars which offered only snacks to accompany drinks, low-class eating houses, and others. Many of these restaurants were kept by men who had been students, and who did their best to imitate the imperial cuisine.[24] We must not forget that Hangchow was also the empire's intellectual center, and that the nearly 2,000 students housed by the university and its colleges did not always, or immediately, succeed in obtaining an official post.

Let us now visit one of the chic establishments, with such promising signs as "The Happy Meeting," or "The Seduction," or "The Pleasures of Novelty." In front of the entrance are placed red and green palings and above the door hang garlands of multicolored silk and gilded red gauze lanterns. The main room, and the arcades at each side which are divided up into small cubicles containing tables and very comfortable chairs, are decorated with a forest of flowers and shrubs. "Toward evening," says our cicerone, "lanterns and candles are lit, spreading a blaze of light everywhere. A dozen prostitutes, luxuriously dressed and heavily made-up, gather at the entrance to the main arcade to await the command of customers, and have an airy gracefulness like that of the Immortals." [25]

These singing-girl-waitresses, about whom I shall say more presently, were required by the owner of the restaurant to suggest special dishes to inexperienced customers "so that the bill would mount up." In all the restaurants, if one desired to gain esteem as a customer, the thing to do was first of all to choose one's place, consult the menu, and order the wine. Only then did one proceed in an unhurried manner to make a careful selection of several choice dishes, whereas "gentlemen from the provinces who, not being yet acquainted with the ways of the capital, began eating right away, were a laughingstock in the eyes of the proprietor." [26]

The waiters had a hard time of it, for there was a fantastic choice of dishes. The author of the *Meng-liang lu,* a veritable Brillat-Savarin,

---

24. *Mll* 16.141 (paragraph *fen-ch'a-chiu-tien*) and 15.131 (on the number of students).

25. *Mll* 16.140.

26. *Mll* 16.141 (paragraph *chiu-ssu*).

lists about 400, each more enticing than the last for those who know Chinese cooking, and describes the manner of serving them as follows:

> When the clients have chosen where they will sit, chopsticks are handed to them and they are asked what they want to eat. The people of Hang are extremely difficult to please: this one wants something hot, that one something cold, a third something tepid, a fourth something chilled; one wants cooked food, another raw, another chooses roast, another grill. The orders shouted out by the customers, each making his own choice, are all different, there being sometimes as many as three separate orders at one table. Having received the orders, the waiter goes to the kitchen and sings out the whole list, starting with the first one. The man who replies from the kitchen is called the Head Dishwarmer, or the Table-setter. When the waiter has come to the end of his list, he takes his tray to the stove and then goes off to serve each customer with the dish ordered. He never mixes them up, and if by any unlikely chance he should make a mistake, and the customer complains, the proprietor of the restaurant will launch into a volley of oaths, and will make him stop serving immediately, and may even dismiss him altogether.[27]

What seems so striking about these excerpts is not that they convey a sense of the unusual, the picturesque, the exotic, but on the contrary that they make the customs of a Chinese town of seven centuries ago seem so ordinary. Is it not something to marvel at, an ever-new miracle, to find that human nature has the same characteristics in all latitudes? The exotic side of Marco Polo's adventure is too often over-stressed.

While we are on the subject of familiar features, perhaps I might mention another which could be regarded as the most typical of all. Hanging around all the establishments I have been mentioning were the usual waste products of town life: unemployed persons, who cautiously approached the tables and sang out their shoddy wares to the rich young people sitting there drinking; obliging fellows, known as "low-down commission agents," who busied themselves round the tables pouring out the wine or offering fruits and perfumes; those

27. *Mll* 16.144–45.

"distributors of extras" who operated in a more subtle way, dispensing to the astonished customers refreshments, fruits, or trinkets, and coming round afterward to collect the money for their goods; finally, the low-class prostitutes, singing girls who demanded a few cents and then, as soon as the trumpery sum was obtained, simply vanished.[28]

This is perhaps the place to say a few words about prostitution—not ordinary prostitution, that endemic complaint of large towns, but the special phenomenon of state prostitution. At the beginning of the Southern Sung, after the exodus, troops from the North were stationed at Hangchow. Since the soldiers were far from home, the government, in order to provide some cheer for them, established places for selling alcoholic liquor as a sideline to the state distilleries and installed prostitutes in them to augment the sale of liquor. In addition, they built about a dozen brothels—or, if you prefer, licensed houses—near the barracks.[29] It is clear from all the contemporary texts that this prostitution, although socially disreputable, was encouraged and organized by the state for fiscal reasons, for all the texts agree that the tax on alcoholic liquors was one of the Treasury's biggest sources of revenue. The names of the most celebrated courtesans of the time—highly cultured ladies who were the friends of powerful ministers—have been preserved for us in the descriptions of Hangchow; but it was in the taverns and public houses that the shock troops of waitresses-singing-girls-prostitutes were to be found, "waiting there," as the author of the *Meng-liang lu* puts it, "for the young men of fashion to come and buy a smile from them, and busy themselves in the pursuit of pleasure." [30]

Though it was inconceivable in the Confucian moral code that any groups outside the four basic social classes could exist, it is nevertheless a fact that this whole upstart world did indeed exist, and it included all those belonging to doubtful professions and those without employment: beggars, commission agents, loafers, peddlers, trainers and exhibitors of fighting animals like cocks and crickets, professional storytellers, mountebanks, dancers, acrobats, jugglers, singers, actors.[31]

28. *Mll* 16.141 (paragraph *jen-ch'a-chiu-tien*).

29. Hsü I-t'ang, pp. 257 ff.

30. *Mll* 16.140; cf. 1.3 and 10.85, where the same expressions recur.

31. *Hsien-jen;* this is the title of the paragraph dealing with this social category in *Mll* 19.181.

Emerging from the interstices of the social structure, they filled the *wa-tzu*, those "pleasure grounds" which must have contributed so greatly to the rise of the two new, bourgeois, literary genres: the novel and the drama. Even if we do not know the precise origin of the term *wa-tzu*—for which the writers of the descriptions of Hangchow provide a rather forced etymology, saying that the people in the pleasure grounds assembled and dispersed again as quickly as tiles (*wa* meaning "tile")[32]—if, as I say, we do not know the origin of the term, we nevertheless have enough parallels in the history of Western literature to be able to recognize at once a certain causal link between the underlying phenomena. The social ferment taking place in the towns produced at one and the same time the need for amusements, a public with sufficient leisure to enjoy them, and the people to provide the amusements—writers, theater people, actor-authors, and the like. The professions of this latter group remained dishonorable for a long time, and their practitioners belonged to the lower strata and remained unrecognized and unappreciated.[33] It is now well known that the Sung and Mongol period is synonymous in the history of Chinese literature with the spread of the drama and the beginnings of the novel proper.

We cannot describe in detail here Hangchow's festivals, such as the gay and noisy feast of lanterns at the beginning of the year;[34] or the excursions, in the spring, into the hills, where incense was burnt and offerings were made to the hill spirits;[35] or outings on the West Lake, which provided escape from the summer heat—occasions when the lake was covered with pleasure boats, and there were merrymaking, music, and sumptuous nautical combats;[36] or, in the autumn, the spectacle of the tidal bore that everyone went to see—in carriages, on horseback, or on foot—booking in advance a good place to see it

32. See *Mll* 19.178, which repeats the definition given by the *Tu-ch'eng chi-sheng*. While the term *wa-shih* ("market") and *wa-tzu* were used to designate fairs, such as the one held in the temple of *Hsiang-kuo-ssu* at Kaifeng, and pleasure grounds in general, the expression *wa-she* (*she* meaning "house") seems to have had the more restricted meaning "houses of prostitution." The *Mll*, in the same chapter, lists 17 *wa-tzu* in Hangchow, the *Wu-lin chiu-shih* adds six more. On prostitution see also the texts referred to by Hsü I-t'ang, pp. 257–61.

33. See *Mll* 20.189–96.

34. *Mll* 1.2–5.

35. *Mll* 1.6–7; 2.9 and 13–14; 4.23.

36. *Mll* 2.11–12, and *Wu-lin chiu-shih* 3.1a–4a and 8a–9a.

from in one of the houses of the neighborhood.[37] The city was as noted for its charitable institutions as for its pleasures. There were public hospitals, nurseries, old people's homes, free cemeteries, help for the poor, and state institutions from which the officials benefited more often than the poor. The poor were sometimes the object of private charity on the part of rich merchants who wanted to make a name for themselves by doing good works.[38]

One final word concerning the financial importance of Hangchow. This was the aspect that made such a vivid impression on Marco Polo, who as a traveler interested himself in everything. His interest in this particular feature had, however, another and more direct motivation, for we must not forget that the object of his visit was to inquire into the resources of the regions under the rule of the great Khan. The total revenue of the Southern Sung, although subject to fairly wide variation, was accounted for in the main by the following items: receipts from the salt tax, 50 per cent; rights concerning alcoholic liquors, 36 per cent; tea monopoly, 7 per cent; tolls, customs, and commercial tax, 7 per cent.[39] Since these sources of revenue consisted mainly in taxes on articles of consumption, there is no need to explain why a town like Hangchow played such a preponderant role in contemporary finances.

We do not know whether Marco Polo—who, as an emissary of the Mongols, was doubly a stranger—made any contact with the ordinary inhabitants. The town was lying under the yoke of the conqueror, and, so shortly after its capture by the barbarian horsemen, was still in mourning for the fallen national dynasty; as a result, it cannot have had the same atmosphere of general gaiety, luxury, and beauty as before. But those of us who have had some experience of enemy occupation know very well that it is impossible to change the character of a people or of a town from one day to the next, and

37. *Mll* 4.26–27; cf Moule, "Marco Polo's Description of Quinsai," p. 114, and, by the same author, "The Bore on the Ch'ien-t'ang River in China," *T'oung Pao,* 22 (1923), pp. 135–88.

38. Moule, "Marco Polo's Description of Quinsai," pp. 124–26, where the interesting passage on private charity from *Mll* 18.172–73 is translated.

39. See *Chien-yen i-lai ch'ao-yeh tsa-chi* A 14,187–203, and Hsü I-t'ang, pp. 278–79. Cf. Ch'üan Han-sheng, "T'ang-Sung cheng-fu sui-ju yü huo-pi ching-chi ti kuan-hsi" (The Relation between Public Revenue and Money Economy during the Sung and T'ang periods), *Academia Sinica Bulletin,* 20 (1948), 189–221.

even if some things are changed, they soon revert to old ways. Although Hangchow may no longer have enjoyed all the splendors of the past, it remained after all the true capital of China and still must have made a profound impression on Marco Polo. It is perhaps not too fantastic to suppose that, as he walked about the town, the words that came oftenest to his lips were: *Questa ricchezza!* And so I think I may say, in finishing off the picture of Hangchow I have built up (if in somewhat rough-and-ready fashion) from material provided by Chinese sources, such—*grosso modo*—was the greatest town of the Far East at the moment when it received within its walls the world's greatest traveler.

EVOLUTION OF

LANDOWNERSHIP

IN FOURTH-AND

FIFTH-CENTURY CHINA

During the course of Chinese history, the free peasant was frequently reduced to servitude as a result of the formation of large estates, and whenever this threatened to occur, voices were raised warning the government against the fatal consequences of the latifundia, and demanding a return to the *ching-t'ien* system.

The *ching-t'ien* system was traditionally regarded as an ancient system of communal ownership, in which the land was supposed to have been divided in the form of the Chinese character *ching* ("water well"), with a central field, belonging to the lord and worked in common, surrounded by eight square fields (*t'ien*) of equal area, each measuring 100 *mou* (six *mou* are about one acre). Whether the tradition was actually based on historical fact has been, and will long continue to be, a topic of debate.[1] But however difficult it may be to sift out the *Dichtung und Wahrheit* of the matter, there is no doubt that the poetry became more important than the truth; for, whatever significance the *ching-t'ien* system may have had in the past, the de-

1. On communal ownership of land, see Henri Maspero, *La Chine antique,* pp. 109–10, and *Etudes historiques* (Paris, 1950), pp. 124 and 199; Swann, *Food and Money in Ancient China,* pp. 116–20. For current discussion of the question, see L. S. Yang, "Notes on Dr. Swann's *Food and Money in Ancient China,*" *Harvard Journal of Asiatic Studies, 13* (1950), 531–42.

This article originally appeared under the title "Transformation du régime de la propriété dans la Chine tartare et dans la Chine chinoise aux IVe–Ve siècles," *Cahiers d'Histoire Mondiale, 1* (1953), 417–26.

mand to return to it was a way of expressing a Utopian demand for greater social justice through equal distribution of land, and this Utopian ideal became much more significant than the vague memories that had been handed down of how the system had actually operated.

This is a paradox that can be more readily understood if two points are taken into consideration. First, the Chinese literati, traditionalists by inclination as well as necessity, were unable to formulate any program of social reform without cloaking it in a reference to the golden age of antiquity. Chinese reformers, unlike their Western counterparts, never projected their ideals into the future. They would have found it not only meaningless and frightening to do so, but unpractical as well; for since public opinion was formed by scholar-officials like themselves, equally steeped in tradition, their only hope of finding support for their programs was to give them a halo of historicity, and thus lend to their demands the prestige of the past. They did this in all good faith, themselves believing in the ideal society vouched for by scholastic reconstructions of a bygone age. Second, the same habit of referring to the past is found in imperial decrees, which were designed to express ethical postulates rather than to lay down rules for administrative practice. Imperial edicts, couched in the most florid style and packed with classical allusions, were often no more than exhortations to the officials pointing out what they *ought* to do. Thus, whether the magic words *ching-t'ien* were used to formulate a Utopian demand or to express an ethical postulate, their real meaning can faithfully be interpreted as "equal distribution of land," and over the centuries their connotation was quite simply "agrarian reform."

This becomes clear when it is realized that the question of reestablishing the ancient system agitated the leading spirits and became a hotly debated topic in government circles (the only circles whose opinion is known to us) at certain particular moments—namely, when an economic crisis was brewing. The essential features of such economic crises were as follows. As a result of increases in population and in the number of large estates swallowed up by the rich and powerful at the peasants' expense, peasant landholdings became so small that the peasants could no longer maintain their independence and were forced to become tenant farmers, agricultural laborers, or serfs attached to a large landowner. The situation was usually further aggravated by famine or floods, by the precarious state of public finance (the large landowners being exempt from tax), and by profound social unrest—in short, a crisis that made it imperative for the ruling classes to consent to a reform that would include limitation or breakup of the large estates, under the threat of seeing their land seized, and perhaps even their rule brought to an end, by the forces unleashed in the eruptive violence of a peasant revolt.

Crises of this kind were part of a recurring social and economic cycle, the stages of which are clearly mirrored in the agrarian policies of the Former Han (206 B.C.–A.D. 9). Toward the end of the second century B.C. a celebrated Confucian scholar-official took the ancient system of land distribution as his authority when putting forward a proposal for "limiting private estates" (*hsien ming-t'ien*). His proposal was never carried out, but it dominated agrarian policy until the end of the dynasty. In 7 B.C. a similar proposal was adopted, aiming to limit private estates to 3,000 *mou,* but came up against the opposition of the influential large landowners and could not be put into effect. When the usurper Wang Mang, imbued with ideas of the past, attempted to carry out a more equitable distribution of land under the guise of a theoretical nationalization, it was already too late. The reform, promulgated in A.D. 9 and abolished three years later as inefficacious and impossible to carry out, was stillborn, and the revolt of the "Red Eyebrows" not only put an end to Wang Mang's clumsy attempts, but also brought to a close both his reign and the reign of the Former Han dynasty.[2] The bloodletting of this tremendous peasant rising having to some extent re-established a balance between available land and population, the Later Han (25–A.D. 220) followed a moderate policy aimed at restricting the size of large estates. This continued until the next large-scale crisis arose, when the revolt of the "Yellow Turbans" made a holocaust of China, burying in its ruins city and countryside, great landowner and expropriated peasant, rulers and ruled.[3]

The situation changed considerably after the fall of the Han. For one thing, a return to some degree of feudalism can be discerned,

2. The economic treatise of the *Han-shu,* Ch. 24 A, trans. Swann, pp. 183, 200–04, 210–11.
3. See Chapter 13, "Political Philosophy and Social Crisis at the End of the Han Dynasty."

along with a general impoverishment of society as a whole, both in the partitioned empire of the Three Kingdoms period (220–280) and during the ephemeral restoration of the dynasty under the Western Chin (265–316). For another, there were vast tracts of uncultivated land, either abandoned after the civil wars and the barbarian invasions in the North, or never yet put under cultivation in the sparsely colonized South.

The land regulations of the period traditionally known as the Six Dynasties, or the division between South and North (third to sixth century), must be viewed in the light of the two major problems of the Chinese Middle Ages: the insufficient amount of land under cultivation, and the formation of new latifundia. Both led to the same result—the phenomenon of tax evasion, which, from the government's point of view, meant a shrinkage in the number of peasant landholders liable for corvée and tax. Behind the regulations of all the various dynasties can be found the same dual concern: how to bring as much land as possible under cultivation while at the same time preventing its being appropriated (*chien-ping*) by the large landowners, and how to guarantee the peasant a minimum standard of living so that he would not seek the protection of these landowners. "Protection" meant in effect that peasants who had become tenant farmers or serfs of a large landowner in order to escape their military and fiscal obligations continued to pay to their new master as much as or more than they had paid the government he was powerful enough to "protect" them against.

The first land law known to us, that of the Western Chin, is dated A.D. 280, the year in which the empire was reunified. It consists of two parts. The first fixes the age limits of persons enjoying normal rights, which is tantamount to saying persons liable for tax and corvée: all adult men from 16 to 60 years of age had the right to 50 *mou* of land, women to 20 *mou*, adolescents and old men to 25 *mou* (the women of these latter two age groups, 13 to 15 and 61 to 65, receiving nothing). The term used to describe this land (*k'o-t'ien*) appears to indicate that it was agricultural land regularly allotted to enable the recipients to meet their fiscal liabilities. A preamble does, however, make a vague declaration regarding the right of a man and a woman to possess 70 + 30 = 100 *mou* (about 12½ acres) of land over which they had rights of possession (*chan-t'ien*).[4] Here can be seen emerging the classic area of 100 *mou* found in the *ching-t'ien* system—the ideal family holding, which would provide the necessary minimum of subsistence for a family consisting of five members. In spite of the ambiguous terms in which it is expressed, it is clear from the context—which, as I have already said, refers to those liable for tax and corvée—that the purpose of the decree was to ensure that the peasant should have a minimum subsistence level and thus provide the state with a broad enough basis for taxation.

The second part of the decree, concerning privileged persons (nobles and officials), seems to have been much more important. It consists of a series of measures designed to restrict the number of "protected" persons and to limit the size of large estates belonging to the aristocracy. Officials were restricted to holding, according to their rank, from 1,000 to 5,000 *mou* of land (about 125 to 625 acres), to having on their estates only a certain number of tenant farmers (up to a maximum of 50 families, or about 250 individuals) and of servants fed and clothed by them, and to protecting at the maximum nine degrees of their relatives—all these people being exempt from tax and corvée.

That the emphasis fell on that section of the decree concerning restrictions is proved by the fact that it is the only part mentioned during the reign of the Eastern Chin (317–420), throughout which the policy of limitation of large estates was maintained, with one or two minor alterations in the figures here and there.[5] It is obvious, however, that this policy merely set an ideal standard, or perhaps did no more than voice a vague Utopian idea, and could never have been carried out; those whose task it was to apply the law would have had to despoil themselves in doing so, being at the same time officials and large landed proprietors. As for the allotment of land, the law of 280 had not specified any methods for carrying it out, and nothing more was heard of it.

Indeed, from soon after 280 there was no longer any question of being able to enforce the law.[6] Already torn with bloody internal strife,

---

4. Economic treatise of the *Chin-shu*, Ch. 26, trans. Yang Lien-sheng, "Notes on the Economic History of the Chin Dynasty," *Harvard Journal of Asiatic Studies*, 9 (1946), 123 ff. and 167–68.

5. E. Balazs, *Le Traité économique du Souei-chou* (Leiden, 1953).

6. Yang, "Notes," p. 121, quotes a memorial (of about A.D. 290): "Since there are *no restrictions on people's fields and houses,* the number of slaves owned should not be regulated in particular" (my italics).

North China was invaded by the barbarians at the beginning of the fourth century, and both the court and the aristocracy emigrated south of the Yangtze and established themselves at Nanking. There, in hostile surroundings inhabited by barely civilized people—a kind of Far West to be conquered and colonized—the limitation of landowner-ship no longer made economic sense. All that remained of it was the political struggle waged by the royal power to maintain its prerogatives against the barons (the feudal princes). Similarly, the concern regard-ing the allotment of land to the taxpayer faded in the overriding anxiety with which all governments were perpetually beset: how to prevent large landowners from encroaching upon land from which tax was normally raised. The historical sources seldom mention the agrar-ian question, and such references as there are reveal the inconsistency and weakness of government policy. In 518, for instance, a decree of the Liang (one of the Southern dynasties) grants three years' exemp-tion from rent to returned taxpayers who had taken flight, and prom-ises to distribute land and houses belonging to the state to those who had lost everything. Another edict (541) sadly states that "the rich and powerful families have occupied most of the public lands" (*kung-t'ien*) and prohibits this abuse, at the same time making an exception for land already appropriated and for estates worked by tenant farmers under the control of large landowners.[7] The favorite ruse of one of the biggest magnates of the times was to chase his debtors off their mortgaged land, and since he happened to be a full brother of the Emperor Wu of Liang, one might well be skeptical of the efficacy of the prohibitions reported in the official histories.[8] We must remember, too, that several documents survive from the Han-Six Dynasties period that bear witness to the purchase and free sale of land. These are con-tracts drawn up for the purchase of land for graves, buried with the deceased (hence their preservation), and, whether they are genuine or not, it is permissible to draw the conclusion that the alienation of land belonging to the peasants was not seriously impeded by the law.[9]

7. *Liang-shu* (*T'u-shu chi-ch'eng* edition of 1888), 2.10a and 3.8b.

8. *Nan-shih* 51.8a–b.

9. N. Niida, "Documents of Sale and Purchase of Land during the periods of the Han, Wei, and Six Dynasties" (in Japanese), *Tōhō Gakuhō, 8* (1938), 33–101. Some of these documents are translated into French in Henri Maspero, *Les Régimes fonciers en Chine* (Paris, 1950).

In North China, the area of the barbarian invasions, landownership underwent a slightly different development. The conquerors, who had come from the steppes, were nomad tribes whose mode of life, customs, and social organization offered a sharp contrast to those of the indigenous subject peoples. After coming to power, the Hsien-pi were fully occupied in digesting the prey they had devoured. The energies of the T'o-pa chiefs were entirely absorbed in waging wars to bring the other Turco-Tartar hordes under submission to their confederation, in conducting raids to augment their herds, in securing pasturage for their numerous cattle, and in reducing the Chinese urban and rural population to a state of powerlessness; and these activities continued long after the foundation of their dynasty, known in Chinese style as the dynasty of the Later or Northern Wei (386–534). It is clear that during this initial heroic period agrarian questions played no more than a secondary role as far as the conquerors were concerned.

It was not until the middle of the fifth century that social developments similar to those found under native Chinese dynasties began to make themselves felt. But monopolization of land by the powerful and tax evasion by the poor were here affected, and indeed singularly complicated, by factors peculiar to the territory ruled over by the Northern dynasties. In the first place, there was the usual antagonism between nomad pastoralists and agriculturalists, the conquering Hsien-pi and the conquered Chinese, on the one hand, and on the other, an increasingly marked distinction between the tribal aristocracy, who made common cause with the Chinese gentry, and the ordinary warriors, herdsmen, and serfs composing the backward and impoverished tribal masses. In the second place, once the wars had ceased, the demographic structure of the North—which had been violently disturbed by the invasions—began to pose the same problem as before and with even greater force. This was the problem of the continuous pressure exerted by a rapid increase of population in the most fertile part of the Great Plain (Honan, Hopeh, Shantung). In these comparatively overpopulated areas a distinction was made between "restricted districts," where there was not enough available land for the population density, and "broad districts," villages with a scattered population and plenty of land.

All these features presented the government with acute problems.

These were particularly critical during the reign of the Emperor Hsiao-wen (471–499), an emperor who had boldly taken the decision to sini-cize his people by means of a series of reforms—the adoption of Chi-nese language, dress, customs—even if this meant sacrificing the special privileges hitherto enjoyed by certain sections of the tribesmen to his aim of fusing into one whole a nation that would be Chinese to all intents and purposes (the vast majority of his subjects never having ceased to be Chinese from the ethnical point of view). It is in this con-text that the Emperor's most celebrated reform, the agrarian reform known as "equalization of land" (*chün-t'ien*), must be viewed.

Before examining this land regulation, it may be useful to recall the preamble that the instigator of the reform, the Chinese Li An-shih, placed at the head of his proposals. In his view, the aims of agrarian reform[10] should be to have no land out of cultivation, and no hands left idle; to ensure that the best agricultural land should not be mo-nopolized by the rich; and to ensure that the poor should reach a minimum subsistence level. At present (485–486), he says, a landless peasant can never re-enter into possession of land he has had to leave, because he has long since had to sell all his acres, and the powerful families know how to make use of their influential connections and see to it that their title deeds are regarded as valid. In this way, law-suits drag on and the land remains uncultivated. Li An-shih therefore proposed the equalization of landholdings, to be effected by redistribut-ing the land, taking away from the large landowners all land in excess of the norm. Furthermore, land that was the subject of dispute was to be assigned to the occupier. This latter point seems to refer to the conflict between new occupants and the Chinese gentry who laid claim to former ownership.

The decree of 485, which almost exactly reproduces the text of the memorial I have just been quoting from, and proclaims the priority of the poor in the allocation of land, allows for considerable diver-gences from the principle of "equal landholdings." Every man has the right to a certain amount of land for himself, his wife, his children, his slaves, and his cattle. There are two kinds of tenure: (a) holdings granted with hereditary or perpetual titles of ownership (*yung-yeh*), being land for planting mulberry trees, elms, and fruit trees, known

10. *Wei-shu* 53.4b–5a; naturally, the author does not use a term for "agrarian reform," but speaks of the *ching-t'ien* ("well-field") system.

under the Wei as "mulberry fields" (*sang-t'ien*); (b) holdings granted on a nonpermanent form of tenure, or "personal shares" (*k'ou-fen*), being the arable land known under the Wei as "dew fields" (*lu-t'ien, that is, fields bare of trees and houses*). In principle, every man over 15 and under 70 years of age was to receive 20 *mou* in perpetuity, and 40 *mou* as personal share, women receiving half that amount; masters of male and female slaves were to receive on their account the same amount of arable land as that granted to free men; finally, owners of cattle were to have a supplementary allowance of 30 *mou* a head of cattle up to four head. These amounts, which were of land of the best quality, were usually doubled, and sometimes (in the "broad districts") even tripled. The decree also allows recently established cultivators 0.33 *mou* for each adult and 0.2 *mou* for each slave or child as land for house and garden. The personal share, that is to say the arable land, reverted to the community for redistribution on the death of the tenant or when the tenant reached the age limit (70). Reallocation was carried out during the first month of the year, so that changes in family circumstances (such as death, the legal coming of age of an enrolled member, or the sale or purchase of slaves or oxen) were not acted upon until the first month of the following year.[11]

Careful examination of its clauses shows that, in both its positive aspect of equalization and its negative aspect of restriction, the 485 law was dictated by fiscal considerations. In the first place it can be seen that, in the normal run of events, holdings of average productivity consisted of the ritual amount of 100 *mou* as the minimum required by one adult (the personal share doubled, which is to say 80 *mou,* plus the 20 *mou* of land held in perpetuity). The leveling process can also be seen in the two other clauses of the decree. The land frequently confiscated from deported criminals, and land belonging to families that had died out, became public land once more (*kung-t'ien*); the sale and purchase of land held in perpetuity was prohibited (that there could be none of land allotted as personal shares is self-evident), although it was permissible to buy and sell land held in excess of the legal amount, a provision that considerably weakened the effect of the official allotment scheme. But what allowed the most latitude to the authorities in charge of allotment was the distinction between the "restricted" and the "broad" districts. The decree provided for a propor-

11. *Wei-shu* 110.3a–b (economic treatise).

tional reduction in cases where the official amount was not available. In the villages of dense population it was provided in the first place that there should be no allotment of land held in perpetuity; then, if land was still scarce, the amount allotted to secondary adults in a family that had already had its main allotment was to be reduced.

A still better indication of the fiscal preoccupations of the legislators is supplied by a contemporary law (of 486) which, for the purpose of reorganizing the tax system and preventing tax evasion, established the system of the "three heads" responsible for rural areas. In place of the former tribal organization, the three heads (*san-chang*) of groups of 5, 25, and 50 families, themselves exempt, were made responsible for the regular payment of taxes and for carrying out the corvée. They were probably also given the task of allotting land. At all events, this law was closely connected with the land law.

The land law[12] assumed that a typical household was a family consisting of father and mother, four children under 15, four male slaves employed as agricultural laborers, and four female slaves employed as weavers: a total of 14 persons, and, in addition, 20 oxen. If the amounts allowed to adults, children, slaves, and oxen are added together, the total is 465 *mou,* or about 62½ acres (according to the theoretical figures); and if the usual doubling of the amount of arable land is taken into account, it becomes 112½ acres, which was doubtless regarded as the normal maximum. But it is not these more or less theoretical amounts (which I have mentioned simply to illustrate the elasticity of the "equalization" concept) that provide the chief interest. Much more significant is the fact that the historical sources introduce the legislation of the years 485–486 (concerning the system of responsible heads, the reorganization of taxation, and the land law) with the following remark: "At the beginning of the Wei, most people sought protection. The protected did not do service (corvée), but the rents exacted by the powerful (the large landowners) were double the amount of the government tax."[13]

Finally, let us make a rapid survey of land regulations introduced by the successors of the Wei, particularly the Northern Ch'i, regarding which we have the most information.[14] Disregarding land owned by

12. *Wei-shu,* 110.3a–b and 53.7b–8a.
13. *Wei-shu* 110.3b; cf. *Tzu-chih t'ung-chien* 136 (year 485), 7b.
14. See Balazs, *Le Traité économique du Souei-chou.*

privileged people (nobles and officials), which came under special regulations, and uncultivated land upon which there were no restrictions, the amounts of land allotted to the common people—according to the land law of 564—are shown in the following table.

TABLE I

	Personal Share of Arable Land		*Land Held in Perpetuity*	*Total*	
Man	80	*mou*	20 *mou*	100 *mou*	(about $17\frac{1}{2}$ acres)
Woman	40	"		40 "	
Household					
4 oxen	240	"		240 "	
60 slaves	4,800	"		4,800 "	
Total, max.	5,160	"		5,180 "	(about 645 acres)

Thus the average peasant family had the right to 300 *mou* (about $47\frac{1}{2}$ acres), divided as follows:

Father	100 *mou*
Mother	40 "
Adult son	100 "
Daughter	— "
Other child	— "
1 ox	60 "
	300 "

The figures must have been the same for the northwest part of China, under the Later Chou (557–580).[15]

To what extent were these regulations carried out? It is very difficult to say. I have stressed the normative aspect of all these regulations. In addition, we have seen how much latitude the law allowed to local authorities in the actual distribution of available land. Even if the regulations had been carried out according to the letter of the law, there was no annual reallocation of the whole amount of land in any one district, but only of land that had become available during the course of the year, this being only a minute proportion of the total amount. In practice, there must have been wide variation in the methods of distributing land, each district following traditional local customs that corresponded better with local conditions than the generalized regulations of the imperial decrees.

15. The economic treatise of the *Sui-shu* says (24.4b in *T'u-shu chi-ch'eng* edition) that a household had the right to 140 *mou*, adults to 100 *mou*. See Balazs, *Le Traité économique du Souei-chou*, p. 37.

All land regulations had a triple aim, which in the last analysis was fiscal: to augment the amount of land under cultivation; to prevent the expansion of latifundia and protect the independent peasant; and to distribute land as a primary source of production. The last objective, the attainment of which was inherently improbable, must have had the least practical result, to judge by a contemporary document.[16] This document, the author of which was not a member of official circles, was written about 577, and is fortunately preserved in an encyclopedia. It deplores the fact that land allotted to rich families for their oxen is not given instead to poor families, and speaks of the sale and mortgaging of small peasant landholdings of all categories. The following sentences from this indictment speak for themselves:

> Although some temporary measures have been introduced in our time, they were not enforced for long. There have been lawsuits concerning land which remain unsettled after thirty years, owing to the lack of any system in the distribution of land . . . Since 550 it has begun to be permissible to buy or sell holdings allotted in perpetuity . . . In addition, all the fertile arable land lying along rivers, on slopes, or by the side of lakes, has either been appropriated by the large landowners as payment of debts contracted by the peasant holders, or conceded to them by the authorities in compliance with a request, and not one solitary crumb of it has been acquired by the common people.

16. Balazs, *Le Traité économique du Souei-chou,* appendix 3.

LANDOWNERSHIP

IN CHINA FROM

THE FOURTH TO THE

FOURTEENTH CENTURY

The agrarian problem, of primary importance in any agricultural society, has always been China's major problem. Its solution determined
the well-being of the peasant masses and of the ruling minority, the
fate of governments and, in the last analysis, the rise and fall of dynasties.

The Han (206 B.C.–A.D. 220), who ruled over the whole of China,
never succeeded in restricting the size of large landed estates, and the
attempts of the Chin (265–420), which were interrupted by the barbarian invasions, were not likely to meet with any greater success. The
national catastrophe that divided China into North and South for three
centuries had profound repercussions on agrarian questions. The incessant wars leading up to it resulted in widespread destruction and a
fall in population which, even if it has often been exaggerated, did
nevertheless greatly ease population pressure. Agrarian problems were
somewhat different under the barbarian dynasties of the North from
those in the South, where national dynasties continued to rule. The
South was a vast territory not yet fully colonized, with any amount of
uncultivated land, where small nuclei of Chinese settlers lived amidst
a scattered population of indigenous peoples; whereas in the North the
Yellow River basin had a dense population of Chinese farmers under

This article originally appeared under the title "Le Régime de la propriété
en Chine du IVe au XIVe siècles. État de la question," *Cahiers d'Histoire
Mondiale, I* (1954), 669–78.

the yoke of the barbarian nomads, who were warriors and herdsmen. The contrast between the North and the South was not, of course, so clear cut as this might suggest, but I have purposely emphasized those aspects that help to explain why it was a Northern dynasty that inaugurated the era of agrarian reform.

The celebrated agrarian reform of the Later Wei (the dynasty of the house of T'o-pa, 386–534), known as the "equalization of land," was part of a whole series of reforms carried out by Emperor Hsiaowen (471–499) with the purpose of placing his state upon a definitively Chinese basis. It was proclaimed in 485–486, its main object being to protect the peasants against encroachment by landowners who had begun acquiring large estates as soon as the T'o-pa conquerors had consolidated their position. It was accompanied by a reorganization of the tax system, necessitated by the fiscal requirement of providing a broader basis for taxation. With the assimilation of the tribal aristocracy at the end of the wars of expansion, the old Chinese gentry exerted a growing influence, and the ancient ideal of "equal distribution of land" (*chün-t'ien*) once more came to the fore. The land reform allotted to each family a certain amount of land in perpetuity, and to each individual a quota of arable land that had to be handed back when the owner reached the age limit. The reform was sufficiently flexible to allow for regional variations; it distinguished between owners who did and owners who did not possess cattle; and it granted a special status to the privileged classes (nobles and officials). Because of these variations in its application, the law may be regarded as primarily normative in character. In fact, legislators at the end of the fifth century were not so much haunted by Utopian visions of equality as concerned with counteracting existing inequalities, and the fame acquired by Emperor Hsiao-wen's decree was due less to its intrinsic merits than to the fact that its clauses served as model for all later enactments, the expression "equalization of land" winning a prestige that still clings to it today.

The Ch'i (534–577) and Chou (534–581) dynasties that succeeded the Wei as rulers of the northern part of the still partitioned empire maintained a policy of allotting land, but it is evident from the few surviving contemporary documents that hereditary holdings, supposed to be inalienable, did nevertheless change hands; soon, even land allotted to individuals was sometimes exchanged, mortgaged, or sold.

The amount of land available for allocation was correspondingly diminished by such transactions, a process that probably began even in its earliest stages to undermine the land regulations of the Middle Ages. Before discussing the nature and causes of the process, let us note the significant fact that when the Sui (581–617) came to power, even though the empire was once again unified, an adult peasant had difficulty in obtaining a holding as small as 20 *mou* (about 2½ acres), at least in the "restricted districts," where the available land was inadequate for the density of the population.[1]

Throughout the early part of the T'ang period (618–906), land continued to be distributed much as it had been during the Middle Ages. Every adult peasant received in principle 100 *mou* (about 13½ acres) of land: an "individual portion" (*k'ou-fen*) of 80 *mou*, in which was conceded the right of usufruct, and a "hereditary portion" or a portion held "in perpetuity" (*yung-yeh*) of 20 *mou*, which was planted with mulberries for rearing silkworms, and with fruit trees. A smaller amount was allocated to women, adolescents, widows, the infirm, and the old. The individual holding returned to the community (again in principle) when the holder died or reached the age limit (60 years), and was redistributed to those villagers who had a right to it; the hereditary portion passed on to his family. Each family received an additional portion of one *mou* for house and garden.

As under the Wei and their successors, the statutory allocations could be carried out only where land was plentiful—that is, where there was waste land, in either uncultivated or devastated areas, or in outlying or sparsely populated regions. In each hamlet the village heads annually drew up the "book of contributions," based on the "veracious declarations" of the heads of families, which indicated the amount of land due and the amount actually received. These lists were the basis for tax assessments and census returns. Now the fragments of census returns found at Tun-huang, which bear such eloquent testimony to how much in advance of the times the T'ang administrative practices were, show that the rights to allocation of land were often no more than a legal fiction. Thus we find that, out of the 453 *mou* due to them as individual portions, a family of seven persons was un-

1. See Balazs, *Le Traité économique du Souei-chou.* On medieval agrarian laws, see preceding chapter.

able to obtain more than a fifth of this amount. In another case, two honorary mandarins, who had a nominal right to 6,000 *mou* and an effective right to 153 *mou*, did in fact possess 243 *mou*, of which 14 were land they had bought.[2]

Leaving aside for the moment all the departures from the law made with regard to the appanages of nobles or the status of privileged persons, the normative character of the regulations for the distribution of land at once becomes apparent if we consider them in conjunction with the whole tax system, which was closely bound up with the land laws. T'ang military power was founded upon the peasant soldier; and the upkeep of a peasant militia, combined with a taxation system based on a land tax that consisted of prestations in kind and corvée labor, presupposed a theoretical equality of landownership. The central government, for political, military, and fiscal reasons, was anxious to bring as much land as possible under cultivation, while preventing, as far as possible, the formation of latifundia; for if the experience of the preceding dynasties throughout the Middle Ages was anything to go by, the large landowner was always able to evade his own obligations, and could also prevent rises in taxes paid by the poor peasant, who sought his "protection" by becoming his client, serf, tenant farmer, or agricultural laborer. The T'ang rulers maintained the principle of equal distribution of land primarily in order to protect the independent peasant in the interests of the state, for if the peasant was guaranteed a minimum subsistence level he could pay his taxes and fulfill his military obligations.

Since taxes were divided into nine categories, the supposed equality of rights and obligations was inherently improbable; and it grew more and more illusory as the distribution of wealth, contrary to the intent of the legislation, became increasingly unequal. Because of the special treatment accorded to the mandarins and other privileged people, the restrictive measures of the land regulations fell into desuetude long before the principle of equal distribution was abandoned. It was the very provisions of the law that did most to favor the formation of large landed estates.[3]

2. Henri Maspero, *Les Régimes fonciers en Chine,* pp. 168 ff.; Wang Kuo-wei, *Kuan-t'ang chi-lin* (1923), 21.9a–11a.

3. For agrarian laws under the T'ang, see E. Balazs, *Beiträge zur Wirtschaftsgeschichte der T'ang-Zeit,* and Maspero, *Les Régimes fonciers en Chine,* pp.

Officials in office had the right to "land owned in perpetuity" in amounts varying between 200 and 6,000 *mou* (about 27½ to 835 acres), and to a "service portion" (*chih-fen-t'ien*), namely, land granted to the holder with rights of usufruct, varying in area between 200 and 1,200 *mou* according to the official's rank. In addition, they had rights to a part of the produce of government-owned land (*kung-chieh-t'ien*), reckoned according to an area ranging from 100 to 4,000 *mou* depending upon the importance of the office held. An official was not allowed to cultivate his own land, so he rented it to tenant farmers, or had it cultivated by agricultural laborers. The same applied to monasteries, often richly endowed, for many landholders made a gift of their holdings to the monks, who enjoyed the privilege of being exempt from tax. This method of indirect cultivation of land, obligatory for officials, was soon extended to other kinds of private property, largely because official status remained the chief avenue to the acquisition of landed estates; and mandarin families, retired officials, and descendants (or those who claimed to be descendants) of officials all invested their savings in land. Such privileged people were exempt from tax and from labor service. In 754, on the eve of the rebellion of An Lu-shan, which overthrew the empire and its institutions, there were only 7,662,-800 people liable for tax and corvée, that is to say, 14.5 per cent of a population of 52,880,488.

More important however than the status enjoyed by the privileged were the actual social and economic developments reflected in these significant figures. The situation that was typical of the Middle Ages is repeated: the small peasant, so deep in debt that he cannot meet his obligations, seeks the protection of "the powerful," and becomes the tenant farmer or serf of a large landowner. Whether he does so voluntarily or involuntarily, the cause always lies in the overheavy burden of the government taxes, of official and unofficial corvées, of legal and illegal exactions, of pressure from the tax collector and demands from the usurer. From the end of the seventh century incessant complaints were made that the independent peasant had disappeared. Tax evasion and the flight and vagabondage of peasants who should have supplied corvée labor and taxes had a cumulative effect, because those liable for

---

167 ff. Cf. R. Des Rotours, "Les grands Fonctionnaires des provinces en Chine sous la Dynastie des T'ang," *T'oung Pao, 25* (1928), 272–73, 321–23, and *Traité des fonctionnaires,* 72–74, 126–27.

tax who remained in the villages found their burden augmented by the amounts due from those who had taken flight. The administrative and military machine was burdensome and costly enough in times of peace, but when the government was faced with the necessity for extra expenditure in times of war or rebellion, the situation became critical, and the difficulty of maintaining legal fictions became insurmountable.

This difficulty was particularly acute during the eventful period between the middle and the end of the eighth century. Two contemporary texts will throw more light on the state of affairs than could the subtlest of analyses. A decree of 752 contains the following statement:

> Officials and rich families vie with each other in founding villas [on this term, see below]; they silently compete with each other as to who will swallow up the most land. They have no fear of the regulations; they all pretend to own waste land, and their fields are all cultivated . . . As for lots for distribution, they buy and sell them against the rights of inheritance and against the law; or they change the titles in the registration lists; or they take the lots as pledge for debts. The result is that the common people no longer have any land of their own. Further, they get hold of men from other parts and hire them as agricultural laborers, and take possession of land belonging to local inhabitants.[4]

Forty years later, after the celebrated fiscal reform of 780 had confirmed the breakdown and exposed the fictitious nature of the principle of equality of rights and obligations, a great writer gives the following description of the plight of the tenant farmers:

> When the peasant is ruined, he has to sell his field and his hut. If it happens to be a good year, he may just be able to pay his debts. But no sooner has the harvest been brought in than the grain bins are empty again, and, contract in hand and sack on back, he has to go off and start borrowing again. He has heavier and heavier interest to pay, and soon has not got enough to eat. If there is a famine, he falls into utter ruin. Families disperse, parents separate, they seek to become slaves, and no one will buy them . . . The rich seize several times ten thousand *mou* of land,

4. Maspero, *Les Régimes fonciers en Chine,* p. 175

the poor have no land left, and attach themselves to the big power-ful families and become their private retainers. They borrow seed and food, and lease land as tenants. All the year round they work themselves to death without a day's rest, and when they have paid all their debts they live in constant anxiety whether they will be able to make both ends meet. The large landowners, however, live on the rents from their land, and are trouble-free and carefree. Wealth and poverty are clearly separated; this is why the stage has been reached where rents [on privately owned land] are much higher, and collected in a more pitiless way, than the government tax. In the regions surrounding the capital, each *mou* of land pays at present [i.e. 794] a tax of five *sheng,* while the landowner re-ceives a rent of up to one *shih* [or 100 *sheng*] per *mou:* that is to say, twenty times the amount of the government tax. If one goes down the scale to land of medium category, the rent may be half as much, but is still ten times the amount of the government tax.[5]

The civil war that followed upon the rebellion of An Lu-shan put the finishing touch to the breakdown of the land regulations. From the end of the eighth century we witness the spread of a different system of landownership.

The new system was a manorial system of "villas." It appeared at first sporadically, and was tacitly tolerated. But by the end of T'ang times and throughout the reign of the Sung dynasty (960–1279) it had become the predominant system of landownership.

The first "private villas" were in the nature of a gentleman's country seat with garden, and were known as "separate" land or country (*pie-shu, pie-yeh*). Later these developed into proper farming estates which consisted of the owner's country house, outbuildings called "guest quarters" (*k'o-fang*) for housing the farm hands, and fields and gar-dens (*t'ien-yüan*) worked either by the "guests" or, as they were also called, the "villa families" (*chuang-k'o, chuang-hu*), or possibly by tenant farmers (*tien-k'o, tien-hu*). The owners, usually officials and hence exempt from tax, were often absent, and so employed a bailiff

5. Lu Chih (754–824), "Criticism of the Large Landowners," trans. Balazs, *Le Traité économique du Souei-chou,* pp. 204–05.

(*chuang-li, chien-chuang*) to manage the farming of their estate, at
any rate on the larger estates. The bailiff supervised the farm workers,
and also the tenant farmers if the fields were much dispersed and the
land let out in small parcels. He was in charge of all the farming
operations, of getting in the harvest and selling it, of seeing to the upkeep of the estate, and probably also of recruiting the "people of the
villa" from among those "wandering guests," the strangers in the
village who, not being on the census list and owning no land, had no
tax to pay, no corvée to perform, no military service to fulfill. These
estates bore the name of the owner's family or office, or were sometimes known by the name of the place where the villa was situated.
They were usually regarded as a unit, and passed, along with animals,
equipment, and farm workers, into the hands of the new owner in
the event of sale or inheritance. Many a village or small town of Sung
times had its origin in a villa.

It is difficult to say whether the security gained by the tenant farmers
and agricultural laborers at the expense of their independence was
any real compensation for their lost liberty, or, to put it another way,
whether their lot was any more enviable than that of a peasant vege-
tating on his own little plot of land. The ground rent or farm rent
(*chuang tsu*) paid to the owner was usually 50 per cent of the harvest,
and on an average came to 1.2 *shih* (about 1.7 bushels) of grain per
mou. This was many times more than the government land tax, and
there were other prestations that had to be made. S. Katō, the chief
expert on the manorial system of landownership, admits that the comparative productivity of free and serf labor depended on the treatment
meted out by the public authorities on the one hand and the private
owners on the other; nevertheless, he maintains that the continuous
increase in both population and area cultivated from the tenth century
onward proves the superiority of the system of large estates.[6] This may
be true insofar as the total amount of agricultural production and national revenue was greater in Sung times than in T'ang times. But the
picture changes if one inquires into the price paid for the progress
achieved.

If the testimony of contemporary accounts is to be believed, in Sung

6. Katō Shigeshi, "Organization of the Chuang-yüan or Manors during T'ang
and Sung and Their Development into Communities," *Mélanges Kano* (Kyoto,
1928), pp. 244–45 and 256 ff.

times both serfs and peasants lived under equally appalling conditions. Here is a description of the former by a well known writer of the eleventh century:

Those who till the fields do not own them, and those who own the fields do not till them. . . . The men at work are urged on with whip and cudgel, and the master treats them like slaves. He, on the other hand, sits at his ease and sees that his orders are carried out . . . Of the produce of the fields, he takes half, although there is but one owner and ten laborers. Hence the owner, his half daily accumulating, attains wealth and power, while the laborer, his half merely providing his daily fare, falls into poverty and starvation.[7]

Ssu-ma Kuang (1019–1086), the famous historian and conservative minister, speaks of the peasant in these terms:

He is exposed to periodic catastrophes such as floods, droughts, frost, hail, locusts and other insects. If the harvest happens to be good, public and private debts [to the tax collector and the usurers] use it up between them. Grain and silk have ceased to belong to him before they have even left the threshing floor or been removed from the loom. He eats the husk, wears coarse cloth, and remains neither nourished nor clothed.[8]

Two special categories of large estates, although similar to the private estates, deserve special mention because of their increasing importance during T'ang times: the domains belonging to the church, and those belonging to the state.

The Buddhist monasteries (and to a lesser degree the Taoist temples) played an extremely important economic role by virtue of the prestige, the good organization, and above all the privileged status of the clergy. Their wealth and power increased as private donations and imperial acts of liberality mounted up. Their temples, being protected places, often acted at one and the same time as business agencies for the rich and places of refuge for the poor. Peasants often preferred the

7. Su Hsün (1009–1066), *Chia-yu chi* 5.7b, trans. Maspero, *Les Régimes fonciers en Chine,* p. 178.

8. *Sung-shih* (Official History of the Sung Dynasty) (*T'u-shu chi-ch'eng* edition of 1888) 179.3a–b.

"protection" of the church to that of private landowners, and in order to escape taxation, corvée, and military service, they handed over their plot of land to a monastery and entered its service as tenant farmer, domestic servant, or agricultural laborer. The church, having acquired too much power, drew upon itself the hostility of the state. But several attempts at secularization failed to change the situation. In 845, 4,600 monasteries were destroyed, and 265,000 bonzes and 150,000 slaves were laïcized, that is to say, registered as taxpayers; in 955, another 30,336 monasteries were closed. Yet a century later (in 1034), 90,000 Buddhist and 20,000 Taoist monks are recorded. This gives some indication of how extensive the ecclesiastical domains must have been. Sometimes a contemporary local gazetteer provides more exact information about the comparative amounts of ecclesiastically owned and privately owned land.[9] For instance, in the Southern Sung period (1127–1279), in the regions of Fuchow, Taichow, and Ningpo, the average holding of privately owned land was 14 to 16 *mou* per family, while for the Buddhist clergy it was 50 to 60 *mou* per person!

Government-owned land (*kung-t'ien, ager publicus; kuan-t'ien,* land belonging to the state, or, more precisely, to the public authorities, the officials) had its origin in the military colonies of T'ang times. In these, uncultivated or fallow land, usually in the border regions, was cultivated under state control by soldiers who paid rent as tenant farmers instead of paying the land tax. During the twelfth and thirteenth centuries, and more in the conquered territory in the North than in the South under the Sung, the public domains were continuously augmented by frequent confiscation of ecclesiastical estates. When the state adopted the method of cultivation used on the large private estates, it received more revenue than it would have received through taxation. In Honan, for instance, under the Chin (about 1215), there were 24 million *mou* of state-owned land rented out to tenant farmers who paid an annual rent (*tsu*) per *mou* of 6.5 *sheng,* whereas the land tax was only 5.3 *sheng.*[10]

The agrarian policies of the conquerors from the North—the Ch'i-tan (Liao dynasty, 907–1125), the Ju-chen (Chin dynasty, 1125–1234),

9. See Aoyama Sadao, "Historical Materials of Social and Economical Studies in the Geographical Monographs of the Sung and Yüan periods," *Tōyō Gakuhō,* 25 (1938), 281–97 (in Japanese).

10. *Chin-shih* (Official History of the Chin Dynasty) 47.5a and 6b; cf. Maspero, *Les Régimes fonciers en Chine,* p. 183, where the figures require correcting.

and the Mongols (Yüan dynasty, 1280–1367)—were characterized by the general adoption of the system of large landowners and tenant farmers found under the Sung, while allowing for an increase in the ecclesiastical and state-owned sectors. There were, however, several special factors in the North that affected the position of the privileged, if not the agrarian system as a whole. These were the special privileges of the tribal aristocracy, and, for a certain length of time after conquest, the favors shown to war veterans; the special favors enjoyed by the clergy;[11] the preponderance of slave labor.

A useful statistical document of the year 1183 survives (giving information about the Ju-chen section of the population only; the Chin empire at that time had 45 million inhabitants, 85 per cent Chinese and 15 per cent Ju-chen) that enables us to distinguish between three different kinds of property: peasant holdings, large private estates owned by the high aristocracy, and state domains.[12] The data are presented in the following table.

TABLE 2

	Tribesmen	Aristocracy	Military Colonies
Families	615,624	170	5,585
Individuals	6,158,636	28,790	137,544
Free	4,812,669 (78.2%)	982 (3.4%)	119,462 (86.9%)
Slave	1,345,967 (21.8%)	27,808 (96.6%)	18,081 (13.1%)
Land (*mou*)	169,038,000	368,375	4,602,417
Oxen	1,154,313	912	15,198
Per family			
Land (*mou*)	275	2,166.9	824
Slaves	2.2	163	3.3
Oxen	1.8	5.3	2.7

From this can be seen the relative importance of the role played by slave labor, particularly on the large private estates. The considerable number of slaves owned by commoner Ju-chen families indicates the privileged situation of the tribal section.

11. For the Liao, see Karl A. Wittfogel and Feng Chia-sheng, *History of Chinese Society, Liao (907–1125)* (Philadelphia, 1949); for the Chin, Maspero, *Les Régimes fonciers en Chine,* pp. 181 ff.; for the Mongols, Paul Ratchnevsky, *Un Code des Yuan* (Paris, 1937), pp. lxviii and lxxi ff., and Meng Ssu-ming, *Social Classes in China under the Yüan Dynasty,* Yenching Monograph Series, 16 (Peiping, 1938), pp. 130 ff. (in Chinese).

12. *Chin-shih* 46.4a and 47.10a; Maspero, *Les Régimes fonciers en Chine,* p. 182, mistakenly regards the figures as referring to the whole population, instead of to the tribal section only.

Under the Mongols there was an even more nebulous distinction between slave and free labor than under the preceding dynasties. The North had a greater number of slaves, and the South a greater number of tenant farmers, but their status was more or less identical. The tenant farmers on state domains (*kuan-t'ien*) enjoyed, comparatively speaking, the best conditions. They paid a rent of about 1.5 to 3 bushels (*tou*) of grain per *mou* (the statutory land tax for the free population was only a tenth of this), whereas tenant farmers of private landowners or of officials in their private capacity (on their service land: *chih-t'ien*) paid their masters up to 30 bushels per *mou,* in good years and bad, not to mention prestations and corvée. But the tenant farmers on state domains could easily be reduced to the level of their less fortunate fellows through the exactions of officials, or because the land they cultivated was sublet or given away. Agricultural laborers who tilled the land let out to a wealthy tenant farmer seem to have suffered the hardest treatment of all. They worked under the supervision of bailiffs, and had to conform to the same metayage system as that under the T'ang and the Sung (50 per cent of the harvest). Repeated interventions by the government to reduce tenants' rents on private estates by 20 per cent—the decrees of 1285, 1304, and 1354—only serve to demonstrate how ineffective such measures were.[13]

Both tenant farmers and agricultural laborers, free in theory, were in practice at the mercy of the landowners. They were bought and sold like slaves, their private life was one of total dependence, they were often punished, and they had no rights before the law. A report of 1302 states:

> At present, all those who have become ruined and impoverished, of whom there are very many in Chiang-che (the modern provinces of Kiangsu and Chekiang), go into service under a master and till the land as tenant farmers. Now, in the period before the fall of the Sung dynasty, whether the tenant farmer lived or died was of no more importance to his master than the withering of a blade of grass. Although since the submission of the country [to the Mongols] these former abuses have to some extent been sup-

13. Meng Ssu-ming, *Social Classes in China under the Yüan Dynasty,* pp. 136–41 and 195–206.

pressed, there is still room for measures to prevent the abuse committed by large landowners who kill innocent tenants.[14]

Our present information concerning the changes in landownership in China is still very defective. Only a thorough comparative study of the official histories, of private documents, and of the wealth of epigraphic material that has so far been little used, will enable us to fill in the gaps in our knowledge. It can however be said, in concluding this brief summary, that the research so far undertaken permits us to draw two definite conclusions. The first is that the medieval regulations for a fictitious equal distribution of land lapsed from the middle of the eighth century; the other is that the large estates that predominated from that time on usually took the form of domains let out in lots and cultivated by tenant farmers. This form of landownership and this method of cultivation were determining factors in later developments of landownership until modern times.

14. Ratchnevsky, *Un Code des Yuan,* p. xcvi.

PART II

HISTORY

HISTORY

AS A GUIDE TO

BUREAUCRATIC

PRACTICE

What is the distinctive feature of Chinese historiography as a whole, when compared with that of the West? The answer a Western historian would give, even after thinking about the matter carefully and doing his best to rid himself of prejudice, would be: its stereotype character. And "stereotype" would imply two apparently contradictory things. It would imply that Chinese historiography lacks the personal touch, and that it also lacks the kind of abstract thinking required for reaching a synthesis; for when it deals with people, they appear not as individuals but as representative members of a group in which their individual characteristics are merged; and when it deals with events, it merely states detailed facts, and although the same facts may be constantly repeated, this does not amount to generalization about them.

Of course, it is only to the Western historian that these negative aspects of Chinese historiography would appear as defects. Nevertheless, they require some explanation, and it seems to me that there are three main factors that have prevented the development of our kind of historiography: the habit of cutting history up into dynastic slices; the official status of Chinese historians, who were the salaried dependents of the state; and the traditional art of using quoted passages—a handicap imposed by the nature of the language.

This study first appeared under the title "L'Histoire comme guide de la pratique bureaucratique" in W. G. Beasley and E. G. Pulleyblank, eds., *Historians of China and Japan* (London, 1961), pp. 78–94.

The traditional art of quotation, still in use today, consists in quoting from documents instead of summarizing the contents; and since it would be tedious to quote the whole document, only key passages are given. If a historian wants to convey the essential points of a document, he never does so in his own words, but tries to make a significant selection of extracts from the text, which he cuts up into separate words and phrases, thus reducing it to a small number of characters providing striking or expressive statements. Economy of expression by the use and abuse of documents from which authentic but truncated extracts have been culled can be achieved only because of the nature of the Chinese language (ideogrammatic characters, the minimum role of grammar, the natural conciseness of the written language).[1] Ingenious though the exercise may be, it is also a formidable drawback, for it bogs the mind down in what has already been said and kills all creativeness. It favors the letter at the expense of the spirit, and the traditional texts and textual traditions become a vast sea of paper and ink which drowns all spontaneity. Always to be copying—adroitly, ingeniously, but always copying—eventually stifles the mind.

The art of quotation may depend for its very existence on the nature of the language, but there are other things besides to account for it. The magic of the word (the charge of intrinsic and associated meanings carried by each written character) undoubtedly has a lot to do with it, and the attitude of pious respect toward everything that is written makes texts sacrosanct and has no doubt helped to encourage the habit of leaving them unaltered. In addition, everyone was brought up to recite texts by heart, and had an unconscious and instinctive horror of changing something that had been said once and for all, and well said when it was a question of the classics. And then, the habit was such a convenient one! The historian who indulges in it can wear the borrowed plumes of a great writer, is spared the bother of thinking, and gets the job done more quickly.

The constant use of this traditional approach results in repetitiousness and verbosity. The historian, carried away on the torrent of his sources, is unable to achieve the conciseness of his classical models, and

---

1. For numerous examples of this procedure, see A. Fang, *The Chronicles of the Three Kingdoms* (Cambridge, Mass., 1952); cf. the reproduction of two pages, one of original text and the other of extracts made from it, in *Mitteilungen des Seminars für Orientalische Sprachen, 36* (1933), 2 ff.

with his ingrained habit of reciting and re-citing, he tends to be as prolix as a teller of anecdotes. For example, he will never say "at one and the same time three peasant revolts broke out in the south of the province." He will say: "On the day *d* of the month *m* of the *n*th year of the period *p-r,* Chang X, son of Chang Y, captured the sub-prefect Z," and then the same thing for Li and for Wang. No one will deny the value of information of this kind, but the trouble is that the writer has so many names, dates, and titles to cope with that he usually omits concrete descriptive details. If the document from which he is quoting should happen to give the precise amounts of land owned by the peasant and the subprefect, it would be safe to bet that the figures would be omitted in both cases, the first lot of figures being perhaps replaced by "a small amount" and the second by a cliché such as "his fields stretched out in an endless row." In short, the procedure retains conventional details and sacrifices descriptive ones.

It is often argued that the mania for copying encouraged the use of clichés. That question aside, we should note that the "copyist" side of the Chinese historian's work—the handing down of documents by continuous grinding out of quoted passages—was inseparable from his function as official historiographer.

Each dynasty maintained an office of historiographers, whose first duty was to record the deeds and doings of the emperor and the acts of government, to make daily notes of public events, to collect and preserve reports and documents, and to draw up the archives.[2] They might or might not reach the stage of condensing these materials into a history of the dynasty, for this was a task—primarily one of preservation—that had to be postponed until the history of the preceding dynasty had been completed. And this was likely to be a lengthy undertaking, for to make judgments and draw moral lessons from the past for application to the present (and history, in the Chinese view, would lose all its sense if instruction and guides for action could not be drawn from it) could be done only bit by bit, and required a thorough knowledge of the documents. Hence it was a task for future generations of historians to assume the role of judge and examine the dossier

2. See the articles in Beasley and Pulleyblank, eds., *Historians of China and Japan* (London, 1961) by Yang Lien-sheng, "The Organization of Chinese Official Historiography," and by W. Franke, "The Veritable Records of the Ming Dynasty (1368–1644)."

of an earlier period—a dossier that had been drawn up and handed down for examination, and that contained papers left more or less intact though to some extent processed in the quotation mill. The motto of Confucius himself—"Transmit!"—presided over this activity, and in principle each document had its own intrinsic value as evidence before eternity. To have one's name preserved and to have traces of oneself handed down to posterity in this way assured survival at least as effectively as was possible by means of the ancestral cult. Whence the almost religious character of the duty of recording facts.

While an excessive love of texts has some positive value, yet it can scarcely be denied that the piling up of unadorned facts and retransmitted sources does not exactly help in making either an analysis or a synthesis of the historical process. Certainly the greatest defect of the office of archivists and historiographers was its narrowly dynastic character. Its occupants were paid to glorify their masters and vilify the defunct dynasty, without in the least believing what they wrote, though there were a few honorable exceptions who refused to comply. Writing history according to the "praise and blame" (*pao-pien*) method was comparatively easy when the reign or dynasty in question had been a long one. Distant founders or the mighty who were long since dead could be lauded or criticized without embarrassment. Again, it was accepted as fact that the last emperors of a dynasty are always decadent, and axiomatic that the "mandate of heaven" had had to be taken from them, either by forcing them to abdicate or by an act of revolt, which on such an occasion was to be regarded as an act of supreme loyalty. Not the least of the drawbacks of official historiography was its double standard of measurement according to whether claimants to the throne had been successful or not, according to whether a house was regarded as legitimate or not, or according to how influential the family of such and such a person was. The resulting hopelessly confused logical contradictions always demanded perilous mental acrobatics, in spite of conventions tacitly followed, and acceptance of the slogan "my dynasty (my family) right or wrong."

The worst drawback of all, however, was not the fact that historian-officials were dependents of the reigning power, nor was it their lack of objectivity (indeed they often evinced a degree of objectivity that was remarkable in the circumstances), but the fact that they were unable to escape from the dynastic framework because of the very nature of their office. The necessity for conceiving of history in dynastic terms, for cutting up the flow of events into clearly separated slices, was of poor service to Chinese historians, forcing them to keep their ideas in watertight compartments. Moreover, the cyclic principle and the lack of continuity swayed the balance in favor of amassing disconnected series of isolated facts, and discouraged attempts to find any system of relations or any sequence in these facts. Hence to arrive at any over-all view demanded a very great effort.

It was difficult for Chinese historians to realize that their art was impeded by the obstacles I have just mentioned, and almost impossible for them to rid themselves of these obstacles. For, in the last analysis, the obstacles derived from the very nature of the society in which the historians lived, and from the specific nature of the ruling class that had dominated that society for over 2,000 years, whose mouthpiece they were.

Yet in spite of all this, the narrowness of the dynastic framework was fairly soon realized,[3] and was frequently discussed after Ssu-ma Kuang (1019–86) had had the courage to go beyond these limitations in writing his famous "Complete Mirror for Aiding Government" (*Tzu-chih t'ung-chien*), the first general history of China since the "Historical Memoirs" (*Shih chi*) of Ssu-ma Ch'ien. But neither Ssu-ma Kuang nor, following him, Yüan Shu (1131–1205) succeeded in doing away with the traditional annals form (*pien-nien*). Their respective merits lay elsewhere. The first inaugurated critical historiography,[4] while the second created a method of writing history which endeavored to give a complete account of one particular topic or question, or of a series of events linked by one particular topic (*chi-shih pen-mo*). It is characteristic that this method, which comes nearest to methods adopted in the West, has a hybrid character. Works of the *chi-shih pen-mo* type really do no more than regroup accounts of events according to subject matter, a strictly chronological order being

3. At least it was realized as early as the time of Liu Chih-chi (661–721) and his *Shih-t'ung* (710). On Liu Chih-chi and Ssu-ma Kuang, see E. G. Pulleyblank "Chinese Historical Criticism" in *Historians of China and Japan*.

4. I am thinking in particular of his "Examination of divergences" (*k'ao-i*), an integral part of the *Tzu-chih t'ung-chien*.

maintained within these groups. It is also significant that the progress made in this sphere under the Sung (960–1279) had no sequel.

There was one other way to shake off the fetters of the dynastic framework—namely, to develop to its logical conclusion the procedure (adopted in one section of the official histories) of viewing history from the angle of certain permanent features of an impersonal nature: this section dealt with things, or the structure and composition of things. Ma Tuan-lin (ca. 1250–1325), who was extremely clearheaded, was well aware of the value of this approach. In the preface to his great encyclopedia (ca. 1317), to which I shall come back later, he says: "Since Pan Ku [the author of the History of the Former Han, ca. 90 A.D.] and his successors, since history has been written in dynastic segments, there has been no general principle which would supply an all-round explanation of the whole and a link of continuity." Then, after paying tribute to Ssu-ma Kuang's work, which covers more than 1,300 years of history, he continues: "Nevertheless, this book is detailed in matters of order and disorder, of rise and fall, but summary as regards statutes and institutions . . . Now, in my opinion, order and disorder, rise and fall, are facts that have no continuity and no reciprocal relations (*pu hsiang yin*) . . . [Whereas] statutes and institutions do have continuity and reciprocal relations." [5]

In other words, the history of events, which are subject to chance, is not very interesting. The only history worthy of the name is the history of institutions, in which it is possible to discern a sequence, a continuity, an evolution or development of some kind. It is hardly an exaggeration to put this interpretation upon Ma Tuan-lin's ideas, for in the same preface he quotes a saying of Chiang Yen (444–505): "Nothing in historiography is more difficult than the writing of monographs," and adds: "true enough, for monographs have to do with state documents and cannot be undertaken by anyone who has not familiarized himself with institutions over a long period." [6]

One may well ask how it was that Ma Tuan-lin had arrived at this comparatively modern idea, but a long detour must be made before an answer can be found. His reasoning obviously presupposes a lengthy period of past history, as well as a fund of experience accumulated by generations of historians.

5. *Wen-hsien t'ung-k'ao*, author's preface (*Shih-t'ung* edition, 1935), 3a.
6. Ibid., 3c; cf. Cheng Ch'iao, preface to the *T'ung-chih*, 2a.

THE MONOGRAPHS

Faced with the enormous mass of Chinese historical writing, the first question one must ask—the crucial question for all forms of literature —is this: who was writing for whom? Who is the author and who the readers? The answer here is a clear one: *history was written by officials for officials*. Right up until modern times, this is a rule with few exceptions. Even the independent writers were officials (in retirement), or men who wanted to make an official career; and the entire body of historical writings (including historical anecdotes, genealogies, historical novels, regional histories, and encyclopedias) was addressed to the same public, an educated public consisting of officials and future officials. Hence there was a community of interests between author and readers—an obvious corollary, but one whose importance cannot be sufficiently stressed. There was no problem of communication between those who wrote and those who read, for having undergone a similar education, they had a common framework of reference and shared the same outlook, tastes, functions, and interests.

Now this fact, important enough whatever branch of history was concerned, was particularly significant with respect to the history of political, social, and economic institutions, for these were closely connected with government. Moreover, the fact that both writers and readers of history were officials accounts not only for the general slant of works dealing with institutions, but also for the very selection of subjects treated in them. Certain subjects were an obvious choice in the world of officials, while others were either automatically eliminated as being without interest, or were taboo. The particular preoccupations of each period introduced a certain limited variety,[7] but otherwise, since the tasks of the ruling class never varied, each generation of historians dealt with the same topics, usually under the same traditional headings.

There are four categories in the branch of historiography devoted to institutions. Taking them in the chronological order in which they arose, they are: monographs, encyclopedias, collections of state documents, and local gazetteers. Actually the gazetteers (*fang-chih*) form a

7. Very little existed, in actual fact. An instructive example is the essay on Buddhism and Taoism in the *Wei-shu* (Ch. 114, *shih-lao chih*), which, precisely because it is not a subject normally treated, is not included in my table. Another example is the treatise on tribal organization in the *Liao-shih*.

class apart, and I do not intend to discuss them here. It should, however, be noted that within the local (regional or district) framework of reference, they adhere to the monographic treatment of certain traditional subjects, extending this treatment to new categories of subjects where necessary. They represent what may be regarded as the terminal point of traditional historiography, the point that is a negation of the whole process.

It was Ssu-ma Ch'ien, the father of Chinese historiography, who initiated the quadripartite division of histories into annals (*chi*), biographies (*lieh-chuan*), tables (*piao*), and monographs. To these last he gave the name *shu* (which might be translated as writing, book, document, treatise, or dissertation), a title that was changed, from the *Ch'ien Han shu* onward, to *chih*. This descriptive term, probably of very ancient origin, means in the first place "registry," "description," and, in a more general sense, "history." It was only after Pan Ku's adoption of it that the word became the name of a category.

What subjects were dealt with in the first monographs? They comprise, either in embryonic form or already quite fully elaborated, almost all subjects found, under the same titles, in later monographs. It is not possible here to explore in detail the genesis of each kind of treatise, or to indicate the creative contributions of various historians, for this is a complicated matter that would require a special study. I shall confine myself to making some comments on the order in which the monographs are presented, and to giving an outline of the subjects dealt with and a statistical table showing the arrangement of topics and the order of precedence traditionally ascribed to them.

It can almost certainly be assumed that the ancient manuals of ritual (for the most part preserved in the classical books) served as model for the first monographs. Hence the treatises on the rites (*li*) and on music (*yüeh*) come at the head of the list. One reason for this— possibly an even more cogent reason than the fact that the manuals of ritual were already in existence—is that, because of the growing influence of Confucianism under the Han, questions of ritual were more highly elaborated than any others, and the rules of etiquette (ceremonies and customs) and hierarchical regulations were regarded as of primary importance for maintaining social order. Each time one comes across the title "Rites," he must remember that the character *li* covers three aspects: the religious, the customary, and the social. The religious aspect is dealt with at length in the chapters on the sacrifices and the great state ceremonies (*chiao-ssu* or *chi-ssu*), while to the customary aspect are devoted an ever increasing number of special monographs on court ceremonial practices (*li-i*) and on sumptuary regulations, insignia, and costume (*yü-fu* or *ch'e-fu*).

Second on the list (although the order that had been traditional was later changed),[8] we find subjects that might be described as natural "sciences." These included observations of phenomena in the heavens and on earth, and the regulations arising from them that were indispensable for agriculture, found in the chapters on astronomy (*t'ien-wen*) and on the calendar—calculations concerning the seasons (*lü-li*). The kudos for pioneer work in this field undoubtedly belongs to Ssu-ma Ch'ien, who was not only a court historiographer, but also court astronomer, a profession with a long written tradition. Incidentally, he gave his treatise on astronomy the revealing title of "Heavenly Functionaries." But Pan Ku, who naturally came under the influence of the cosmological speculations of his age, inaugurated the very wide rubric of unusual phenomena (*wu-hsing,* the "five elements") like floods, droughts, and other "signs and omens."

No need to enlarge the scope of science was felt until Sung times, and even then it was only occasionally that a wider field was covered by the second group of treatises; for the lines laid down by tradition were by then too rigid to allow for innovations.[9] "Science," therefore, was very much science in quotation marks, and emphasis must be laid on its prescientific character. It was purely empirical and strongly tinged with superstition.

Since all the monographs—indeed one could say the histories as a whole—were conceived as being guides to administrative practice,[10]

8. The "sciences" take first place in: *Wei-shu, Chin-shu, Chiu Wu-tai shih, Sung-shih, Chin-shih, Yuan-shih, Ming-shih,* and *Ch'ing-shih kao.*

9. Cheng Ch'iao (1104–62) devotes one of his summaries (*lüeh,* another word for *chih,* a term he reserves for the title of his encyclopedia: *T'ung-chih*) to plants and animals, among other innovations such as those on onomastics, linguistics, cartography, and archaeology. It is not that there were no natural sciences at this time, but simply that they were not included in the monographs.

10. We may recall here the final title of Ssu-ma Kuang's work: "Complete Mirror *for Aiding Government.*" The original title was also significant in another way: *T'ung-chih,* "General History," the title Cheng Ch'iao chose for his encyclopedia.

administrative matters proper were bound to occupy a central position. It was essential for the servants of the state to know how it
worked. The elite must be briefed on such matters of vital importance
as the functioning of the apparatus of civil and military administration
and the titles, attributes, and hierarchy of officials (to be found in the
pai-kuan, known as *chih-kuan* from Later Han onwards, and in the
ping, the monographs on the military system dating from T'ang
times); or the avenues to power, the conditions and methods of
selection, appointment, and promotion of officials (*hsüan-chü*), the
educational system, and, from T'ang times onward, the inner workings
of the examination system. All such information was to be found in
the relevant treatises.[11] Then, in order to prepare officials for their
work, it was necessary to provide them with information about geography in general and the territorial administration of the empire
in particular (*ti-li*), and about the hydrographic system and everything to do with transport and canals (*ho-ch'ü*). They also had to
be given some idea of political economy (*shih-huo*) and of legal institutions (*hsing-fa*) so as to become acquainted with the fiscal and
judicial matters that would form part of their daily official duties.
Monographs of this kind, dealing with state institutions, formed the
third group, and it goes without saying that they tended to grow in
number as the area of state control increased and its bureaucratic basis
became consolidated.

Finally, in order to round out the store of information required by
the educated man (and one can never sufficiently stress the fact that
every official was by definition an educated man) a bibliographic
guide was helpfully placed in his hands. The bibliographies (*i-wen*
or *ching-chi*) were simply catalogues of the books in the imperial
library—for a long time the only, and always the biggest, library in
the empire—and were arranged in such a way that all the various
branches of literature could be taken in at a glance. Their compilation
depended on circumstances. It was felt to be particularly suitable at
times when the editor combined the functions of historiographer and
imperial librarian, or when an accumulation of written or printed

11. The introduction to the section on bureaucratic organization (*chih-kuan
lei*) in the Imperial Catalogue of 1782 (*Ssu-k'u ch'üan-shu tsung-mu t'i-yao,* Ch.
79, Commercial Press edition, 2, 1667) says: "Indeed, the establishment of official
functions is the basis of all institutions."

books, following upon a long blank period unfavorable for acquisitions, indicated the advisability of making a new inventory.

Although the monographs are arranged in a different order in each of the official histories, the changes in arrangement do not seem to me haphazard ones. On the contrary, the same general principle seems to be at work both in the grouping of the monographs and in the amount of space devoted to the various topics treated. In all the official histories the monographs are consistently grouped into four categories, a convenient arrangement making it possible to include them all in one table in order to compare the amount of space assigned to each category in the various histories. The percentages are no more than approximate, because they are calculated on the basis of the total number of chapters, not of pages as would be necessary for arriving at a more accurate figure. Even so, the figures give sufficient indication of certain pronounced trends.

Table 3, below, gives first the title and date of completion of each

TABLE 3. *The Monographs in the Official Histories*

Title	Date of Completion	Total Chapters	Total Mons.	Percent Mons.	I	II	III 1	III 2	III 3	III 4	IV
Shih-chi	90 B.C.	130	8	6.5	49.5	30		4.5	17		
Han-shu	A.D. 90	120	18	15	16.5	44		16.5	11	5.5	5.5
Hou-Han-shu*	300	130	30	23	26.6	40	16.6	16.6			
Sung-shu	488	100	30	30	49.9	36.5	6.6	13.3			
Nan-Ch'i shu	537	59	11	19.1	36.4	36.4	9	18.2			
Wei-shu	554	136	20	14.7	25	40	5	15	5	5	
Chin-shu	644	130	20	15.4	30	45	5	10	5	5	
Sui-shu	644	85	30	35.3	33.3	26.6	10	10	3.3	3.3	13.3
Chiu T'ang-shu	945	200	30	15	40	20	10	13.3	6.7	3.3	6.7
Chiu Wu-tai-shih	974	150	12	8	33.3	25	16.6	8.3	8.3	8.3	
T'ang-shu	1060	225	56	25	27	26.6	14.5	14	9	2	7
Sung-shih	1345	496	162	32.7	35.2	22.8	18.5	8	8.6	1.9	5
Liao-shih	1345	115	32	27.8	31.2	9.6	31.2	15.6	6.2	6.2	
Chin-shih	1345	135	39	29	41	10.3	23	10.3	12.8	2.6	
Yüan-shih	1370	210	58	27.6	24.3	17.2	27.6	15.5	8.6	6.8	
Ming-shih	1736	332	75	22.6	29.4	20	16	17.3	8	4	5.3
Ch'ing-shih kao	1927	536	142	26.4	16.9	24.7	18.3	28.2	7	2.1	2.8

Columns I, II, III (1, 2, 3, 4), and IV show the Distribution of Space among Categories (%).

* Date of the monographs.

official history; then its total number of chapters (*chüan*), its total number of monographs, and the percentage of monographs (out of the total number of chapters); finally, the percentage of space devoted to each of the four categories within the monographic section.

The four categories are as follows:

    I. *Rites and customs* (rites, ceremonial; music and liturgy; sacrifices; insignia and costume)

    II. *"Sciences"* (astronomy-astrology; calendar; unusual phenomena, cataclysms)

    III. *Government institutions* (of the centralized state)

        1. Civil and military administration; selection of officials (examination system); education

        2. Administrative geography

        3. Economy (fiscal administration)

        4. Law (judicial administration)

    IV. *Bibliography*

What conclusions can be drawn from these statistics? Let us first of all take note of the factors that qualify the data in the table. Percentages are based on the number of chapters instead of on the number of pages; the marked variation in the number of monographs means that the relations between the established categories vary; the fact that I have deliberately put ceremonial and insignia under "rites" greatly adds to the amount of space devoted to the ritual category and lessens the amount devoted to the institutional category. But in spite of the drawbacks of this rough-and-ready method, certain trends can clearly be distinguished. There is a decrease in the amount of space occupied by the rites (from one-half to about one-third) and by the "sciences" (from two-fifths to one-fifth), and an increase in the amount of space devoted to institutional matters in general (amount doubled) and to officials and geography in particular (amount trebled). In other words, we can observe a displacement of attention from the irrational to the rational, from the ritual to the functional, from the speculative to the factual—in short, emerging secularization, rationalization, bureaucratization. It will be found that these trends are confirmed when we examine the methods used in compiling encyclopedias and collections of state documents.[12]

12. A different view is expressed by J. Gernet, "Economie et action en Chine," *Critique, 103* (Paris, December 1955), p. 1099.

What value do the monographs have? The answer will vary according to whether one adopts the system of ideas of the age that produced them, or judges them from a modern point of view. There is no question of their usefulness for the readers on whose behalf they were conceived: they formed a compendium of the whole body of knowledge available to, and required by, the average scholar-official. By "the whole body of knowledge" is meant a smattering of each branch of knowledge such as might be useful to a gentleman (*chün-tzu*) in the exercise of his profession. And this profession, we must remember, did not require any specialized knowledge or particular technical skills, but only skill in governing. The general instruction provided by the treatises was aimed, and successfully aimed, at producing not scholars but statesmen and administrators who were knowledgeable about all government activities, and who would be useful members of the ruling class.[13]

The aim of providing a general education for political purposes, which underlies all the treatises without exception, also explains their style and method of handling material. The introductions do not deal exhaustively with the topic under consideration, but give a summary of it that is steeped in the orthodox philosophy and ornamented with quotations from the classics. The main body of the monograph is presented in the form of an outline of rules to follow, illustrated by historical examples. The more technical the subject, the more the author has recourse to original sources, incorporating long passages from them in his text, and limiting his own contribution to that of editor. In this capacity, whether he is making cuts here or additions there or doing a certain amount of embellishing, he is simply practicing that art of quotation so dear to the hearts of Chinese compilers which I have already discussed in the introduction to this paper. This amounts to saying that the treatises are a mosaic of texts and extracts of texts, of actual passages from calendars, astronomical and mathematical calculations, manuals of ritual, liturgical texts, laws, and census returns, together with passages from innumerable memorials, requests, and petitions. These last are important not only because they are so numerous, but because their inclusion determined the value of the

13. This was comparable to the European practice whereby young girls of good family used to take singing or piano lessons, not in order to become professional, but to acquire accomplishments that would enhance their value as brides.

monograph both for the past and for the present. It was, of course, an accepted procedure to quote large numbers of requests and memorials to the throne. But since the society that produced them was a highly literate as well as a bureaucratic one, these official pieces—while providing a main source of reference—were also highly prized as examples of literary style.

The procedure of quoting original texts, which is but another aspect of the combination of bureaucracy and literacy, is responsible for the main interest the monographs have for the modern historian. The greater the number of ancient texts contained in the treatises and the smaller the possibility of access to the original documents, the greater is the value of the materials thus put at our disposal. Often the monographs are our only source of information concerning institutions. But in order to extract the full and proper value from this wealth of material, the incomplete quotations must be constantly checked against other contemporary texts (annals and biographies) and, even more important, against such original documents as are preserved elsewhere (archaeological materials, inscriptions, law codes, collections of state documents, complete works of writers, and so on). This method, fruitful even for the Han period and the Six Dynasties, is essential from T'ang times on, when there are ever increasing numbers of independent sources and parallel texts available. It should in addition be noted that sometimes the treatises contain information or documents that have been overlooked by the compilers of other supposedly more complete works—such compilations as the Veritable Records (*shih-lu*) or the collections (*hui-yao*).

Finally, apart from the mode of presentation and the historical perspective of the monographs (both of great interest to the modern historian), the kind of historical material they provide is more convenient to handle than any other, and they should form the basis of all serious work in the near future. That is why time is better spent in getting as much out of them as possible by making special studies, annotated translations of parts or of a whole treatise, or indexes, rather than indulging in pipe dreams of making a complete translation of all twenty-four official histories. It is enough of a dead weight having it all in Chinese.

THE ENCYCLOPEDIAS

There is such an abundance and such a variety of Chinese encyclopedias that some general remarks are called for. Various categories can be distinguished according to the uses for which they were intended. There are general encyclopedias containing classified information on all subjects; lexicons for literary composition; manuals of political science; and lastly, collections of texts serving as a storehouse of learning. The various categories overlap, of course, and all have a common denominator: passion for quotation and classification. The tendency of the Chinese mind to think in categories (it is typical that the encyclopedias should have been known as "books of classification" *lei-shu*), and the habit of compiling works containing extracts of texts, provide an explanation for the uniform method used in this vast branch of literature.[14] But there are special historical reasons for the proliferation of such works from T'ang times (618–906) on.

Introduction of the system of selecting officials by examination created a demand for, and a growing supply of, handy manuals containing information of any kind likely to be useful to competitors. Since candidates had to write essays and poems according to traditional canons of style, the need arose for anthologies providing models for themes, prose style, or versification. And since they also had to know the classics and the histories, particularly those sections relating to questions of government, in the widest sense of the word, and were required to write a piece upon political and administrative problems and be prepared to answer questions on it, it was found desirable to produce manuals containing a summary and a historical outline of all the relevant topics, classified into categories.

To say that the examinations, which were literary and bureaucratic in character, gave a strong impulse to the production of encyclopedias is tantamount to saying that historiography was oriented toward the compilation of compendiums of political economy by the continuous need to produce scholar-officials. Examinations and manuals alike are simply complementary expressions of the bureaucratization of Chinese society.

Both the general and the specialized varieties of encyclopedias covered much the same ground as the monographs in the official histories,

14. See Teng and Biggerstaff, *An Annotated Bibliography of Selected Chinese Reference Works* (Cambridge, Mass., 1950), pp. 106 ff.

since all were designed to supply scholar-officials with a general humanist education and with training in literary and political matters. A glance at the tables of contents in the encyclopedias will bear this out.[15] The growing interest in the political sciences, in economic problems, and in the history of institutions to which they testify, was a true sign of the times. One would have to be blind not to see the connection between the crisis in the middle of the eighth century and the rise of this form of literature.

The first encyclopedia of political economy, now lost, was called "Government Institutions" (*Cheng-tien,* ca. 740, in 35 chapters), and was written by Liu Chih, the son of one of China's greatest historians, Liu Chih-chi (661-721).[16] The date of this work closely coincided with the date of completion of the huge manual of "ritual of the K'ai-yüan period" (*Ta T'ang k'ai-yüan li,* 732, in 150 chapters) and of the T'ang administrative code (*T'ang lü-tien,* 739, in 30 chapters). But to my mind, more important than its date was the influence it had on other works. When Tu Yu (735-812) wrote the first general history of institutions, the famous *T'ung-tien* (801, in 200 chapters), he based it on the *Cheng-tien* as well as borrowing copiously from the other two collections of administrative topics; and the *T'ung-tien* was a model for all future political encyclopedias.[17]

Its characteristic feature is the emphasis placed on the political sci-

15. Ibid., p. 110: "The following is a rough summary of contents . . . of most later encyclopaedias: celestial phenomena, geography, emperors and empresses, human nature and conduct, government, rites, music, law, officialdom, ranks of nobility, military affairs, domestic economy, property, clothing, vehicles, tools, food, utensils, crafts, chess, Taoism, Buddhism, spirits, medicine, and natural history."

16. On Liu Chih, see *Mitteilungen des Seminars für Orientalische Sprachen, 34* (1931), 64-65, and the description of the *T'ung-tien* in the Imperial Catalogue (Ssu-k'u, Ch. 81, 2, 1695).

17. On these works, see R. Des Rotours, *Le Traité des examens* (Paris, 1932), pp. 84, 99, 149. The classification of the political encyclopedias has set a problem for Chinese bibliographers. That of the Imperial Catalogue is logical enough. All the general encyclopedias are classified as *lei-shu* (*Ssu-k'u,* Chs. 135-39), while political encyclopedias such as the *T'ung-tien,* collections of state documents (*hui-yao*), and collections of statutes (*hui-tien*) form a separate class called "books on government" (*cheng-shu,* Chs. 81-84). The *T'ang liu-tien,* however, is regarded as belonging to a third class, that of books on the "administrative system" (*chih-kuan,* Chs. 79-80). Disregarding the various minor anomalies that occur, it must still be admitted that it is a mistake to class together the handbooks and the collections of documents.

ences. It is in nine parts, arranged as follows: (1) political economy (first in order of precedence); (2) examinations; (3) officials; (4) rites; (5) music; (6) army; (7) laws; (8) the administrative geography of China proper; (9) the border regions. Looked at from the angle of the categories of subjects treated in the monographs, it can be seen that Tu Yu has omitted "science" and bibliography (Nos. II and IV of the categories), given priority to government institutions, and assigned rites and customs to a secondary place. This is nothing short of a revolutionary step.

The brief summaries, placed at the head of each section, bear witness to a historically-minded interest in the development of institutions. The method adopted—quotations in chronological order within each section—remains, however, the same as in earlier works. Needless to say, the idea of treating political science in this encyclopedic manner sprang from the brain of a high official: Tu Yu was a government minister.

The *T'ung-tien* created a precedent and Tu Yu's imitators and successors were legion. Among them are three or four names that deserve to be remembered. I have already mentioned Cheng Ch'iao in passing.[18] For the past thirty years it has been customary to sing his praises. Certainly he had an inventive mind; but the original ideas in his work are buried under a mound of platitudes. Li Hsin-ch'uan (1166–1243), who belonged to the famous family of Sung historians renowned for their clarity and meticulously critical spirit, brought out, as companion volume to his well documented chronicle of the early years of Southern Sung,[19] a work with the ponderous title "Various notes on the court and the people since the period Chien-yen" (*Chien-yen i-lai ch'ao-yeh tsa-chi*, 40 chapters, written in 1202 and 1216), which gives a very good picture of Sung institutions. Wang Ying-lin (1223–96), a writer on a variety of subjects and author of the best general encyclopedia, the *Yü-hai* (in 200 chapters), undoubtedly had the most encyclopedic mind of all the compilers. He deserves mention here be-

18. See note 9 above.

19. This was the *Chien-yen-i-lai hsi-nien yao-lu*, a chronicle of 36 years (1127–62) in 200 chapters. It was a sequel to the chronicle of the Northern Sung, *Hsü Tzu-chih t'ung-chien ch'ang-pien* (1174, originally in 1063 chapters) by Li Tao (1114–83), which in turn was a continuation of Ssu-ma Kuang's work. I feel sure that there will be growing appreciation of the works of Li Tao and Li Hsin-ch'uan.

cause his encyclopedia, which became the viaticum of candidates for the highest examination, faithfully mirrors the main interests of the times (see the Table of Encyclopedias).

I have already spoken of Ma Tuan-lin, worthiest follower in the tradition of Tu Yu in the sense that he also was an originator. For his encyclopedia, the *Wen-hsien t'ung-k'ao* (ca. 1317, in 48 chapters) —a vast single-handed effort—is not only a general history (*t'ung*) of institutions, but also a critical examination (*k'ao*) of original documents (*wen*) and of related texts and dissertations (*hsien*). This free debate between different expressions of opinion taken from both earlier and contemporary writers that Ma Tuan-lin introduced into his work makes him a quite exceptional figure. His own voice can always be clearly heard expressing his own opinion with combative warmth, and his prefaces and commentaries abound with perspicacious views and carefully considered judgments.[20]

It would be tedious to enumerate all the works that followed upon the *T'ung-tien*, the *T'ung-chih*, the *Wen-hsien t'ung-k'ao,* and other encyclopedias. There is scarcely any variation in their general methods and layout. Several factors should be mentioned, however, that from Sung times onward acted in favor of the compilation of compendiums. The invention of printing made possible a general diffusion of knowledge hitherto impracticable, and made books available to the most modest of purses. The resultant increase in the number of libraries reinforced the bookish nature of education, fixed the literary character of the examinations, and helped Neo-Confucianism to inculcate the precepts of traditional conservatism and to disseminate respect for antiquity and interest in history. These factors increased the demand for digests and inventories. They also explain the steadily growing importance of bibliography (for instance, the *Yü-hai* and the *Wen-hsien t'ung-k'ao*).

Another point worth mentioning is the decline in private initiative. It became more and more difficult for a man to master all the branches of literature, and the compilation of large encyclopedias passed into the hands of anonymous editors sitting on imperial commissions. Individual efforts were replaced by collective and official enterprises (often at the expense of quality). The same is true of the collections

20. It is surprising that no translations have been made of them, nor any study of Ma Tuan-lin's personal contribution.

of official documents and statutes, the compilation of which required access to the state archives. Table 4 shows the amount of space assigned

TABLE 4. *Encyclopedias (Percentages)*

	T'ung-tien (801)	Wen-hsien t'ung-k'ao (1317)	Yü-hai (1290)	Sung hui-yao (1044–1242)
I. Rites, customs	50.2	25.6	21.5	22.5
II. "Sciences"		9.7	9.5	1
III. Institutions				
1. Administration	22.8	17	36.5	41
2. Geography	16.8	9.7	6	6.5
3. Economy	5.9	8.5	5.5	21.5
4. Law	4.1	3.5	2	4
5. Politics		8.7		3
IV. Bibliography		17.3	19	

to the various categories of subject matter in several encyclopedias and one collection of documents. The categories are the same as those in Table 3 above, except that I have added a subheading for political institutions (such as feudalism and imperial genealogies) that cannot easily be fitted in elsewhere. The calculation of percentages remains approximate (based on the number of chapters) for the *Yü-hai* and the *Sung Hui-yao*, but is more precise for the *T'ung-tien* and the *Wen-hsien t'ung-k'ao* because it is based on the number of pages in the *Shih-t'ung* edition. It will be seen that the relative amount of space devoted to the various topics bears out the statements regarding the trends disclosed by a study of the monographs.

COLLECTIONS OF DOCUMENTS AND STATUTES

When we come to the collections of documents, we leave the domain of historiography proper. The encyclopedias were already somewhat different from the histories, but they presented their material within a historical framework, and a clear distinction must be made between them and works in which original texts are assembled as raw material, linked merely by a system of classification. It is easy to see why the two have sometimes been confused, for both result from the habits of quotation and classification (the same classification being used as in the monographs). It is also true that a few works fall between the two categories (such as the *Ts'e-fu yüan-kuei,* which I nevertheless classify as a collection of documents).

The characteristic features of these compilations are as follows. (1)
They are impersonal works carried out by official commissions, usually
produced by the office of historiographers. (2) They contain nothing
but official documents from the state archives: imperial edicts and
decrees, laws, statutes, regulations, and, above all, reports made by
officials (of all ranks, but mostly high officials). (3) They reproduce
the documents verbatim and, in principle, at full length, without any
trimmings or stylistic changes. This is why these works, although not
in themselves histories, are the best source material for the modern
historian of China. Their documentary value cannot be sufficiently
stressed.

The first "collection of important documents" was the *T'ang hui-yao*
(100 chapters). Three different compilers worked on it at different
times (804, 852, 961), and it was completed by an editor who also
undertook the collection of documents relating to the period of the
Five Dynasties, the *Wu-tai hui-yao* (961, in 30 chapters). The documents, although classified under a number of headings, mostly concern
political, economic, and social institutions. To give but one illustration
of the usefulness of the *T'ang hui-yao,* anyone who wished to study
usury under the T'ang would find all the relevant documents assembled
in one chapter.

The two *hui-yao* mentioned served as models for compilers who
attempted to do the same for dynasties of a much earlier period by
gathering material from ready-made sources like the official histories.[21]
But these imitations, although useful, cannot compare in value with
the models. The reverse is true with the *Sung hui-yao,* a monumental
source work of the highest value that only became available in 1936.
Official commissions under the Sung dynasty had from time to time
made collections of documents, some of which had been used in the
various compilations ordered from the office of historiography and
some of which had not. There were ten of these collections (or it
might be better to say there were ten stages in the process, for some
of the consecutive editions were rearranged) whose titles are known.

21. Cases in point are the *Hsi-Han hui-yao* (1211, 70 chapters), and the *Tung-
Han hui-yao* (1226, 40 chapters), both compiled by the same author under the
Sung. Similar works are the *hui-yao* concerning the Three Kingdoms period and
the Ming, which were not collected together until the end of the nineteenth
century; cf. Teng and Biggerstaff, *An Annotated Bibliography of Selected Chinese Reference Works,* pp. 158 ff.

They were compiled between 1044 and 1242, and the total number of chapters was 2442! Of these, only 460 survive, all relating to the period 960–1224.[22]

After showing the amount of space devoted to institutions in this collection (see Table 4, p. 147), all that need be said further about the *Sung hui-yao* is that it is a mine of information where one can find the original text of most of the documents that are extracted in other sources, as well as many documents not found elsewhere.

Finally, a word should be said about the huge collections of statutes and administrative regulations compiled during the last two dynasties, examples of which are the *Ta-Ming hui-tien* and the *Ta-Ch'ing hui-tien*.[23] These provide an inexhaustible source for the specialist in details of administration, and the general historian will regard them as massive monuments to the bureaucratic state. The many editions, each one larger and more detailed than the last, conjure up a striking picture of the cumbrous, gigantic machinery of government, with its red tape, its hitches, and yet despite these its efficient functioning. No trace of the great steam-roller's many victims is found here. All that can be heard is the muffled sound of a precision machine of improved design, the end product and the perfect expression of those scholar-officials who have dominated—and also written—China's history.

22. See Teng and Biggerstaff, p. 162, and T'ang Chung, *Sung hui-yao yen-chiu* (Shanghai, 1932). Cf. the convenient table of successive stages in Wei Ying-ch'i, *Chung-kuo shih-hsüeh shih* (Shanghai, 1947), pp. 176–77, and the table of contents of the section on economics drawn up by Konuma Tadashi in *Shigaku Zasshi, 48* (1937), 886–901.

23. On these works, see W. Franke, *Preliminary Notes on the Important Literary Sources for the History of the Ming Dynasty* (Chengtu, 1948), p. 42, and J. K. Fairbank, *Ch'ing Documents* (Cambridge, Mass., 1952), *1*, 59–60, 66–71.

TRADITION

AND REVOLUTION

IN CHINA

To attempt, in a few pages, to assess the forces of tradition and revolution in China is a presumptuous task. Indeed, the very idea is quite absurd, for if the task were to be carried out at all adequately, familiarity with various specialized branches of knowledge, a mastery of world history, and a global point of view would be required, since the problems involved have eventuated in the complete recasting of one of the greatest and most ancient of civilizations and in the violent upheaval of a quarter of mankind—an event that will have incalculable consequences and will alter the balance of forces in the world as we know it. I am fully aware how complex the problems are and how ill equipped I am to deal with them, and all I can hope to do is draw attention to one or two aspects of the present extremely serious situation.

I shall begin by telling a story. One evening in A.D. 731 a poor peasant and an old Taoist called Liu met together in an inn on the road to Han-tan. In order to forget how hungry they were, they started to chat while the innkeeper prepared a bowl of gruel for their supper. The peasant spoke of the cares and anxieties of his poverty-stricken life, but when the strange old man offered him a curious porcelain pillow, scarcely had he laid his weary head upon it than he was transported to a wonderful land of dreams, where he possessed a house of his own, was married to a daughter of one of the best families, was rich, looked up to, and respected, and had passed the civil service ex-

The material in this chapter originally appeared as an article, "Tradition et révolution en Chine," *Politique Étrangère, 19,* No. 3 (July 1954), 291–308.

aminations with distinction. After filling a number of important posts, he was appointed governor of the capital, and in this capacity, conquered an army of barbarians. As a reward, the Emperor made him a minister; but a rival faction was successful in its plot to bring about his downfall, and his headlong plunge from the heights of power to the depths of a dungeon nearly ended in his being decapitated. Only at the last minute did he escape execution, and he was then restored to office, and given a title to make up for the injustice he had suffered. His five sons, all high officials, provided him with numerous descendants, and he had come to the point of contemplating retirement, happy to end his days in peace, and looking forward to a final resting place with his ancestors, when he suddenly wakened to find himself once again in the vile inn, where the pot of gruel was still heating on the stove, and the old Taoist was smiling at him and saying, with a wink: "That's the way life passes, quick as a flash."

This little tale, known in Chinese as "The Yellow Millet Dream," dates from the end of the eighth century,[1] and later supplied the theme for a number of stories and plays. The story is remarkable, because it contains the dream of happiness shared by all Chinese, and expresses it with the utmost conciseness yet without leaving out a single salient feature. It is as if the writer had striven to put all his experience into a nutshell, and in doing so he has summarized two thousand years of history, during which the ideal of every Chinese had always been to become an official, this being regarded as the height of power and the sum of happiness. It was, however, an ideal that could be realized only by a tiny minority of the elect, and the fate of the vast majority was to remain a peasant, an artisan, or a merchant—in short, one of the *misera plebs,* the humble subject of those remote, haughty, flesh-and-blood divinities of the terrestrial universe, the officials.

Is it possible that a thousand-year-old tale should contain a valid image of the past and present of a society so vast in extent both in space and in time? Is it no more than a fantasy to imagine that a constant feature can be detected throughout such a broad and lengthy development? The answer to these pertinent questions brings us to the fundamental problems of China's history.

Nothing is further from the truth than the picture of China as a

1. Cf. E. D. Edwards, *Chinese Prose Literature of the T'ang Period* (London, 1938), 2, 212–15.

calm, unchanging, smiling land suddenly transformed into a blazing inferno by the flaming torch of twentieth-century social and nationalist revolutions; of China as an amiable giant, torn from three thousand years of somnolence amidst gracious works of art, sophisticated customs, and mystical wisdom, by the shrill call to arms of foreign emissaries and agitators. For just as false as that other legend of her immobility and impassivity is the extremely tenacious legend of the social harmony that prevailed in the old China. If even a minimum of objectivity is to be attained when speaking of tradition and revolution in China, it will be necessary first to rid ourselves of the tissue of falsehoods arising from gross ignorance and deep-seated prejudice.

Our own eventful eighteenth century formed an idealized picture of the distant Celestial Empire as an idyllic, stable society, well balanced and well content, automatically following a rhythm similar to that of the recurring seasonal cycle. This was a Utopian vision that had more relevance to those who invented it than to the unknown country that served them as model; for, however dear it may be to harassed Westerners in search of ideals, it will not stand up for an instant under serious examination. The smiling landscape is found to be a veil which, when torn asunder, reveals a craggy vista of precipices and extinct volcanoes, reminiscent of the visions with which most Chinese landscape painters were obsessed.

It is, however, by no means true that the idealized picture of the Chinese landscape was pure invention. It had some element of historical truth. The force of inertia in a social mechanism whose driving power is generated by conflicting pulls easily gives the impression of a pre-established harmony. Tensions are kept under control by force, and thus tend to cancel each other out, so that the internal dynamic force appears to be in a state of constant equilibrium.

What were the factors that were responsible for the continuity of one of the most stable social structures ever known? This question must be asked, in view of the fact that the old order lasted for over two thousand years—if the abolition of the ancient form of feudalism by Ch'in Shih-huang in the third century B.C. is taken as the beginning of the period occupied by the Chinese Empire, and the irruption of Western civilization in the nineteenth century as the end. Convenient though it is to make vague generalizations, it would nevertheless be simplifying in the extreme if, by omitting every detail that might detract from such a generalization, one were to say that Chinese society never changed and always followed the same pattern. The only excuse for doing so would be to facilitate comprehension of the essential otherness of the old China, in order to distinguish it both from the West and from the new China. It would be a device for taking a mental stance that might provide a point of departure. Let us, then, adopt such a stance for a moment and attempt to compress China's history in order to bring the main trends into relief.

Traditional China was a well articulated agrarian society divided into four sharply demarcated classes, each following a hereditary occupation. The largest of these classes was the peasantry, forming the wide base of the social pyramid. The peasant's life was hard but honorable, for the well-being of the entire community depended upon his labors. Hence his was regarded as a fundamental occupation, honored in the national pantheon in the form of the Divine Farmer. Once a year, the Emperor dutifully rendered homage to him by personally plowing a symbolic furrow. The peasant family was self-sufficient, for apart from its agricultural tasks, each peasant household did its own spinning, weaving, and all the work required for making its tools and utensils. This self-sufficiency explains why the other two occupations— craftsmanship and commerce—were regarded as much less important. Merchants and craftsmen not only lagged far behind numerically, but their social position was also less respectable. Although they had a far better life than the peasant from every point of view, having less hard work, more wealth, and more chance of rising in the social scale, their prestige was incomparably lower—was, in fact, almost non-existent, because they were looked upon as people who practiced an intermediary occupation. The profession of craftsman, and even more that of merchant, since both were dependent on the fundamental classes, traditionally bore the stigma of being superfluous and parasitical.

When we come to the apex of the pyramid, we find a small social group such as has never been known in the West. We must examine this group more closely, for it is this social stratum—tiny, but of considerable specific gravity—that determines the total structure. By exploring the nature and role of this peculiar class we may find the key that will explain the structure of every regime, past and present, of eternal China.

It was a class that was unproductive, or rather not directly productive, but which possessed aristocratic privileges and, as a rule, landed property. Nevertheless, it was not landownership, nor even heredity, that conferred upon it its special position and its extraordinary power; it was its indispensable social function. The Chinese official—the dominant, central figure of the old regime—may have found a certain amount of material security in having a country estate and useful kinship relations, for this enabled him to be educated, and facilitated his passing the examinations and attaining a career in the service of the state. But it was only by being in office that he was able to make full use of his privileges, for then he no longer had to pay taxes and was exempted from corvée and, usually, from military service. The mere fact of being in office guaranteed to officials and their descendants the monopoly of education that provided such an inestimable source of prestige amidst a sea of illiterates. It also conferred special rights which in practice amounted to complete immunity before the law, in a country where the ordinary subject was deprived of all legal rights and at any moment was in danger of being sentenced to deportation, banishment, or decapitation by judges who could only be described as guardians of the law in the interests of, and by virtue of being, officials— "official" and "magistrate" being synonymous terms. Moreover, official status allowed those who enjoyed it to enrich themselves by every means, legal or illegal, and to acquire new lands, or enlarge the family estate. The combination of these factors enabled the scholar-official gentry to continue in office and perpetuate themselves as the mandarinate that remained the ruling class until recent times.

Thus we find that, at bottom, Chinese society consisted of a vast majority of illiterate workers without legal rights, and a tiny minority of cultivated literati who planned, directed, supervised, and officered the work of others—in short, who assumed all the tasks of organization, coordination, and administration, and without whom the social organism could not have functioned at all. A passage from Mencius, who gave popular form to Confucian thought, will give a much better idea of the general picture than any amount of sociological discussion: "Great men have their proper business, and little men have their proper business . . . Some labor with their minds, and some labor with their strength. Those who labor with their minds govern others; those who labor with their strength are governed by others. Those who are governed by others support them; those who govern others are supported by them." [2]

The necessity for government if the cohesion of a vast agrarian empire was to be maintained explains why the ruling class was able to cling so tenaciously to their prerogatives and last for such an astonishing length of time. Without strict fulfillment of its coordinating function by the mandarinate, China with its mixture of races and tribes would quickly have disintegrated and fallen prey to the dissensions of particularism. It was only constant supervision and harmonization of individual efforts that prevented the system of communications from becoming disorganized, the vital tasks of water conservation and utilization from being neglected, and roads, canals, dikes, and dams from falling into a state of disrepair. The calendar, too, depended upon the mandarinate, and without it all the agricultural tasks of the peasantry would have fallen into indescribable chaos. But the Chinese people had to pay an exorbitant price for all this. The bureaucracy was a hard taskmaster, and its tentacles reached everywhere. It marked every member of society and every sphere of life with its stamp. Nothing escaped it; for the least deviation from prescribed paths had to be kept in check lest it should lead to rebellion, and any dislocation, however slight, was a threat to the system as a whole.

After much hesitation, the officials adopted the Confucianist doctrine as being the ideology that best expressed their way of life, since, in spite of preaching respect for others, justice, and reciprocity, these virtues were reserved for relations between educated people, whereas for the ordinary subject, the cardinal virtue was absolute obedience. Its unalterable aim was to maintain the status quo of the social hierarchy. Ancestor worship, divested of its earlier religious character, geared the social mechanism, regulating every detail of social relations. Respectfulness, humility, deference, docility, complete submission and subordination to elders and betters—these were the dominant features of the Confucian ethic that helped to cement the hierarchy, creating a patriarchal, paternalistic world in which gradations of rank, from the sovereign downward, were marked by the reciprocal relations of favor and obligation, and individual rights, initiative, and liberty were entirely lacking. In the Confucian view, the family was the main pillar

2. *Mencius* III A, 4.

of society. Not only was it the smallest social unit in which relations of dominance-subservience obtained (although here somewhat tempered by kinship solidarity), and hence regarded as the very embodiment of the moral code, but it was also, on the administrative level, the vector of the system of collective responsibility, for the whole family had to expiate for a crime committed by one of its members.

The picture I have drawn of Chinese society as it used to be is, of course, incomplete and one-sided—if you like, tendentious. I have deliberately omitted the brighter side, left out all the nuances, passed over the humor, the easy-goingness, and all the other pleasant characteristics that graced Chinese life. For it is my firm conviction that they flourished not because conditions were favorable, but as by-products of a harsh reality that would have justified a more tragic outlook on life.

It is inconceivable that a society as regimented as this one was, with every member obliged to conform from the cradle to the grave, should have remained permanently content to follow the prescribed patterns of behavior. Indeed even its privileged members sometimes suffered under the pressures brought to bear by its institutions, for although as a class they were both masters and the main prop and stay of the state, as individuals they were its humble servants and often its victims.

State ceremony and the rules of propriety were as far as Confucianism went in the direction of religious feeling (it is indeed doubtful if anything so sober and so lacking in feeling as Confucianism can be described as a religion at all), which was scarcely enough to satisfy the human desire to transcend circumstances and move toward a worthier destiny. This must be borne in mind when we try to understand why Taoism (the other basic attitude open to the Chinese that ran parallel with Confucianism) maintained a permanent appeal. It was the philosophy adopted both by peasant revolts and by frustrated individuals. Its basic ideas were in direct contrast to those of Confucianism: spontaneity, nonintervention, nonaction (*wu-wei*), and a return to nature, as against duty to the state, regulations, propriety, and moral obligations; nature as the absolute, spontaneous and untrammeled, the primal autonomous and self-sufficient community, characterized by metaphysics, mysticism, and meditation, as against the works of man, represented by civilization, order, the state, rationalism.

It was, however, not only on the plane of ideas that the subjects of the state withheld their obedience. They rebelled in practice whenever the officials exerted too much pressure on them, and the moment when this would inevitably occur was determined by time and patience, or, to apply the measurement used by Cocteau in his definition of courage, by knowing when one has reached the end of one's tether. China's history is one long chain of peasant revolts, and it is not surprising to find that their ideology always had pronounced Taoist features. Every time the amount of land under cultivation was reduced through floods, drought, or overpopulation, and the fiscal screw was tightened; every time the usurers began foreclosing on mortgaged plots of land, and exploitation and exactions reached the point where they could no longer be endured—a leader arose and gathered round him bands of peasants in revolt. The smouldering resentment of the ragged, ill-organized masses then burst forth, and, like some elemental force, they hurled themselves upon the country, charging blindly against each and every representative of authority. The devastation and de-population brought about by civil war then frightened the forces of law and order into declaring a remission of taxes and a redistribution of land, which restored some measure of equilibrium, even if it was only a compromise that would last until the next revolt broke out.

After the Northern Sung dynasty had fallen, waves of fugitives poured southward with the cavalry of the Ju-chen barbarians at their heels, and the country was once again sufficiently out of control to provide opportunity for a peasant rising. The central government was powerless to prevent bands of peasants from roaming the country, and local authorities did not know whose orders to obey—the usual state of affairs during times of disorder. A peasant leader then arose in Honan and proclaimed himself king. A contemporary account tells us:

> For twenty years he has been leading the masses astray with his heresies. He calls himself the "Great Celestial Saint," and claims that his spiritual powers enable him to get into communication with Heaven and to heal the sick. But in secret he says to his followers: "The law that divides commoners from nobles, that separates the poor from the rich, is not a good law. The law which I shall introduce will confer equality of rank on commoners and nobles, and level degrees of poverty and wealth." It is with words such as these that he rouses the common people. So that within an area of several hundred leagues, the common people in their

ignorance follow him, keep him supplied, and call him Revered Father.[3]

The account then describes how the partisans of the thaumaturge, originally recruited from the regular peasant militia, turned their arms against the authorities and set fire to government offices, monasteries, towns, and landowners' houses, and massacred everyone who might—however vaguely—be regarded as an official.

There are a number of other examples I could have chosen instead, but this one gives a good enough idea of the usual stages peasant revolts went through and of how their social demands were expressed in religious terms. Nor was the name this rebel gave to his ephemeral kingdom a fortuitous one. He called himself the King of Ch'u, because the area over which he reigned had once formed part of the powerful ancient kingdom of Ch'u. Ancient names, hallowed by history, were often revived in China. It is a familiar feature of Western history as well to disguise something new in historical costume, but in China the habit went much further, and might almost be described as something organic—a visceral reflex, as it were. Utopias were always placed in the distant past, in the earliest times of the Sage Kings. This golden age provided a meeting place for the Confucianist reformer, who had to clothe his proposals in historical precedents in order to get them accepted, and the Taoist dreamer, who longed for the lost paradise—the primitive stateless community, where there were neither lord nor servants, and everyone lived in peace and contentment. This archaistic tendency set severe limitations on peasant movements. The eyes of the rebels were always firmly fixed on the past, and no new horizons opened up for them. No one could escape these limitations. The unprecedented filled the guardians of tradition with terror, but even those who wanted to make changes were unable to go beyond the sacred ideas of the past. "He who succeeds becomes Emperor, he who fails is a bandit" is a Chinese proverb that expresses this attitude with all the ripe wisdom of practical experience.

In point of fact, few of the innumerable bandits in Chinese history succeeded in founding a dynasty, although most dynasties fell as a result of agrarian crises. For instance—to name the most important—

3. *Chien-yen i-lai hsi-nien yao-lu* (Chronicle of the Period 1127–1162) 31.613 (*Ts'ung-shu chi-ch'eng* edition).

the Former Han dynasty perished in the anarchy created by the rebels who called themselves the "Red Eyebrows," and the Later Han went down in one of the bloodiest of all peasant wars, the revolt of the "Yellow Turbans," under its banner of the "Great Peace" (*T'ai-p'ing*). The T'ang fell under the blows of a rebel who combined in his own person all varieties of the humiliated and dispossessed: he was the son of a peasant, a candidate who had failed the examinations, and a smuggler. The Mongol conquerors were expelled by a movement that had at first a social and later a national character; its leader founded the Ming dynasty, which, in turn, was removed by a peasant rising, whereupon the vacant throne was occupied by the Manchu conquerors. This last dynasty never recovered from the blow dealt it by the T'ai-p'ing, those peasants who rose, inspired by a chiliastic faith half Taoist and half Christian, who ruled over the greater part of China for about a decade, and whose exploits have now become a favorite subject for study in present-day China.

Thus we find that, until recent times, there has always been a combination of traditional and revolutionary elements at those turning points in Chinese history when a latent agrarian crisis accelerated events and all problems had to be solved at once within a few feverish years or decades. Nevertheless, it was seldom the same person who stayed the course from the fall of the old regime to the establishment of a new one. Rarely were the grave diggers of a decadent dynasty able to fulfill their promise of founding the next. Leaders falling by the wayside and upstarts who know how to profit from the occasion are phenomena typical of times of upheaval found in our own history as well as in China's, with this difference only: in China, whether a new dynasty was founded by an adventurer or carried to victory by the peasants, sooner or later it was taken over by the literati, the traditional intelligentsia, who, being both staunchly conservative and experienced as administrators, always brought the revolutionary forces under control, canalized them, tamed them, and rendered them harmless. Whence the awkward paradox that while revolutionary features marked the founding of every new dynasty (and heaven knows the Confucian high priests of history had plenty of difficulty in justifying the unforeseen leaps taken by their god, and in endeavoring to interpret disobedience—*post festum* and because of exceptional circumstances—as the most sacred of duties), yet the founding of a new dynasty after the fall of an old one, its rise to prosperity and subsequent gradual deterioration, was a pattern that repeated itself so monotonously that it became like a series of ritual gestures where no deviation is permissible, or the movements of a ballet in which the choreography is always the same. I would even go so far as to say (with certain reservations to which I shall return presently), that in the last of the great and victorious peasant wars—the one that led to the founding of the empire of Mao Tse-tung—historical parallels have, either consciously or unconsciously, played as important a part as the new foreign doctrines, although in very different circumstances. The peasant's son, poor and unknown, who finally succeeds after many misfortunes in overcoming his rivals and, despite the wiles of his enemies, mounts the imperial throne in the role of magnanimous conqueror, and reigns as the wise Son of Heaven, surrounded by a circle of counselor-companions—this is an epic conception of the founders of dynasties that has entered so deeply into Chinese consciousness, thanks to popular historical novels, that striking parallels must constantly emerge. Even the most Westernized of intellectuals must find it difficult to resist the temptation of drawing them.

So far I have spoken only of the traditional forms of revolution, or rather simply of tradition, emphasizing the features common to the past and the present. Now it is time to turn our attention to the uprooting of traditions that has taken place—the revolutionary transformation of all accepted values that has been mainly brought about by a truly revolutionary revolution. I assume there is no need for me to repeat facts that are known to everybody, nor any need to rehash events which, in many different ways, all illustrate the same basic theme: the irruption of the West in China. (And an irruption it certainly was: the abrupt entry of Western technology, economic institutions, habits of thought, and ways of feeling, into a pre-industrial subcontinent.) For, although it is not yet ended, the world conflict that arose from the dynamic expansion of Western capitalism confronted with primitive communities or with societies that were perhaps dormant or at all events static, is now a matter for school textbooks. The steam engine and Gauguin, impersonal technology as against the Russian or the Chinese or the Negro soul (one or another to be chosen at random), material well-being as against spiritual joys, unrelenting progress coupled with hygiene on the one hand and passive contemplation accompanied by vermin on the other—such were the facile terms in which awareness of the immense and potentially tragic conflict was expressed.

The stages in the Chinese version of the conflict can be labeled as follows: the Opium War, the imposed treaties, the extortion of foreign concessions, consular jurisdiction, the Sino-Japanese War, the Boxer Rising, the Republic, Sun Yat-sen, Chiang Kai-shek, the Manchurian incident and the Japanese invasion, the Soviets and Mao Tse-tung. What lies concealed beneath these headlines of recent history? What is the underlying trend of events that began with the violent opening of China's ports, and has finally made this most civilized of great nations close her frontiers against the West and remain entrenched behind them? To answer these questions briefly, it is necessary to oversimplify and do violence to historical facts.

The inborn xenophobia of the Chinese marked their first reaction to the interminable series of humiliations inflicted upon them. But since they were the inheritors of a civilization that had either repulsed or else swallowed and digested so many different barbarians, they felt they could afford to greet such happenings with a smile that was haughty rather than indignant. But these new barbarians from the West were made of different stuff from the others. Not only did they refuse to become assimilated, but they continued to carve out for themselves larger and larger slices of Chinese territory. What was worse, the competition among them, which prevented any one of the great powers from swallowing the whole indigestible morsel, did not stop them from combining to nibble away the very substance of China, changing the lives and innermost being of the Chinese people with their corrosive, disintegrating influence.

I should like to mention here, parenthetically, that the powers of resistance of one of the higher civilizations, when confronted with an industrialized civilization, are quite different from those of a primitive people. The higher civilization is at once more resistant and more easily contaminated: more resistant, because it has something solid for the corrosive forces to work upon; more easily contaminated, because it has more sensitive organs whose receptivity favors the possibility of contamination. The relations between China and the West might be compared with those of Russia and the West, if only one century instead of two lay between Peter the Great and Stalin. In any case, it was the Russians themselves who asked the foreigners for help, and they always remained their own masters, whereas China became a mere chattel in the hands of foreigners who came uninvited and arrogated to themselves extraterritorial rights within the country. While we are on the subject of the instructive comparison between Russia and China, it should also be mentioned that, apart from the forced industrialization of the last twenty years, the Europeanization of Russia has been a slow process similar to the blending of liquids, whereas the bombardment of China's atoms by Western influences is like nothing so much as the nuclear disintegration that takes place in a giant cyclotron.

The second phase of China's conflict with the West was resignation in face of an unavoidable evil, and might be given the descriptive label "learning from the barbarians." After the bitter experience of the 1895 war with Japan, the Chinese were anxious to imitate the barbarians, to see through their tricks and adopt their techniques and their technology without however in any way damaging their own institutions. This was a period of investigation and of travels abroad for study purposes, of tentative reforms and of struggles against the ultraconservatives; it gave rise to some remarkable men who, with touching naiveté, attempted to grapple with the insoluble problem of trying to borrow from the West what was technologically useful, and combine it with all that was of permanent value in the East. The problem was insoluble because it very soon appeared that what was thought to be of value was perhaps not so sound as it seemed, and that it was clearly impossible to attach new hands and feet to the old torso without also renewing the head. Every attempt at adaptation failed. On the one hand, the dynasty, with senile obstinacy, refused to countenance even the most inoffensive of reforms. On the other, technology proved to have a voracious appetite, and engulfed a far wider sphere than had been expected. It was simply not possible to go on studying the classics, observing the rules of propriety, respecting one's ancestors, and condemning all specialists, and at the same time be busily occupied in constructing railways. The old civilization was totally unable to withstand the shock of the introduction of a textile industry, of artillery, and of blast furnaces, once the decision had been taken no longer merely to endure them as evils introduced by hostile foreigners, but to make active use of them and integrate them into the life of the country.

From this time on, traditional ways were perceptibly in retreat. Within the space of two generations, from the middle of the nineteenth century to the beginning of the twentieth, the West, on its irresistible march, captured one stronghold after the other of China's three-thousand-year-old culture. Once the field of technology had been conquered, those of economics, science, the arts, and even the old conception of the universe all had to capitulate. As retreat followed upon retreat, all hope of holding the lines of defense had to be abandoned. The two generations concerned were mercilessly pulverized in the process. Only future historians will be able to do justice to the tragic greatness of the men of these condemned generations. Their tragedy consisted in the rapidity with which the efforts of Chinese progressives became outdated. It took more courage to declare oneself a constitutional monarchist in 1890 than to become a republican in 1910, or confess to being a Communist in 1930.

The hard apprenticeship, which had been nearly completed toward the end of World War I and the beginning of the Russian Revolution, can thus be seen to have brought about profound changes. The degree of change varied considerably according to whether the situation was viewed from Shanghai or from a village in the depths of the country. But since the history of the countryside has so far been little studied, while that of the treaty ports will continue to occupy historians for some time to come, it is from this angle that I shall attempt to show how values were transformed and how tradition and revolution exercised an alternating influence on events.

The greatest upheaval of all must undoubtedly have been the painful collapse of the old world view, the conception of the Chinese Empire as the universe, the *t'ien-hsia,* with China at its center, and all other peoples grouped around it ranked according to their degree of participation in the one civilization worthy of the name—the Chinese civilization. Now, China had become merely one among many other countries, and could not even claim a place in the concert of nations, having been reduced to helplessness—a mere bone of contention between the great powers. The shift in the center of gravity and the changed view of the world (the Chinese world having shrunk, while the world of the West had been enlarged) had one inevitable consequence: the birth of nationalism. The Chinese had formerly had a certain pride in their civilization, a firm awareness of its exclusive value, and a feeling of vocation for governing the world, which after all was simply the *t'ien-hsia*. But a prickly, touchy, demanding kind of nationalism, all the more virulent because of the mortal wound to their former feeling of superiority, was something entirely new to them.

After many avenues had been explored, nationalism finally found expression in the noisy demonstrations of the student movement. The universities and colleges became the hotbed of feverish agitation, reminiscent of the patriotic student movement of the "people's springtime" in 1848. The younger generation was strongly opposed to all that was reactionary, and wanted to emancipate everything—in the first place, themselves, from the tutelage of their fathers, and secondly, the Chinese language, from the shackles of the literary style (which played a role similar to that of our dead languages), so that they could express their ideas in journals and reviews in a way that everyone could understand, thus enabling them to speak to the people. But there could be no real freedom from the yoke of tradition until family ties were loosened and the emancipation of women was achieved, just as the national shame of the iniquitous unequal treaties could not be wiped out until riddance was made of the puppets of the foreign powers, those shady war lords, governors, and generals whose names are now forgotten but who, in the years around 1920, exercised a wide influence and were responsible for much bloodshed. Thus it was through the linguistic reform of 1917 and the famous May Fourth movement of 1919—a protest from the universities against the megalomaniac demands of Japan—that nationalism was brought to birth. Soon a wave of nationalism was to flood the whole of China.

Before long, however, it was realized that national resurgence could not take place without the accompaniment of a social revolution—another feature reminiscent of Europe in 1848. Hence the fanatical champions of independence for China became eager apostles of social emancipation. At the beginning of the eventful twenties, scholars were turning from translating *Werther,* Dickens, and John Stuart Mill to translating Maupassant, Chekhov, and Karl Marx, and education by missionaries was being replaced by university lectures given by men of the caliber of Bertrand Russell. Anticolonialist America, the champion of the "open-door" policy, was still regarded as the disinterested friend of China, although the recent October Revolution in the great neighboring country was already arousing eager echoes. This was the time when the Chinese Communist Party came into being. It was founded by a professor, and its first members were students.

That a revolution that would be both nationalist and social was next on the program was a belief shared by all progressives, whether they belonged to the Nationalist People's Party (the Kuomintang) or were members of the tiny Communist Party. They were also unanimous in proclaiming the slogan that united everyone without exception: the struggle against imperialism! The only thing the intellectuals disagreed about was who was to carry out and direct the revolution. At first the question was a purely academic one, for on both sides power was still in the hands of the intelligentsia, and relations between the Kuomintang and the Communists were still those of friendly collaboration. But the revolution of 1926–27 was a prompt catalyst of events. A military march was planned, such as had never before been seen, and was expected to conquer the whole country. But General Chiang Kai-shek, who led the northern military expedition, turned against his Communist companions-in-arms, whom he succeeded in duping, and hoped to exterminate. The massacre of the Communists fixed the fronts for the next twenty years. The dividing line ran through the little word "and," the copulative conjunction linking the nationalist *and* social revolution. The Kuomintang more and more confined itself to being the mouthpiece of the nationalist cause, and proved to be not only set upon maintaining the established order, but, because of its niggardliness, certain to preserve all the traditional ills of poverty. The nationalist bourgeoisie of the Kuomintang equaled the officials of the Celestial Empire in corruption, nepotism, bureaucracy, and inefficiency, and it was only to be expected that this national-socialist police state should finally restore Confucianism and inscribe the ancient Confucian virtues upon its flag. Those who resent this realistic assessment as being too harsh, or who do not find it convenient to subscribe to it, place themselves in a position from which it is impossible to form a cool, dispassionate judgment about either the present or the future.

On the other side of the dividing line, the Communist Party—decimated, proscribed, and forced to go underground—grew rapidly. Although, in spite of many internal crises, it continued to preach the social and nationalist revolution, it adapted its doctrines to the necessities of the situation and changed from being a party representing the interests of a minute urban proletariat (without, however, renouncing any of its Marxist jargon) into a body of political and military cadres for organizing a mass movement of peasants. The striking thing about the civil war that shook China during the years between 1930 and 1950 was that it invariably recalls the peasant risings of former days, in spite of the modern techniques used. The red partisans were described as bandits, whose extermination was triumphantly announced by the government month after month for years on end. These same bandits, while ceaselessly harassing their enemies (whom of course they also described as bandits) with guerrilla warfare, also found time to set up a countergovernment in the territories they had gradually succeeded in occupying, known as Soviet districts, and to organize an army and stubbornly prepare themselves for the final struggle. But of course when drawing these historical parallels, we must not forget the modern context, which was something quite new. The pious legend—half believed in, half invented according to the ends in view—which represents Mao Tse-tung in the reassuring guise of an ordinary agrarian reformer, does not become true by constant repetition on the part of people anxious to be persuaded of its truth.

Indeed, all the analogies I have suggested are no more than approximations, and can be justified only as part of an attempt to understand the new complex situation by bringing out certain constant factors. For example, if one were to compare the Chinese revolution with the French revolution, the comparison—which is quite a valid one—is permissible only if one bears in mind the fact that making a revolution in a Europe of absolutism and stagecoaches is one thing, and making the same sort of revolution in mid-twentieth century, in a highly industrialized world of interdependence and atomic bombs, is quite another. Those who wish to see Mao as nothing more than an agrarian reformer must ask themselves whether it is still possible to carry through a simple agrarian reform nowadays without setting off a whole chain of reactions. Not a single one of the measures introduced by the present rulers of China can be regarded in the abstract, leaving other things out of consideration. The same reservations must be made when comparing the aims, methods, stages, and tempo of the Russian revolution with those of the Chinese revolution. Any sociologically minded observer would at once be struck by certain obvious features they have in common. Both revolutions took place in a pre-industrial, underdeveloped country, where existing conditions were the outcome of a long period of autocracy and absolutism. In both countries the overwhelming majority of the inhabitants were peasants. Consequently, the bourgeoisie was relatively unimportant. All the more important, therefore, was the role of the intelligentsia, consisting of the sons of officials, peasants, and petty bourgeois. In addition, both revolutions were made by peasants and soldiers, but directed, in the name of the working class, by the intelligentsia, and it is they who were the first to derive palpable benefits.

These analogies must be borne in mind when we come to consider the sequence of events, the results achieved, and the future prospects of the immense experiment taking place in China today. That this again has salient features in common with the Russian experiment is natural only if account is taken of the direct influence Russia had on the Chinese revolution. On the other hand, many elements in the Russian situation are understandable only if we remember the Asiatic factors common to the development of both countries.

It is unnecessary to linger over the seizure of power by the Chinese Communists, for it is still fresh in everyone's memory, and all witnesses of the great event are in agreement as to its explanation. Their unanimous verdict is simply that Mao owed his triumph to the shortcomings of Chiang Kai-shek. The regime of the Kuomintang, which collapsed like a house of cards, was marked by its inefficiency and muddle, by nepotism and greed, corruption and disorganization; the trumps held by the army known as the "liberation" army were its efficient organization, its discipline, the incorruptibility of its soldiers and staff, and their devotion to the tenets of the movement. How long these virtues will last remains to be seen, but no one can deny that they existed, nor that they were of decisive importance at the crucial moment; and that is what counted. No doubts can any longer be held that the government of the Generalissimo, who was at one time acclaimed as the nation's savior, gradually and irretrievably alienated nearly the whole of the Chinese people. Everything it did seemed designed to lose the support of liberal intellectuals, which would have been such an asset, and to push them into the arms of the Communists. Students deprived of bread, liberty, and hope, professors who had been hauled over the coals for their opinions, starving writers, artists, and teachers, salaried workers without salaries, employees without employment, peasants who bore the brunt of the accumulation of follies and muddles perpetrated by the regime—all nursed a unanimous hatred for the chicaneries of the speculators and the activities of the police, and fell an easy prey to the cunningly modulated song of the Communist sirens. The dust of which Secretary of State Acheson spoke is still far from being laid.

A vast country, backward and poverty-stricken, and in addition ravaged and disorganized by a long civil war; a population of nearly 500 million, 90 per cent of whom are peasants; a working class that is half peasant, scarcely literate, and numerically insignificant; an infinitesimal number of skilled workers, engineers, and technicians; finally, a complete lack of capital and little hope of getting any from abroad—these are the main factors in the present situation. To state them is alone enough to reduce any talk of socialism to its proper value as mere verbiage. But socialism is referred to only in the future tense or the conditional mood; even more than in Russia, it is a far-off paradise. Present reality, since it must be given a name, is called state capitalism. With more of state than of capitalism, the system is marked by the pronounced disadvantages of all state capitalisms: shortages, restraints, and bureaucracy. There is a shortage of everything, of the means of production as much as of articles of consumption. When things are in short supply, regulated distribution becomes a necessity, as even the wealthiest nations discovered during the last war. And when food rationing is unavoidable and a system of priorities has to be operated, in which appropriate shares must be distributed as equitably as possible according to need, bureaucracy is inescapable. The more poverty there is, the more regulations, restraints, and bureaucracy there are. Is this not reminiscent of the former institutions of imperial China?

The economic activities of the present regime consist mainly in grandiose public works on the one hand, and on the other, in state monopolies of all kinds—neither of which, it must be admitted, are exactly a novelty for China. One of the first state farms, now known as "sovkhoz," was established by soldiers on uncultivated land in Turkestan; does this not recall the agricultural military colonies of long-forgotten dynasties? Public works on a gigantic scale, carried out by a servile labor force, have existed in China from time immemorial; nor are state monopolies something new, any more than are their consequences—measures carried through by force, direction of the economy, compulsory saving, red tape, falsified reports, misappropriation of funds, maladministration, top-heavy overorganization, and the inevitable piling up of incidental expenses.

The complete regimentation of public and private life has a long tradition behind it. State officials and party cadres are as privileged today as the mandarins used to be, and prescribe in as much detail the duties of the ordinary mortal, who has not become any more precious in their eyes. The fountain pen is used instead of the writing brush and the Communists have replaced the Confucianists as the official party, but at bottom it is the same intelligentsia that assumes the indispensable function of direction, command, and administration. Even their mentality often recalls that of the autocratic and authoritarian tyrants of former days.

The stifling of all criticism, the muzzling of opinion, the punishment of the slightest sign of opposition as if it were a crime; threatening the faintest suspicion of heresy with serious penalties, deporting political adversaries to deserted regions, terrorizing kin through the system of collective responsibility, extorting confessions by refined forms of torture and elevating suicide to the level of an act of mercy—all such features of totalitarian power do not need to be borrowed from their neighbor by the Chinese Communists, for all are to be found in abundance in the storehouse of their own national traditions.

On the other hand, what does appear as a surprising novelty are the methods of agitation and propaganda used by the official party for taming the masses. Bringing politics into the daily life of the whole population has radically altered their former habits. Innumerable demonstrations, reunions, marches, committees, meetings, and public trials; theatrical performances, dances, public rejoicings; notices, pamphlets, journals—by every possible means official slogans are constantly drilled into every brain. In this way, what was formerly a sluggish, lethargic, undifferentiated mass of people has been shaken up, wakened up, enlivened, turned topsy-turvy, thus releasing an elemental force that will have incalculable consequences. Equally new, and with potential consequences whose importance it is impossible to exaggerate, is the enforced breakup of the traditional form of the family. It has been slowly disintegrating for the past century, but the Communists want to push the process to its logical conclusion. If they succeed in transforming family loyalties into submission to the state, and persuade the individual to transfer his allegiance from the family to the state, they will have accomplished one of those memorable feats that change the course of history, for suppression of the clan spirit at the same time removes the main causes of nepotism and corruption. It is, however, too soon to judge whether the official ideology of collectivism and what can only be described as state slavery will be capable of dislodging deeply ingrained attitudes toward the family. Only one thing can be predicted with any certainty, and that is that in China individual liberty is not yet on the program; for the present it remains the cherished inheritance of the West and the secret dream of the Taoist sages.

I should like to conclude with a declaration of faith that our present Russian-American century will be succeeded by a Chinese twenty-first century. All the potential is there. Is this tantamount to saying that the "yellow peril"—that specter invented by a Victorian generation of Malthusians with a bad conscience—will actually eventualize? No. If peril there be, it is not a yellow one. I hope I have succeeded in giving some slight indication of the very different and far more serious nature of the danger that does actually confront us, and that it is not simply a question of what will happen in China, but of what will happen in the world as a whole.

PART III

THOUGHT

TWO SONGS

BY TS'AO TS'AO

Ts'ao Ts'ao is a name that triggers off an endless chain of associations in the Chinese mind, for few of China's great men of the past are so wrapped in history, poetry, and legend as the man who bore it. In China as in the West, a famous historical figure not only assumes the outsize dimensions of an ideal type, but becomes a receptacle into which the ideas of countless generations are poured, and from which each succeeding generation draws anew. The manifold contradictions in Ts'ao Ts'ao's personality—reflecting the contradictions of his times —have resulted in an entirely different Ts'ao Ts'ao being presented to us according to which aspect of his many-sided personality is spotlighted. Ts'ao Ts'ao the Cunning, Ts'ao Ts'ao the Versatile—the unscrupulous and successful adventurer who fought his way through to the imperial throne—is the hero of legend and folk tale, familiar all over China through the storytellers who gave renderings of anecdotes from the "Romance of the Three Kingdoms" (*San-kuo chih yen-i*), and through the theater, where the epic heroes have been stylized into masks. Ts'ao Ts'ao the successful military commander and expert strategist, who wrote a commentary on the founder of Chinese military theory, Sun-tzu, the strong man who was able to gather the best brains of the age around him, the Machiavellian usurper or the wise founder of a dynasty, belongs to history and the historians. But Ts'ao Ts'ao as one of China's greatest poets is very little known.

This article first appeared as "Ts'ao Ts'ao, Zwei Lieder" in *Monumenta Serica*, 2 (1937), 410–20. The texts of the two songs translated are taken from Ting Fu-pao, *Ch'üan Han San-kuo Chin Nan-pei-ch'ao shih* (1915, 54 chapters); they appear in the section devoted to poetry of the Three Kingdoms (1.4b–5b).

It is impossible, and would in any case be pointless, to crowd into a few pages the colorful events attending the decline of the 400-year-old Han dynasty and the rise of the Three Kingdoms, for the story of the eclipse of a whole world and the dawn of a new age would require lengthy specialized study. All that need be done to make the poems that follow understandable is to single out certain trends and explain certain features of this transition period. Ts'ao Ts'ao (A.D. 155–220) stands on the dividing line between the two epochs, not only because of his deeds as grave digger of the Han dynasty and midwife to the new age that was dawning, which became known in history as the period of the Six Dynasties (roughly 200–600), but also because his surviving works mirror the intellectual trends of the changing times.

From the middle of the second century A.D., there were ever-increasing signs of the troubles to come, and a growing number of critics who, in various ways and from various standpoints and with various aims, all voiced the same thought again and again: "Things cannot go on like this!" The feudal nobility, sunk in scandalous luxury and senseless debauchery, and so degenerated that they were unable to produce a single capable ruler from their ranks, had become a burden that could be borne no longer. The hatred felt for the travesty of a government was directed equally against its executive organs and its hangers-on—the thoroughly corrupt bureaucratic hierarchy and the no less corrupt and perhaps even greedier eunuchs, those lackeys who stopped at nothing. The eunuchs, some of whom were of plebeian origin, formed a caste standing in an intimate, confidential relationship with the harem, and they waged a fierce competitive struggle with the grandees and also with the traditional literati, the gentry, who were steadily losing influence and among whom trouble was brewing on account of their anxieties concerning their increasingly curtailed means of livelihood.

The literati, who formed the intellectual aristocracy, were unanimous in demanding reforms, but were divided by a number of splits of various kinds. Individualists who followed the Taoist path were inclined toward anarchistic ideas, and endeavored to escape from no longer endurable social pressures by looking forward to the untrammeled life they hoped to find by immersing themselves in spontaneous nature, and by searching for the medicinal drugs for attaining it.

They resigned themselves to being quietist hermits, or sought contact with those lower in the social scale who joined in the broad stream of popular unrest. Closely connected with them, and no less radical in outlook, were the activists who, drawing on the ancient School of Law, considered that what was needed was a strong-armed man who would use the sword to cut through the Gordian knot of circumstances. They had close contacts with the armies fighting on the frontiers against invading barbarians, with nothing to gain for their Spartan, self-sacrificing life except perpetual expectation of death at the hands of the barbarians or of public reprimand from the distant court. It was these activists who formed the group to which Ts'ao Ts'ao and his circle belonged. They found plenty of opportunity in the ensuing civil war for performing heroic deeds and winning fame, and the successful ones grouped themselves around the three centers of power that were gradually forming, which later became the Three Kingdoms. (This group was called the *ch'ün-hsiung,* the "group of heroes," by the annalists and writers of tales.)

A group that stood in contrast to the two just mentioned (although the dividing lines were less sharp than they became later) consisted of the tradition-bound Confucianist literati, who only advocated "reasonable" or "justifiable" reforms such as might be sanctioned by holy writ, and who were primarily concerned with winning back the position of power they had lost (or rather, had not yet fully attained). Their movement, in which tens of thousands of students (candidates for office) took part, acquired the character of a political party—the first in Chinese history. This was known as the League of Literati (a league of officials debarred from office), and its subsequent bloody extermination or persecution by the government (*chin-ku* or *tang-ku,* "prohibition against employment of league members"), which took place during the decade from 166 to 176, was the first storm signal. The storm itself was soon to break, but it came from a different direction.

The peasants, who stood to gain little from the fine plans for reform, and who were rotting away in poverty-stricken conditions that all contemporary accounts paint in the darkest of colors, were plotting an organized rising that soon assumed a religious character, known as the "Revolt of the Yellow Turbans." Under Taoist leadership, and fortified by charms of Taoist inspiration, the peasants made their way to the towns and flooded over the whole country like some natural catastrophe. Their aim: "The Great Well-being" (*t'ai-p'ing*); their methods: extermination by fire and sword of everything that might be even remotely connected with authority and the powers that be; their opponents: court circles (now entirely without any kind of leadership) and the disorganized imperial army. The first great rising of 184 was suppressed. But peasant insurgent troops kept cropping up here and there until the middle of the third century.

The Han, whom Ts'ao Ts'ao once described in a poem as "the apes with cap and girdle, full of schemes but lacking in knowledge," never recovered from the blow. They retreated completely into the background until the time of their official demise, and left the field free for various war lords and military dictators. One of them—the greatest of all—was Ts'ao Ts'ao.

Ts'ao Ts'ao the poet is no less a figure than Ts'ao Ts'ao the statesman, and the two cannot be viewed apart. As poet, he exercised the same profound and fruitful influence, and occupied the same position astride two epochs. Han times had produced no great poet, but had given birth to a number of wonderful anonymous folk songs. The lengthy task of building up a state had more need of a sound prose style, and the lyrical torrent that originally sprang from Ch'ü Yüan became a trickle which either disappeared from the surface and flowed in small underground channels, or became a narrow artificial stream. It was only his form that poets borrowed from Ch'ü Yüan, and a formalized version of it at that. The elegiac, rhapsodical Hymns of Ch'u gave place to an erudite, ponderous, stilted kind of prose-poetry (the *fu*). Imaginative outpourings full of a feeling for nature had given way to bloodless philosophical dissertations, lacking in all feeling. Confucianism was as ill disposed toward poetry in its youth as in its old age.

Taoism was another matter. Just as Ch'ü Yüan, the greatest of China's poets of the pre-Christian era, was steeped in Taoist philosophy and legend, so were the host of lyric poets—beginning with, and including, Ts'ao Ts'ao—in the closest relations with Taoism. Two features of the original doctrine now came very much to the fore: the return to nature, which epitomized in both a symbolic and a practical way the idea of freedom from all restraint (and it is to be noted that the Chinese language at that time had no word to express the concept of "freedom" in a positive form); and speculations about the prolongation of life, upon which even greater emphasis was laid because of the general insecurity of the times. The emperor who instituted pilgrimages to the Isles of the Blessed, the hermit who hoped to conserve his vital energies by means of breathing exercises and meditation, the peasant who prayed to the immortals for help against epidemics and calamities, were all engaged in the same search for salvation. And the poets who came after Ts'ao Ts'ao were merely expressing the same trend in another way when they everlastingly sang of the fleetingness of life and endeavored to drown their pessimism in wine. Half a century of wars and civil war, total uncertainty as to what the morrow might bring, and the breakdown of all moral values, had reduced life to being a matter of the passing moment, which some wanted to drink to the dregs and others to stretch out to eternity.

Ts'ao Ts'ao was no stranger to pessimism. But with him, as the particular songs here translated show, resignation was more an artistic device, with wider implications, than an end in itself. And individualism—a new note that made its shy appearance in the poetry of the dawning Middle Ages—was in his case heightened by the gigantic proportions of his historical task, but by the same token weakened as an expression of the egocentricity of the individual personality.

Thus Ts'ao Ts'ao is not primarily an individualist or a pessimist, or even a true Taoist. He lets himself be carried away by his moods (moods we find in most of his contemporaries), but half consciously and half unconsciously he fights against this and hurls himself upon his objective: action. "Now I sing my firm resolve."

The duality of his nature, and the close correlation between his need for action and his secret longings, are manifested in a particularly fascinating way in the first of the songs I have translated. It was composed during the campaign against Chang Lu in A.D. 215. A branch of the Taoist rebels had established itself in Szechwan, where for centuries a Taoist community had been building up, under the leadership of Chang Lu. Ts'ao Ts'ao, if he wanted to unify China or at least attain effective hegemony, had to fight and destroy these Taoist rebels. But upon meeting with the first setbacks in this difficult terrain, he sang of the joys of a hermit's life and of withdrawal from the world—the world in which he was out to destroy the very persons who held and preached ideas of this kind. This is typical Ts'ao Ts'ao: carrying out the aims of the enemy he destroys and saying to him, "Upright and not crafty"—perhaps his opponent will believe him and yield? (Chang Lu yielded.)

So Ts'ao Ts'ao is not a Taoist. Is he a Confucian? By no means. What, then, about the passages which either come from the writings of K'ung-tzu or are attributed to him, and which Ts'ao Ts'ao liked to weave in with his own ideas? There are countless quotations or allusions in early Confucianism that are known to share common ground with Taoism. In a land where quotations are much used, everything depends upon the interpretation put on them. Ts'ao Ts'ao goes back to the line of thought of the "Book of Changes." This is what lies closest to him. And he can take over unaltered the highly compressed mode of expression used by Confucius to express these thoughts. Thus it comes about that even as a poet, Ts'ao Ts'ao is also a strategist. He makes use of the common heritage of Confucianism as a means for disarming an opponent. When he writes: "Dignified by Kindness and Justice, glorified by Rites and Music," he is not the least interested in the Confucian cardinal virtues as such, but is merely using them as a means for "changing" or "civilizing" opponents.

Another strand of traditional thought of an entirely different nature also appears in his poetry. Single expressions, phrases, or even whole lines from the Elegies of Ch'u occur. He goes back, whether consciously or unconsciously is not certain, to Ch'ü Yüan and his school. Thus Ts'ao Ts'ao, although he may not have been quite the first to do so, starts a process of enriching the orchestration of the new poetry by drawing upon the inexhaustible store of images and the imaginative power and modes of expression of Ch'ü Yüan's art.

Only two dozen of Ts'ao Ts'ao's poems survive. Two are included in the anthology called the *Wen-hsüan*, and so are familiar to every educated Chinese. The others are not so easily accessible. Together they provide a rather heavy meal. The two I have selected for translation are to my mind the most representative of Ts'ao Ts'ao's work, and also the most beautiful.

With regard to the translation: already many translations from the Chinese have been made, and a great deal has been written on the subject. It is better simply to try and make good translations than to write about how to do so, but a few words must be said about the main problems. The ideal, of course, is to get as near as possible to both form and content. In my opinion, however, the content should never be rendered in too compressed a manner, and an attempt to keep close to the form should never allow the content to be sacrificed. This rules out the possibility of attaining the ideal as far as translating from Chinese is concerned. On the other hand, if a Chinese poem is forced into the procrustean bed of a European form, either nothing of the original poem is left, or all the life is crushed out of it and it loses its raison d'être. The nearest approach one can hope to make toward producing a satisfactory version is to choose a form that dispenses with rhyme. The most successful exponent of this method is Arthur Waley.

The greatest difficulty of all, however, is to awaken in the mind of the reader the same associations and feelings as are conjured up by the poet in the mind of the Chinese reader. In most cases it is quite impossible to do this directly, for there is such a huge gap between China's and Europe's worlds of thought and all the associations contained in them, that the gap cannot be bridged by such a fragile construction as a lyric poem. There remains the indirect method of providing the reader in advance with some information about the moods, images, allusions, and thought associations forming the soil from which the poem has sprung, so as to enable him to approach closer to the unfamiliar idiom. This is what will be attempted here.

Both the poems translated are songs (*hsing*) composed to a set melody (in the same way as European medieval "ad notam" poetry was composed). The name of the musical theme, which is used as a title for the poems, is *Ch'iu-hu,* or "The mulberry tree on the balk." It is unnecessary to go into the story of Ch'iu-hu-tzu that provided the material for the original folk song.[1] All that concerns us is the form. Each stanza consists of nine lines, in which the number of syllables are as follows: 5, 5, 5, 5; 8, 8 (or 10), 8; 4, 5. The three middle lines, which rhyme with each other, sometimes have an arrangement of 10, 8, 8 syllables. Often, but not always, the opening lines rhyme.

1. The story can be found in *Tz'u-yüan* (under *Ch'iu-hu hsing*) and in *Chung-kuo jen-ming ta-tz'u-tien*, p. 676.

EXPLANATORY NOTES ON THE FIRST POEM

Ts'ao Ts'ao began his campaign against Chang Lu in Szechwan in the spring of 215. In the fourth month he came to the San-kuan pass (in the southwest of Shensi, near the present Pao-chi hsien), which was the strategic key point for the invasion of Szechwan. The hilly country enabled the native Tanguts to defy Ts'ao Ts'ao for two months, and it was not until the autumn that he was able to make his way southward through the Yang-p'ing pass. Chang Lu wanted to surrender immediately, while his brother continued fighting, without success. After the battle near Yang-p'ing, Chang Lu handed over the booty, and the Taoist state came under Ts'ao Ts'ao's control.[2]

The "sad and moving air" is the melody *ch'ing-chüeh,* which (Han Fei-tzu tells us) Huang Ti played on the holy mountain, the T'ai-shan, to the assembled ghosts and demons there. It is so overwhelming that when the music master Shih K'uang at last acceded to the music-loving Prince P'ing's request and played it for him, dark clouds formed, a storm arose, torrential rain ripped open the walls of the tent, and the people who had been listening fled in terror.[3]

In antiquity, several old men were supported and looked after by the state as a sign of the emperor's solicitude. They were called the *san-lao* ("triply ancient"). This institution still existed in Han times. The same title was borne by village elders, the occupants of the lowest grade in the hierarchy of local officials, responsible for public morals and moral education. *San-lao* was also the name given to the master mariners of the Yangtze gorges. Whatever may be meant by the use of the expression here, it remains a fact that the figure of an old man was always used to represent Taoist wisdom and the immortals who personified it.

Shabby clothing was also symbolic for the Taoists. The coarse, unsightly outer covering has a jewel hidden within it. "Few understand me; but it is upon this very fact that my value depends. It is indeed in this sense that 'the Sage wears hair-cloth on top, but carries jade underneath his dress.' "[4]

2. See *Tzu-chih t'ung-chien* 67.7b and 10a–11b; cf. *Hou-Han shu* 105, the biography of Liu Yen, in which that of Chang Lu is included, and Chang Lu's biography in *San-kuo chih* 8; see also *San-kuo chih* 1 (year 215).

3. Cf. *Tz'u-yüan* supplement under *ch'ing-shang.*

4. *Lao-tzu* 70, trans. A. Waley, *The Way and Its Power* (London, 1934).

"True Men" (*chen-jen*), again a Taoist term, is another name for the immortals—men who have reached perfection and become saints, and who are in possession of the *Tao,* the Way.

The K'un-lun mountains of the farthest west played a great role in the myths and legends of Han times. Most of the genii dwelt there, and the Queen Mother of the West (*Hsi-wang-mu*), goddess of the plague and giver of everlasting life, had her realms there.[5]

The inner vision of the Taoists, by means of which they were able to transcend individual limitations and become one with the All, was attained through reaching a state of trance, which, from Chuang-tzu to Ch'ü Yüan, was always described as the ecstatic "Journey into the Distance" (*yüan-yu*)—a blissful experience of hovering above the heights. The soul's voyage of discovery through the landscape of the self was projected on to the natural landscape. All descriptions of this state agree down to the minutest details. The accompaniments of the hermit's life are equally stereotyped: a stone for pillow, the heavens for tent, dew as nourishment, and so on. There are so many passages referring to such things in the literature that it would be tedious to cite them.

The ascent to heaven is a symbol for the soul's being freed from the weightiness of the earthly body, and has very little to do with the attainment of heavenly bliss with which it is associated in the West.

In the first poem of the "Nine Changes" (*Chiu-pien*) by Sung Yü, Ch'ü Yüan's most famous disciple, the following lines occur: "So empty and purposeless! the poor man. With no position, and unfulfilled ambitions. So desolate and forsaken! wanders, loses his way, and has no friend at hand. So despairing and sad! and secretly he pities himself."

Duke Wen of Chin was very arrogant, and when he became hegemon, he forgot about the faithful followers to whom he owed his rise to power. Duke Huan of Ch'i, on the other hand, was wise and generous, and succeeded in attracting to his court the greatest statesman of the time, Kuan Chung. The Analects of Confucius has the following passage: "The duke Wen of Tsin was crafty and not upright. The duke Hwan of Ch'i was upright and not crafty."[6] Ts'ao Ts'ao uses this saying, which Confucius had intended as a reproach

5 Cf. M. Granet, *La Pensée chinoise* (Paris, 1934), pp. 357 f.

6 *Lun-yü* XIV, 16; translation by James Legge, in *The Confucian Analects.*

against the twelve unenlightened rulers who had not appointed him to office, in order to compare himself with the wise and generous ruler of Ch'i. When he becomes hegemon, he will not forget those who have helped him, but will honor all of them by drawing them round him to devote their energies to building up the state.

The "writings" are the holy writ of the Confucian canon, and "the West" signifies the place of origin of Taoist legends.

EXPLANATORY NOTES ON THE SECOND POEM

It is not known whether the second song was written at the same time as the first one.

See above for explanations of the Taoist expressions translated here as "wandering to the utmost limits" (*yüan-yu*) and "godlike beings" (*chen-jen*).

The Great Hua mountain, so called to distinguish it from the Little' Hua mountain to the west of it, is the holy mountain of the West, in Shensi. One of its peaks is called "The Immortal's Palm." P'eng-lai is the "Isle of the Blessed" where the herb of immortality grows.

Po-yang is another name for Lao-tzu. Ch'ih-sung-tzu, Master Red Pine,[7] and Wang Ch'iao were legendary immortals. Master Red Pine (the pine tree is a symbol of long life) was rain controller in the time of Shen Nung, dwelt in the K'un-lun mountains, and served as emblem for Chang Liang, the famous Taoist of the Former Han dynasty. Wang-tzu Ch'iao was supposed to have been a son disowned by King Ling of the Chou dynasty. He lived as a hermit on the Sung mountain for thirty years. One fine day he sent word to his family that they could expect to meet him on the seventh day of the seventh month on the K'ou-shih peak. True enough, he appeared at the appointed time riding on a white crane. But he could only be seen from a distance, and could not be approached more closely. He stretched out his hands, bade farewell to the world, and disappeared. A sorcerer called Wang Ch'iao, who in the time of the Emperor Ming-ti (58–75 A.D.) astonished the court with his arts, is supposed to have been a reincarnation of this prince. On the first and the fifteenth of every month, he would suddenly appear at the capital having come all the way from his distant native district. Once the Emperor had observers

7. Cf. P. Pelliot, "Meou-Tseu ou les Doutes levés," in *T'oung Pao, 19* (1918–19), 406–07.

posted, when it was time for one of his visits, to find out what means of transport the magician used. A pair of wild ducks on the wing was seen approaching. One of the ducks was shot and turned into a shoe—and so on.[8]

The "Two Powers" are the elemental powers of Heaven and Earth. The phrase "throughout the world, every man is the king's subject" comes from a passage in the *Shih-ching* that is particularly well known because it is quoted in Mencius.[9] In Ts'ao Ts'ao's poem the meaning is slightly altered. What was stressed originally was that all land belongs to the king, but here the emphasis is on the contrast between nature and society: all earthly matters are the work of political man. The poet's basic idea—that man, who controls nature, is of primary importance—comes out very clearly in the following stanza. The whole passage from the "Book of Changes," in which the key phrase occurs, runs as follows in Legge's translation:

> The great man is he who is in harmony, in his attributes, with heaven and earth; in his brightness, with the sun and the moon; in his orderly procedure, with the four seasons; and in his relation to what is fortunate and what is calamitous, in harmony with the spirit-like operations (of Providence). He may precede Heaven, and Heaven will not act in opposition to him; he may follow Heaven, but will act (only) as Heaven at that time would do. If Heaven will not act in opposition to him, how much less will men! How much less will the spirit-like operation (of Providence)! [10]

It should be noted that Heaven is equated with nature.

TWO SONGS ON THE AIR *Ch'iu-hu*

1.

At break of day I climbed the San-kuan mountain,
How full of perils is the way!
At break of day I climbed the San-kuan mountain,
How full of perils is the way!

---

8. All these legends come from the popular collection *Lieh-hsien chuan;* cf. *Chung-kuo jen-ming ta-tz'u-tien,* pp. 507, 77, 125; *Hou-Han shu* 112.1 and 3b–4a.
9. *Shih-ching* II, vi, 1; *Meng-tzu* V A 4.
10. *Texts of Confucianism,* Part 2, p. 417.

Oxen halt, can go no further, wagons hurtle to the depths.
High upon a crag I sat, softly fingering the strings,
Played a sad and moving air, troubled and confused in mind.
Now I sing my firm resolve.
At break of day I climbed the San-kuan mountain.

Then there came a triply ancient man,
He suddenly appeared by my side.
Then there came a triply ancient man,
He suddenly appeared by my side.
On his back a hairy garment—no mortal man was he.
"Sir," he said, "why be so troubled? Why accuse yourself so harshly?
Why be full of hesitations, when thus far you have arrived?"
Now I sing my firm resolve
Then there came a triply ancient man.

"My abode is in the K'un-lun mountains,
And one of the True Men am I.
My abode is in the K'un-lun mountains,
And one of the True Men am I.
My Way leads far, and has led many to behold the high mountains,
Wander to the utmost limits, resting on stones, bathing in brooks,
    drinking from springs . . ."
Musing I sat, still undecided, while he ascended into heaven.
Now I sing my firm resolve.
My abode is in the K'un-lun mountains.

He disappeared beyond my following gaze,
I felt as if my heart were torn with anguish.
He disappeared beyond my following gaze,
I felt as if my heart were torn with anguish.
Night after night, how could I sleep? Despairing and sad, I pitied
    myself.
"Upright and not crafty," thus I shall be, according
To what the sacred writings said, and what was told from out the
    West.
Now I sing my firm resolve.
He disappeared beyond my following gaze.

2.

I long to climb the Great Hua mountain's peak,
And there with godlike beings wander far.
I long to climb the Great Hua mountain's peak,
And there with godlike beings wander far.
Traverse the K'un-lun mountain range, all the way to P'eng-lai,
Whirl away to the utmost limits together with the godlike beings,
So as to find the holy herb: ten thousand years' duration then.
Now I sing my firm resolve.
I long to climb the Great Hua mountain's peak.

Heaven and Earth, how long they last!
But man's allotted span is brief.
Heaven and Earth, how long they last!
But man's allotted span is brief.
Po-yang, so they say, never knew old age,
Ch'ih Sung and Wang Ch'iao also are said to have found the Way.
Whether that was so or not, at least they lived long lives.
Now I sing my firm resolve.
Heaven and Earth, how long they last!

Sun, Moon, how bright they shine!
Everywhere is filled with their light.
Sun, Moon, how bright they shine!
Everywhere is filled with their light.
Wondrous works the Two Powers perform, but in man alone true
    worth resides,
In every state, "throughout the world, every man is the king's subject,"
Dignified by Kindness and Justice, glorified by Rites and Music.
Now I sing my firm resolve.
Sun, Moon, how bright they shine!

The four seasons ever die anew,
Day follows night until the year's complete.
The four seasons ever die anew,
Day follows night until the year's complete.
"The great man precedes Heaven, yet Heaven does not oppose him."
Do not mourn that time is fleeting—care about the world's disorder.

Fate decides success or failure, only fools fear the attempt.
Now I sing my firm resolve.
The four seasons ever die anew.

Sad, sad—away with melancholy!
Joy and laughter, let us seek for these.
Sad, sad—away with melancholy!
Joy and laughter, let us seek for these.
Strength, ripeness, knowledge, wisdom, these will not return again,
Grudge time's passing, seize each moment—but who will benefit from
    that?

Plunging into reckless living would be merest foolishness.
Now I sing my firm resolve.
Sad, sad—away with melancholy!

POLITICAL PHILOSOPHY

AND SOCIAL CRISIS

AT THE END OF

THE HAN DYNASTY

I propose to discuss here three philosophers who have a double claim upon our interest. In their capacity as articulate observers of the times they lived in, they have transmitted to us information which either corroborates or supplements the rather meager accounts provided by extant historical sources. As thinkers, they selected from the storehouse of ancient philosophy those ideas that seemed to them most suitable for use as weapons in the social struggles in which they were engaged; in doing so, they not only revived the controversies that raged among the many schools of thought during the third century B.C., but also prepared the way for the intensely active intellectual life that characterized the third century of our own era. They are required reading for anyone who wants to understand the spiritual renaissance of the Middle Ages, those four centuries from A.D. 200 to 600 which totally transformed China.

The last years of the Han and the Three Kingdoms period already contained in embryonic form the salient features of the new age—the impoverishment and refeudalization of society, the sudden irruption of the barbarians, a profound religious feeling that had never be-

This chapter originally appeared under the title "La Crise sociale et la philosophie politique à la fin des Han," *T'oung Pao*, 39 (1949), 83–131. The text was taken almost unaltered from two lectures given in March 1948 at the Institut des Hautes Etudes Chinoises in Paris (Sorbonne). It is the sketch for a larger, uncompleted work begun in 1933.

fore existed, the blossoming of a new kind of lyric poetry, and the creation of a magnificent art of sculpture. Indeed, I think that at the stage we have now reached in our study of the period it is possible to advance the hypothesis that the hundred years from A.D. 150 to 250 exerted on China's future development an influence not less important than that of the third century B.C.

In both periods an age was coming to an end, and in both, philosophical doctrines prepared the way for subsequent political changes. Let me therefore preface my discussion of the three philosophers with a rapid survey of the main events and representative social groups of the age that saw the gradual decay of the Han dynasty.

By the middle of the second century A.D., the vast Han empire had enjoyed many years of comparative peace. The population had almost doubled since the dynasty was restored at the beginning of the Christian era, and the transition from a natural economy to an exchange economy had not only brought an accumulation of wealth, but also intensified the division of labor. The result was a greater inequality in the distribution of wealth, along with changes in the traditional social structure. The most conspicuous sign of social disequilibrium was the weakening of the emperor's power, the effete scions of the house of Liu now ruling only by proxy. The apex of the pyramid had begun to crumble, and a closely fought struggle for the exercise of effective power set in.

What were the forces involved? The aristocracy, who had been privileged in holding all the main government posts, played a progressively less important role. The nobles lived on the revenues from the land they owned, but rather than spend their time looking after their estates, which were cultivated by tenant farmers or agricultural laborers, they preferred the brilliant life at court, and divided their time between the hunt, entertainments of various kinds, and the holding of a sinecure that brought nothing but boredom. Generally deficient in culture and supremely arrogant, they had sunk into a state of apathy brought about by idleness, luxurious living, and the assured continuance of their privileges.

They viewed with distaste the rapid rise of a section of society they despised—a group that was now entering into competition with them and seizing hold, with all the avidity of the parvenu, of every opportunity that came its way. The new section of society consisted of men belonging to the "external clans" (*wai-ch'i*)—that is to say, the kin of each reigning empress. Bitter experience had long since brought home to these men the insecurity of their position, and their greed was accordingly all the more insatiable. The price they paid for enjoying the imperial favor was the risk of becoming victims of changed circumstances in the harem, and they lived always at the mercy of the emperor's caprice. Their opportunities being transitory, they knew that they must make full use of them. So these greedy, unscrupulous "new men" made their fortunes in a very short space of time, only to lose them no less quickly. At the time we are considering it was the Liang clan, the kin of the Empress Liang, whose turn it was to be in favor. The head of the clan was the Grand Marshal Liang Chi. For twenty years he had had the empire in his clutches. During this time he had succeeded in accumulating for himself every conceivable important post, acquired a fortune assessed at 3,000 million cash, put two puppet emperors on the throne, and placed all his relations in lucrative positions. His family could boast of having supplied the empire with two marshals, three empresses, six imperial concubines, seven marquises, and fifty-seven high officials. His pleasure park near Loyang, the capital, contained a zoological garden filled with exotic birds and beasts and set in an artificial landscape; it is described in the literature as of unequaled sumptuosity.[1] But the eventual fate of Liang Chi is typical of the instability of the positions won by these nouveaux riches clans: he was assassinated by a eunuch in 159, and all the members of his clan were executed and all his protégés ruined.

This brings us to the third social group that laid claim to power: the eunuchs. Of plebeian origin, they owed their influential position to the intimate, day-to-day relations they enjoyed with the Son of Heaven, who had come to rely more and more on these faithful retainers to support him in his struggle against being patronized by the grandees, tyrannized by the "external clans," and morally chaperoned by the literati. His closest confidants could count on obtaining government posts and titles through imperial favor and on being able, by fair means or foul, to make a fortune for themselves or their kin. The five eunuchs who carried out the surprise attack against the Liang

---

1. See *Hou-Han shu,* ed. Wang Hsien-ch'ien (1915), 64 and passim, 110A.13b ff.; *Tzu-chih t'ung-chien* (Commercial Press edition, 1917), 53.4a and 8b; 54.5a–8a.

clan were ennobled, each receiving a marquisate that brought with it the right to taxes paid by 76,000 families; in addition they were given a special reward of 56 million cash for services rendered. Naturally the greed of the eunuchs and their low moral standards were in direct proportion to the opportunities available to them. In this respect they were quite on a par with the kin of the empresses, with whom their official functions brought them into contact, and with whom they often had business dealings. Naturally, too, we find that among the people with whom the eunuchs had business dealings were a large number of merchants and industrialists, people who could do business and make profits by contributing to the conspicuous consumption of the imperial court. But it should also be recognized that the eunuchs, though they were mere plebeians who were the tools of the absolute monarchy, were by no means entirely without culture. On the contrary, they endeavored to acquire an education, were greatly interested in technological questions (it was a eunuch who invented paper-making in 105 A.D.) and even had plans for organizing their own educational system—plans that raised indignant protests from the literati at this proposed breach of their monopoly of education.[2]

Thus the literati, who were not yet a clearly defined class, found that they were more and more losing control of the management of affairs. It was they, or rather the more unfortunate among them, who set in motion the train of events that led up to the crisis. Finding themselves out of office, and threatened with losing their ancient privilege of holding office, they now formed a league that was a kind of political party of the intelligentsia. At the capital, the party leaders, consisting of prominent literati and high officials, voiced their criticism of government vices and their vituperations against the misdeeds of their opponents, in a constant stream of remonstrances, memorials, and petitions. They were supported in the provinces by the petty officials and the yamen employees, and by the students, who numbered as many as 30,000, and who were often so poor that they had to earn their living as artisans, agricultural laborers, or petty employees. Living thus among the people, they had first-hand experience of the widespread poverty and distress, and started agitating throughout the empire; their most effective means of rousing public opinion and express-

2. *Hou-Han shu* 8.3b; 84.8a.

ing their criticism of the government were posters displaying seven-character-line epigrams denigrating their political enemies, or slogans either inviting general disapproval of corruption in high places or praising their own leaders in a few trenchant words. This was the "criticism by the pure" (*ch'ing-i*), the full force of which must be measured by the prestige enjoyed by education and the written word in a country of illiterates.[3] The literati class, though internally divided (since, springing from the ruling class, it included among its members large landowners as well as poor students), was thus united in its opposition both to the shocking luxury of the life led by the grandees and the nouveaux riches, and to the exactions, corruption, and venality of the eunuchs and their hangers-on.

As a result of the sharpness of the League's criticisms, the number of its adherents, and the prestige traditionally belonging to any enterprise undertaken by the intelligentsia, it was a redoubtable enemy. The eunuchs, the literati's most serious competitors, had no time to lose, and it was they who opened hostilities. What ensued was a desperate struggle for power, in the course of which the three sections of the ruling class tore at each other's throats. As it moved from one stage to the next, with fortune favoring now one side, now the other, it brought in its train civil war, general impoverishment, the disappearance of the contestants themselves, and finally the breakup of the Han empire.

It was in 166 that the eunuchs went into the attack, arresting and imprisoning the members of the League. In the following year an amnesty was declared, but the League members were sent home to their native districts and prohibited for life from holding public office. The accession of a new emperor a year later provided an opportunity for revenge. But the attempt to exterminate the eunuchs failed; it was they, on the contrary, who assassinated the most prominent literati. The state of unrest reached its peak when the murder of a eunuch gave a pretext for setting up a preliminary investigation into proceedings to be taken against the literati, with the result that the severest measures were adopted to proscribe them. From that time on,

3. Cf. *Hou-Han shu* 97.3a; 98.1a–8b; 104A.1a; 109B.4b and 15a; *San-kuo chih* (*T'ung-wen* edition, 1884), 9.21a; *Chin-shu* (*T'u-shu chi-ch'eng* edition, 1888) 45.1a; *T'ung-chien* 55 (year 166), 13b–14a.

the former members of the League and their relations to the fifth degree of kinship found themselves debarred from holding any government post.[4]

But the eunuchs were not to enjoy their triumph for long. For, while the front line of the battle was loud with the clashes among the various sections of the ruling class, each intent upon carving out for itself the largest possible portion of revenue and all of them deaf to the warnings of the philosophers, the people of the countryside were preparing to rise against intolerable exploitation by the large landowners and vexatious exactions of the mandarins. The agricultural population—that is to say, almost the entire nation—was living in indescribable poverty. The free peasant was in the process of disappearing. With nothing but his little plot of land, faced with the constant threat of famine and with demands for taxes and labor services that could not be met, under pressure from the many exactions made by inadequately paid officials, and sometimes in addition threatened with expropriation by a lord desirous of extending his domain, he was sooner or later condemned to join the agricultural proletariat, either by renting land as métayer of a large landowner, or by hiring himself out as an agricultural laborer if his resources had been exhausted by debts, floods, or drought. Or again, he might flee the land and lead a vagrant life as peddler, artisan, domestic servant, soldier, or bandit. For his children, the only possible openings were slavery or prostitution. He was forced to sell them, and they flocked to the town houses of the aristocracy as slaves, singing girls, actors, and eunuchs.

The vast amorphous mass of starving peasants and vagrants lived in a state of sullen unrest, and for a dozen years or so they had been worked upon by the emissaries of a new faith: the "Way of the Great Peace" (*t'ai-p'ing tao*). The prophets of this millenarian sect, whose bible, the *T'ai-ping ching,* was full of Taoist signs and symbols and magic formulae, did not limit themselves to announcing to their followers the coming of a new golden age of prosperity and equality —the real meaning of the expression *t'ai-p'ing*—or stop at mere promises of a miraculous recovery: they organized them into actual phalansteries, rural communities in which there was public confession of sins and communal repasts held in houses of justice (*i-she*); and

4. *Chin-ku* or *tang-ku;* cf. *Hou-Han shu* 97, a chapter entirely devoted to the members of the League.

they established an astonishing military organization with thirty-six divisions. When these divisions went into action on New Year's Day 184, which was the first year of a new cycle, they proceeded to occupy the country by means of a lightning march. Under the leadership of the three Chang brothers—who bore the respective titles of General the Duke of Heaven, Earth, and Man—the Yellow Turbans (the name by which the sect was commonly known because they wore yellow as a symbol of the earth) then proceeded to put the whole of North China to fire and sword. From the two centers based on the areas of highest population density, the lower Yellow River valley and Sze-chwan, the revolt spread like wildfire, until it covered the whole of inhabited China, consisting at that time of the area between the Yellow River and the Yangtze. Significantly enough, the first actions of this vast half-social, half-religious peasant rising were to storm the prefectures and subprefectures, killing or chasing away the officials in charge and appointing others in their place, and collecting taxes and repairing roads.[5]

All this came as a complete surprise to the government. At first there was stupefaction; but the ruling powers, while accusing each other of being responsible for this unexpected catastrophe, or even of double-dealing, recovered sufficiently to organize punitive expeditions. The repression was ferocious, accounting for half a million victims during the year 184 alone. The people of the countryside were defenseless, some coming under attack from the rebels, and some from the forces of repression. The battles waged between the imperial troops and the Yellow Turbans, who suffered defeat at one point only to spring up in ever larger numbers at others, brought chaos to the entire country. What with the exodus of literati and the wealthy to some safe spot or other, and the desperate flight of refugees and vagabonds, there was a migration of population in all directions.

It was, however, in the vacuum created at the capital that the de-

5. On the Yellow Turbans, see *Hou-Han shu* 84, 85, 87, 88, 96, 101, 102, 104A, 105, 108, and *San-kuo chih* 1, 6, 7, 8, 31, 46; cf. L. Wieger, *Textes historiques* (2 vols. Hsien-hsien, 1922), *1*, 773–89, and Henri Maspero, "Les Procédés de 'nourrir le principe vital' dans la religion taoïste ancienne," *Journal Asiatique*, 229 (1937), 402 ff. On the *T'ai-p'ing ching* see *Hou-Han shu* 60B.9b–11b and *San-kuo chih* 46.6b–7a; cf. Pelliot, *T'oung Pao, 19* (1918–19), 407 ff., and T'ang Yung-t'ung, *Han Wei liang Chin Nan-pei-ch'ao Fo-chiao shih* (2 vols. Shanghai, 1938), *1*, 58 ff., 104–14.

cisive events occurred. Yüan Shao, a typical patrician who was the spokesman of the aristocratic faction opposing the eunuchs, steadily persevered in urging the empress' brother, one of the "new men," to do away with the eunuchs once and for all. This man fell victim to the persuasive delaying tactics of the eunuchs, but Yüan Shao intervened at the crucial moment and with icy determination saw to it that all the eunuchs in the palace were massacred. But the triumph of the nobles and the literati—allies against the common enemy—had come too late. Now it was the military who came into their own in a war of each against all. During the brief reign of the novice dictator Tung Cho a whole series of claimants to the throne entered upon the scene, leading to civil war and the bloody elimination of competitors desperately struggling for power. The struggle lasted the lifetime of a whole generation, and transformed China from a powerful empire into a vast cemetery. Its outbreak provided a golden opportunity for adventurers, swashbucklers, condottieri, and military leaders of all kinds. With their bands of starving and ragged mercenaries, vagabonds, criminals, landless peasants, jobless intellectuals who had come down in the world—men of every variety, with neither creed nor code—they dominated the scene for thirty years. Their careers were all more or less the same. After winning their first laurels in the war against the Yellow Turbans, they roamed about with their bands of freebooters, pillaging now one province, now another; if they were lucky, they succeeded in seizing some fortress or town left standing, and used it as a springboard for the next step toward victory. This new daredevil type finds its personification in Ts'ao Ts'ao, the great strategist, marvelous poet, and clever statesman, who was perfectly described by a contemporary physiognomist in the following epigram: "A vile bandit in times of peace, a heroic leader in a world of turmoil." [6]

This, then, in outline, was the world of the philosophers I shall discuss. They were full of its uncertainties and shot through with its contradictions, but in their own way they exercised a lasting influence through their contribution to the ideas developed during their times.

What were these ideas? It must first be borne in mind that the

6. *Hou-Han shu* 98.7b. On Ts'ao Ts'ao, see above, Chapter 12, and D. von den Steinen, "Poems of Ts'ao Ts'ao," *Monumenta Serica, 4* (1939–40), 125–81.

literati had not yet become a distinct social class, nor had a body of orthodox doctrine yet been formulated. Thus it came about that the best minds, aware of a certain uneasiness, a feeling of confusion and disorientation, sought some framework of reference by which they could set their compass and be guided through the stormy sea of events. As the crisis grew more acute, so the need to make a mental effort to discover the means of salvation became more pressing. All Chinese philosophy is pre-eminently social philosophy, and even when it attempts to detach itself from the temporal world and arrive at some form of pure, transcendental metaphysics, there can be no hope of understanding it without recognizing its point of departure, to which sooner or later it returns. And since it is always fundamentally based on human relations—not individual human relations, but relations between human beings as integral parts of social groups—I would even go so far as to say that Chinese philosophy is primarily *political* philosophy. This explains the common basis, along with the divergences, of the various schools, and also the curious fact that a repeated situation always produced the same ideas, although this amounts to no more than saying that the same causes inevitably produce the same effects.

During the long and comparatively peaceful reign of the Han, there was no need for any of the extremist systems of antiquity. Minds did not seek to inquire beyond the limits of Confucian pragmatism, and the various schools of ritual were absorbed in petty squabbles for priority. But from the beginning of the second century, the systematic doubts expressed by Wang Ch'ung began to bring the official doctrine into disrepute, and even the most rigid of the commentators on the classical texts became uneasy about the irreconcilable contradictions presented and perpetuated by the Confucianist interpretation. Search for a more coherent doctrine was embarked upon, and the long-forgotten theories of the Taoist and Legalist schools, and even of the Sophists and the Logicians, suddenly seemed relevant to the burning questions of the day. Three main trends of thought can be discerned. If, to oversimplify, one were to give a rough indication of their content and of their relation to the climate of the times, it might be said that all three were trying to find a solution for the crisis that had arisen. It was commonly accepted that things were in a bad way and that something must be done. But what? How could the crisis be explained, and where lay the remedy? These questions gave rise to different answers. The three main positions were as follows.

The Confucianists held that the existing intolerable situation had arisen because the precepts of the ancient sages were no longer followed. The world, now so out of joint, would be set right only if the traditional pattern of social relations were strictly adhered to, and everyone returned to his proper place in the social hierarchy, as laid down by the moral code. Hence the key concepts were still *li* and *i*— *li* meaning propriety, custom, rites, etiquette; *i,* which connotes impartiality, standing for equality among superiors, and devotion to duty on the part of inferiors. All this was expressed in moderate, sugared tones.

The Legalists were as interested in maintaining order in the temporal world as the Confucianists, but held that changed times required new methods. They wanted to break with the old methods and discard the traditional ideas of government by virtue, which events had reduced to an absurdity. They proclaimed the necessity for a universal code of law, applicable to everyone equally. In their view, the only hope of salvation lay in the universal and impartial application of a coherent system of rewards and punishments. Only the sword of justice, wielded by an enlightened despot—who, however, would himself be bound by the inexorable rule of law—could cut the Gordian knot of existing difficulties.

The Taoists opposed both these viewpoints. They denied the possibility of improving the world. Not only was the existing situation bad; society itself was impure. They sought to drown their basic pessimism in mystic contemplation of supernatural forces, and regarded the vain efforts of governments as merely leading to man's degradation by removing him from the primal simplicity of the original anarchic community. For this basic evil there was only one sure remedy: a return to spontaneous nature, which knew neither laws nor moral code.

Even such a bare outline as this suggests that the extremes met, and I should like to set forth my own views as to why and how this occurred. I think that the application of modern political terminology to these three schools of thought may help to clarify the differences between them. The Confucianists—traditionalist, reformist, and al-

ways ready to compromise, so long as their own position was not en-
dangered, in the belief that tried ways would prove the best—might
be described as the party of the center, in which case the radicals who
believed in authoritarianism must be placed on the right, and the
radicals who believed in spontaneity on the left. It has already been
noted—I need only mention the names of Duyvendak, Henri Maspero,
and Waley[7]—what a striking similarity there is between the Legalist
doctrine and the totalitarian movements of our own times. The anarchistic leanings of the Taoists are self-evident. It has also been recognized that the idea of an impersonal law brings together the Legalist
school and the school of the Tao—the Tao being the law of the universe. All this has been said. But I think we can go further. Taoists and
Legalists were at one in their hatred of traditionalism, and both proclaimed the need for a revolution. On the other hand, the positive
outlook shared by the Legalists and the Confucianists made both
afraid of the inexplicable exaltation of the Taoists, suspecting that it
held a potential threat that might have far-reaching consequences.
Neither wanted to see the realization of the Taoist Utopian ideal, and
this shared fear, together with a belief—which they held in common
more than is usually supposed—in the utility of severe laws, often
brought them into temporary alliance. Where they vitally differed was
in the answer which each gave to the question: *against whom* were
the laws directed?

The dividing lines between the schools had always been fluid, and
this was particularly so in the period under consideration. There
were Confucianists who leaned toward Legalist doctrines, Legalists
tinged with Taoism, metaphysicians who admitted the necessity for
education through virtue in worldly matters, and so on. I think that
in the last analysis the reason for this fluidity was that all the various
systems were founded upon the same social substratum: the literati
class. In addition, I believe it might even be possible to relate, in rough
fashion, each of the various schools to a certain section of society. In
general, Confucianism was the ideology of the bureaucracy, and in
particular, of high officials when in office. The adherents of Taoism
were in the main recruited from among retired petty officials or of-

7. J. J. L. Duyvendak, *The Book of Lord Shang* (London, 1928); cf. the review of this book by Henri Maspero, *Journal Asiatique,* 222 (1933), suppl., pp.
48 ff.; Waley, *The Way and Its Power,* p. 85.

ficials dismissed from important positions because of their poverty, or from among candidates for office impatiently awaiting the moment when they would start their official career—almost all of whom had their roots in the peasantry. Those radicals who held positivist and realist views came from the same circles, but had strong links with men engaged in practical affairs—military men, merchants, technicians—and were in daily contact with problems of administration, public works, frontier defense, and the like. It is beyond the scope of this essay to provide adequate support for this hypothesis. Perhaps the words of the three philosophers I will now discuss, each representing one of the three main trends of thought, will provide some evidence of its validity.

WANG FU, OR THE SOCIAL CRITICISM OF A HERMIT

The first of the three philosophers is Wang Fu the hermit, whose approximate dates are A.D. 90 to 165. He was a native of present-day Kansu, then a border province on the western frontier of the empire that was exposed to frequent raids from the Tangut barbarians. Being the son of a concubine, he was looked down upon by his fellows and debarred from an official career, but he enjoyed the friendship of some of the most famous men of his time; among these were the grand patrician Ma Jung (79–166), who was the first to write a commentary on the entire classical canon, and the mathematician-poet Chang Heng (78–139). A feeling of social inferiority, accentuated by his failure to obtain office, explains the vehemence of his style and the irascible tones in which he investigated contemporary social processes. It is impossible to overlook the bitter resentment and personal spite that lend a special flavor to his variations on the well-worn theme of the misunderstood Confucianist scholar. In many passages he harps upon the evil counselors, the jealous and incompetent favorites, the servile flatterers, and the protégés of the great families who surround the emperor and bar the way to superior men, condemning them to silence and inactivity in some out-of-the-way hermitage.

Wang Fu himself was one of those who had to live cut off from political life. His biography tells us:

> Since the emperors Ho (89–105) and An (107–125), each generation was set upon obtaining office, and the influential people of

the day all recommended and protected one another. But [Wang] Fu firmly resisted falling in with the customs of the times, and was uncompromising in his integrity. That is why he was unsuccessful in making an official career. Exasperated by the disappointment of his ambitions, he lived in retirement, and wrote a book of more than thirty chapters criticizing the shortcomings of the age. He did not want his name to be known, and so he called his work "Criticisms of a Hidden Man" (*Ch'ien-fu lun*).[8]

Wang Fu is the most important eyewitness of his times, about which we would know very little if it were not for his account. But in addition, his work, which is an amalgam of the main contemporary trends seen from a Confucianist angle, contains many original ideas. He held that the attainment of the Great Peace (*t'ai-p'ing*)—this expression, which was to have a great future, appears again and again in the *Ch'ien-fu lun*—depended upon a return to what was fundamental (*pen,* the root, what is basic) and the suppression of the secondary (*mo,* the branches, what is secondary and unimportant). On the economic and social level, the basic things were agriculture, useful occupations, and the exchange of goods; the secondary ones, the unstable occupations (*yu-yeh,* or, as we might say, occupations engaged in by people who had been uprooted), artificial refinements, and the

8. *Hou-Han shu* 79.2a. The *Ch'ien-fu lun,* now divided into ten volumes (*chüan*), contains 36 chapters or sections (*p'ien*). Several editions exist; I have used the *Ssu-pu ts'ung-k'an* edition. An index has recently been compiled by the Centre d'études sinologiques in Peking: *Index du Ts'ien-fou louen (Ts'ien-fou louen t'ong-kien)* (Peiping, 1945), xxxvii + 95 pp. The incursions of the Ch'iang barbarians into present-day Kansu in 111 and 141 hit An-ting (Wang Fu's native district) particularly badly. His complaints about the weakness the Emperor and his court displayed in the face of the barbarians were occasioned by the fact that the Emperor transferred the administration of the two commanderies An-ting and Pei-ti, and removed the population to the interior (his book, however, was not written until the reign of Emperor Huan, 147–67, whose policy for external affairs was slightly more energetic): see *Ssu-k'u* 91 (Commercial Press edition, 2, 1882), and cf. *T'ung-chien* 49.15b; 51.13a; 52.12b. This has some bearing on the remarks made in A. Forke, *Geschichte der mittelalterlichen chinesischen Philosophie* (Hamburg, 1934), p. 149. The pages devoted to Wang Fu illustrate the basic weakness of this work, namely, that it attempts to explain, judge, and classify writers on no firmer basis than commonplace opinions and a nodding acquaintance with traditional philosophical conceptions, and with no appreciation of the originality of the thinkers concerned. It is as if one were to try to understand Kant through his contribution to geography, or Voltaire through his plays.

sale of luxury goods. Hence for Wang Fu the essential social categories were a peasantry attached to the soil, craftsmen engaged in useful tasks, and merchants whose trade was confined to the exchange of the products of a natural economy. But nowadays, he complains, the situation is quite the reverse. There is a concentration of wealth. "Although this means enrichment for individual families, it brings impoverishment as far as public revenue is concerned." [9] There should be regulations against the manufacture of articles having no practical utility and of shoddy goods, and against the sale of luxury articles, so as to prevent craftsmen and merchants from making illicit profits. The arts suffer from the same decadence. Scholars discuss futile questions and their prose is written in a precious, artificial style, while their poems are overloaded with rare and high-flown expressions, in an effort to show how clever they are and to achieve celebrity.

Wang Fu was tireless in his fulminations against favoritism, and was continually lashing out against high officialdom for its prevarications, venality, greed, and harshness. "The basis upon which the preservation or ruin of the state rests, the controlling mechanism for order or disorder," he says, "is the enlightened choice of officials." [10] Men should, therefore, be selected on account of their qualities and inherent merits, and not on the grounds of kinship, noble birth, wealth, or even nationality, for even barbarians can be as wise as the Duke of Chou, while among Chinese sometimes the worst of scoundrels can be found. [11] But as things are, "someone who has a lot of money is regarded as a man of merit, and someone who is harsh and violent is looked up to as a superior." [12] And he describes how Heaven blinds the eyes of favorites, usurpers, and flatterers, and all the people who belong to cliques and coteries.

> Even though they may, in the days when they were poor and humble, have been gifted with understanding and with a feeling of human sympathy and a sense of justice [*jen* and *i*], as soon as they become wealthy and ennobled, they turn their backs on their kin, slight their old friends, and lose the feelings they had originally. They desert their nearest and dearest and make their

9. *Ch'ien-fu lun* 1.5b.
10. Ibid., 2.10a.
11. Ibid., 1.11b.
12. Ibid., 2.5a.

favorites their intimates; they scorn their old friends and prefer the company of dogs and horses. They are openhanded with their wealth toward servants and concubines, and use up all their salary and emoluments [in giving presents] to their low slaves. They would sooner see strings of cash rot by the thousand or ten thousand than lend someone else a single cash coin, or the stores of grain rot in their granaries than lend someone else a single bushel.[13]

One of the most interesting chapters of the *Ch'ien-fu lun* is the one entitled "On Excessive Luxury" (*fou-ch'ih*). This is a document of capital importance for information about the social conditions and the morals of second-century China. It begins with the following general remarks:

The present generation are abandoning the fundamental occupation [agriculture] and throwing themselves into trade. Oxen and horses, carriages and carts, block the streets and roads. The products of idle hands [of itinerant vendors] fill the towns and villages. The number of those engaged in the fundamental occupation [i.e. the farmers] diminishes, while those who earn their living through some frivolous occupation increase in numbers . . . If one looks at Loyang today, those engaged in one of the secondary occupations outnumber the peasants ten times, and the number of unemployed is ten times as great as those in secondary occupations. Thus one man plows and a hundred people consume the product; one woman rears silkworms, and a hundred people clothe themselves with the silk. How can one single person supply the needs of a hundred? There are in the empire 100 commanderies, 1,000 subprefectures, and tens of thousands of towns and villages, and everywhere it is the same.[14]

One might be listening to a Middle West farmer inveighing against New York as a modern Babel, or to a peasant from the Midi talking political economy.

Now, a disequilibrium between agriculture and the secondary occupations inevitably resulted in famine, crimes, oppression by officials,

13. Ibid., 3.2b and, with some variants, *Hou-han shu* 79.3a.
14. *Hou-han shu* 79.4a and *Ch'ien-fu lun* 3.4b–5a.

revolt, and finally the fall of the dynasty. This led Wang Fu to formulate a maxim in which each term, pushed to its extreme, produces its opposite in a dialectical movement: "Poverty arises from wealth, weakness derives from power, order engenders disorder, and security insecurity." [15] Formerly, moderation and thrift had been held in high regard. "Now, people dress, eat, and drink extravagantly; they are glib of tongue and practice deceits and tricks of every kind." [16] Some are professional swindlers, others strip fools of their money in games of chance. Even peasants abandon the plow and go prowling over uncultivated land armed with bows. Sometimes they fabricate earthen pellets and sell them to hunters, and they have no time to spare to catch thieves and protect the crops against birds and rodents. Sometimes they manufacture all sorts of toys for amusing children: clay carts, pottery dogs and horsemen, and figurines of singers and dancers. The women, instead of attending to household tasks and weaving, go in for the pernicious arts of magic, dancing, and sorcery to entertain the common people, whose superstitious credulity goes beyond all bounds. The sick brave all weathers to put themselves into the hands of impostors; but the worse their illness becomes, the more they believe in magic cures. They refuse the medicines prescribed by the doctors and seek help from the spirits, and if they die, they are not regarded as the sorcerer's victims, but are blamed for having had recourse to magic too late. The finest silk is cut into ribbons on which magic words and incantations are painted. Far from procuring the good fortune which is sought, these practices are actually a means of robbing the people. "Those people," cries Wang Fu, "who eat up the best of the harvest without having worked, who pass their days in idleness and destroy what others have achieved, should be put under prohibition." [17]

The extravagance of the aristocracy at the capital surpassed all bounds. Even the servants and slaves wore clothes such as no one would have dreamed of wearing in the old days. In the great families, marriages provided an occasion for an unheard-of display of luxury: carriages, slaves on horseback, servants of all kinds. And the worst of all was that "the wealthy vie with each other as to who can outdo the

15. *Ch'ien-fu lun* 3.5a.
16. Ibid., 3.5b, and *Hou-han shu* 79.4b.
17. *Ch'ien-fu lun* 3.6b and *Hou-han shu* 79.5a.

other, while the poor are only ashamed that they cannot compete. And so expenditure on one single festivity is enough to ruin the capital for a lifetime!" [18]

It was the same with funerals. In order to find and transport the rare woods from the south that were the only kinds the nobles considered fit material for coffins, labor had to be mobilized throughout the empire, from Lo-lang to Tun-huang; all the skills of the craftsmen were called upon, and manpower was recklessly wasted. "Today, the wealthy aristocracy at the capital and the great landowners in the provinces, although they scarcely trouble to look after their parents during their lifetime, honor them with a sumptuous funeral when they die." [19]

Another of Wang Fu's favorite themes is injustice, or rather the delays and chicanery attending the administration of justice, and the interminable procedures that robbed people of time. The resulting costs and wastage of man-hours impoverished the state. The various ranks of magistrates all kept a check on their subordinates, or were anxious about what those superior in authority might do, and so postponed settlement from spring to autumn and from autumn, again, to spring. The common people were unable to afford the costs and the waste of time involved in procedural methods of this kind, whereas wealthy people could employ an advocate (*k'e,* literally "guest") to represent their interests. On the other hand, amnesties, which were only too frequent, merely acted as an incitement to wrongdoers. In Loyang, there are bands of criminals in league with the authorities, and instigators of murder who have a dozen lives on their conscience and are never punished.

It was in connection with judicial procedure that Wang Fu developed a kind of labor theory of value, one of the most curious features of his work. The passage in question runs as follows:

The existence of the state depends upon the people. The existence of the people depends on nourishment. A plentiful supply of nour-

18. *Ch'ien-fu lun* 3.7a and *Hou-han shu* 79.5b.

19. *Ch'ien-fu lun* 3.8b and *Hou-han shu* 79.6b. Interestingly, the two border towns mentioned by Wang Fu have since become famous as sites of important archeological finds, and many objects of the funerary cult have been found at Lo-lang. Cf. for instance K. Hamada, "On the Painting of the Han Period," *Memoirs of the Tōyō Bunko, 8* (1936), 31 ff.

ishment depends upon the work of men. Work is reckoned by labor-days [*jih-li,* literally "a day's strength," that is, the hours of work and the energy spent]. The days of a well governed state are long, because [men have a sense] of well-being; moreover people have some hours of leisure and a margin of energy. The days of a disorderly state are short, because [people feel] pressed for time; moreover people are stretched to their full extent, and have not enough strength to carry out their tasks.[20]

Wang Fu hastens to explain that that does not mean days can be made longer and hours regulated at will, but that in a well governed state people are calm and the days appear long, whereas in a disorderly state injustice, oppression, corvées, and arbitrary exactions exert pressure on everyone and make the days seem short. And he sums up his conclusions in the following maxim: "Morality and Justice [*li* and *i*] arise from wealth and plenty, pillage and robbery result from poverty and scarcity. Wealth and plenty arise from having free time at one's disposal, poverty and scarcity from having no time at one's disposal." [21]

Finally I should like to mention several passages that anticipate a return to the Legalist doctrine, which was to dominate the thoughts of the succeeding generation. In a chapter on the appraisal of merit, Wang Fu once more denounces privilege: "The marquises of today have inherited their title from their forebears and benefit from the rank of their ancestors. Being themselves of no service to China and of no value to the people, they yet reign as autocrats in their fiefs, and eat their fill in the idleness afforded by their large incomes; they drain the resources of the people and possess all the wealth in the state. This is the height of parasitism!" Radical methods must be adopted to remedy this state of affairs, and Wang Fu is spurred to cry out: "The law, rewards and punishments, are the real pivot of order and disorder." [22] Elsewhere he explains that a personal sense of justice on the part of the ruler is not enough. The law must be observed in the same

20. *Ai-jih p'ien* (The Grudging of Labor Days), *Ch'ien-fu lun* 4.13b and *Hou-han shu* 79.8a. (The literal translation should run: "What makes the state a state" and "What makes the people a people.")

21. *Ch'ien-fu lun* 4.14b and *Hou-han shu* 79.8a. Cf. *Ta-tai li-chi,* chap. *Sheng-te.*

22. *Ch'ien-fu lun* 4.11a and 12b–13a.

way by everyone, rich or poor, wise or foolish. "The law and its regulations are the bit, the reins, and the whip in the sovereign's control, the
people are his chariot and horses." [23] This metaphor, which comes
from Han Fei-tzu, shows how Wang Fu was already impregnated
with the idea of an impartial system of law that must be applicable to
everyone, high or low, without regard to social distinctions. But it is
highly significant that he finds it necessary to excuse himself, and adds
the following remark: "Critics will no doubt maintain that corporal
punishments should not be used, and that it is enough to rely solely
on the civilizing power of virtue. This is far from being the opinion
of those who realize that times have changed." [24]

TS'UI SHIH, OR THE ATTEMPT TO REVIVE LEGALIST DOCTRINES

Ts'ui Shih, the second philosopher to be studied, came from present-
day Hopeh[25] and belonged to a well known family of impoverished
gentry. Born about 110, he was a generation younger than Wang Fu,
who was one of his father's best friends.[26] He was called to office in
151 as one of the "scholars of independent mind," and had the mis-
fortune to be attached to the department of the Grand Marshal Liang
Chi, who, as we have seen, was the most powerful, the wealthiest, and
the most hated man of his time. Although Ts'ui Shih merely worked
as an archivist in the Tung-kuan library in connection with the editing

23. Ibid., 5.5b.
24. Ibid., 5.6a.
25. The subprefecture of An-p'ing, south of Pao-ting. Cf. F. Kuhn, "Das
Dschong lun des Tsui Schi. Eine konfuzianische Rechtfertigung der Diktatur
aus der Han-Zeit (2. Jahr. n. Chr.)," *Abhandlungen der Königlich Preussischen
Akademie der Wissenschaften* (Berlin, 1914), 27 pp. This doctoral thesis contains so many errors that I refrain from enumerating them.
26. The biography of his father, Ts'ui Yüan (78–143), precedes his own in
Hou-han shu 82.12a–14a. We read there that Ts'ui Shih faithfully carried out
his father's last wishes, which were expressed in these terms (13b): "Man is
given the breath of Heaven and of Earth so that he may live. When the end
comes, the essence of his being re-enters Heaven, and his bones return to Earth.
It is unimportant what piece of land contains his mortal remains, so it is not
necessary to take my coffin to our village. You must not accept anything in the
nature of a gift of condolence, nor allow a single domestic animal to be offered
in sacrifice!" This account somewhat contradicts that of the costly funeral Ts'ui
Shih gave his father at Loyang, which used up the whole family fortune. Both
Ts'ui Yüan and Ts'ui Shih were famous as calligraphers; cf. *San-kuo chih* 1.45a
and 21.22a (commentary).

of the official annals,[27] yet, because he was a former client of Liang Chi, he was dismissed and debarred from holding further office. Before the proscription of Liang Chi's followers, he had made himself familiar with the thorny problems arising on the frontiers that were under constant threat of barbarian invasion. He had taught the indigenous population along the upper reaches of the Yellow River, in the region of present-day Sui-yüan, how to use hemp instead of the grass they had formerly used for making clothing, and had bought spinning wheels and looms out of his own funds. He also organized a warning system of beacons for purposes of military defense. I mention these details only to illustrate the fact that adherents of the Legalist school were men of practical experience. Such men, whose life in out-of-the-way places in the farthest corners of the empire had given them a realist outlook, and who were thoroughly versed in everyday practical matters and in military and administrative problems, must have found Confucian homilies intolerably repugnant, and must have felt an implacable hatred against the greedy holders of metropolitan sinecures. They must also have acquired a fairly strong sense of nationality from having fulfilled military or civilian duties on the frontiers of Chinese civilization, and this would make them bristle with anger over the negligence and lack of concern among the high officials at the court, who had no feelings of this kind whatsoever. Whatever their origins may have been, whether lower class or gentry, these knowledgeable men with technological skills were very close to the working classes, and, prizing efficiency as they did, they felt misunderstood and betrayed. Thus muddle and corruption became anathema to them, and they sought to combat them by every possible means.

The incessant attacks of the Hsien-pi barbarians[28] in southern Manchuria around 160 made it advisable to appoint an experienced administrator, and Ts'ui Shih was made prefect of Liao-tung. A little later, when the persecution of the literati was imminent, he had the prudence to refuse the offer of a high post as a secretary of state. Upon the death of his father, he was forced to sell the family estate in order to meet the expenses of the elaborate type of funeral demanded by

27. This work, begun in 151, resulted in the *Tung-kuan Han-chi,* the official history of the Han, part of which has survived; cf. *Ssu-k'u* 50 (II, 1089) and *Hou-han shu* 56.4a.

28. The Hsien-pi conducted raids in 158, in 163, and again in 166; cf. *T'ung-chien* 54.19a and 55.13b.

the extravagant customs of the times. Thus ruined, he earned his living as a distiller and an itinerant vendor, which brought upon him the scoffing comments of his social equals. His biographers, however, hasten to assure us that he restricted the amount of profit to what was necessary for his daily needs, and ended his career as poor as when he started. On his death, which occurred about 170, not enough money could be found within the four walls of his house to provide for a decent burial.

Ts'ui Shih must have written his treatise, entitled "On Politics," shortly after 150. Today, all that remains of it are the fragments that appear in his biography and in an encyclopedia of political writings compiled at the beginning of T'ang, which did not survive in China, but was fortunately preserved in Japan.[29] The authors of the *Hou-han shu* tell us that the treatise was highly valued by his contemporaries, and they quote a remark of Chung-ch'ang T'ung, that "every sovereign should have a copy made to keep by the side of his throne." [30]

It would perhaps be more correct to translate the title *Cheng lun* as "On Government." Nevertheless, it remains true that Ts'ui Shih was determined to find a purely political solution to the problems of his times. They were the same problems that had already appalled the hermit Wang Fu, but they had now become more pressing, and a more radical method of dealing with them was now required. The time for merely voicing complaints was over; what was now needed was a more precise way of thinking that would lead to action. The particular contribution of Ts'ui Shih, who may be regarded as the pupil of Wang Fu and the master of Chung-ch'ang T'ung, the third philosopher to be discussed, was his renewed championship of the old Legalist doctrine. With him, there were no further hesitations. He came down firmly on the side of the School of Law, and viewed every problem from the realist angle.

What is the reason for the present scarcity, he asks. A long period of peace gives rise to slackness, carelessness, and inertia. Morals be-

29. *Hou-han shu* 82.14b–17b and *Ch'ün-shu chih-yao* (*Ssu-pu ts'ung-k'an* edition) 45.1–14b. On this encyclopedia see Juan Yüan, *Ssu-k'u wei-shu shu-mu t'i-yao* 2.1a, in *Ssu-k'u, Ta-tung* edition, Vol. 9, and P. Pelliot, "Notes de Bibliographie Chinoise," *Bulletin de l'Ecole Français d'Extrême Orient,* 2 (1902), p. 315. The Sui bibliographical treatise includes the *Cheng-lun,* in six chapters, in the section on the Legalists, and also lists the works of Ts'ui Shih in three chapters, lost since the Liang dynasty; see *Sui-shu* 34.3a and 35.2a.
30. *Hou-han shu* 82.14b.

come perverted, cunning prevails, and decent men have to keep quiet. But the worst feature of all is the deadening effect of routine.

> The ordinary run of people cling to the ancient books and are entangled in the past. They do not know how to adapt to circumstances, and they overvalue tradition and neglect practical experience. How can one discuss with them important matters of state? . . . What! These dull-witted reactionaries deliberately ignore changing circumstances and complacently accustom themselves to what they see happening. They are incapable of appreciating achievements, and still less able to plan anything new. They simply say that everything derives from ancient institutions, and that is all there is to it! [31]

But "the Sage (*sheng-jen*) takes circumstances into account and adapts institutions to the times." [32] This formulation is characteristic of the realist spirit, as is also the tendency—common to all innovators up to and including Wang An-shih and K'ang Yu-wei—to give their ideas the prestige derived from historical precedent, for which purpose they make Confucius into a reformer, or even a revolutionary. There are two aspects of this antitraditionalist interpretation of venerable tradition. Until modern times, it illustrates both the magic attraction of historical precedent, and the necessity for innovators to clothe their ideas in historical precedent if they wanted to gain a hearing. But all Chinese reformers, even if they referred to traditions only in order to demonstrate their uselessness, remained influenced by them in spite of themselves. This shows the limitations of pragmatic opportunism.

It is unnecessary to go into the historical examples Ts'ui Shih uses to support his thesis. Let us rather consider the political conclusions he draws.

> Since it is at present impossible simply to take as model (*fa*) the eight generations [that is, the Three Sovereigns and the Five Demiurges], it is therefore advisable to turn to the regime of the hegemons [*pa-cheng,* the tyrants of ancient China]. Hence rewards should be augmented and punishments made more severe so that [the people] can be led, and the technicalities of the law (*fa-shu*)

31. *Hou-han shu* 82.15b and *Ch'ün-shu chih-yao* 45.2b.
32. *Hou-han shu* 82.15a and *Ch'ün-shu chih-yao* 45.2a.

should be published in understandable form so that [the people] can be kept within bounds. Since the days when sovereigns ceased to possess supreme virtue [this is a small concession to Confucianism], it is severity that ensures order, while indulgence ends in anarchy.[33]

That seems clear enough. But Ts'ui Shih clarifies his thoughts still further in order to justify the shocking brutality of his proposals.

In the field of historical argument, he strives to prove that the abolition of corporal punishment under the liberal regime of that Confucian paragon, the Emperor Wen of the Former Han, only led to an increase in the incidence of the capital penalty; for the 300 or 500 strokes of the rod, which replaced the cruel punishment of amputation of the nose or feet, invariably brought about the death of the victim. So let no more hymns of praise be heard about the benefits of the charitable reign of Emperor Wen. Incidentally, Ts'ui Shih's opinions on the necessity of re-introducing barbaric forms of punishment in order to intimidate criminals were shared by no less irreproachable a Confucianist than the celebrated commentator Cheng Hsüan. Indeed, the chapter on the penal code in the "History of Chin" informs us that about 163, on the eve of the troubles that were already threatening to plunge the whole empire into a state of anarchy, Cheng Hsüan, together with Ts'ui Shih, proposed a re-introduction of the old forms of punishment, although the proposal was not carried through.[34] This question was not unimportant, as we shall see later. Meanwhile, I shall confine myself here to reporting the characteristic reflections recorded by so eminent a Confucian scholar as Ssu-ma Kuang, the famous historian and conservative statesman of Sung times, upon reading the *Cheng-lun*. In his great historical work, after giving the passage I have quoted here, he says:[35]

The laws of the Han dynasty were severe enough; and yet Ts'ui Shih considered them overindulgent. What is the explanation for this? The fact of the matter is that most of the rulers during the period of decadence were weak and lax, and their foolish coun-

33. *Hou-han shu* 82.16a. *Fa-shu,* "the art of legislation," or "the recipes of the Legalists." Under the Later Han, this term was used for the doctrines of Shang Yang and Han Fei; cf. *Hou-han shu* 58B.8b and *San-kuo chih* 1.45b.

34. *Chin-shu* 30.3b.

35. *T'ung-chien* 53 (year 151), 13b–14a.

selors were only concerned with preserving their accustomed tranquillity. Thus high dignitaries in favor were not called to account for their misdemeanors, nor were wealthy people and rascals punished for violation of the laws. Only to relations and intimates was any sympathy or mercy shown. Scoundrels achieved their aims, but the fundamental principles of justice were not observed. That is why Ts'ui Shih's treatise, while it may have served as a corrective to injustice at a particular time, does not lay down a principle that is applicable to all ages. Confucius said: "If the government is indulgent, the people become negligent. If they are negligent, they must be corrected with severity. If the government is [too] severe, the people are oppressed. If they are oppressed, they must be accorded indulgence. Harmonious government consists in using indulgence to counteract severity, and severity to counteract indulgence.[36] That is the eternal, invariable way of things!

In the ideological sphere, too, Ts'ui Shih proves to be a thoroughgoing Legalist, and the way he defines his standpoint as against that of the visionaries of Taoist persuasion is of the greatest interest. Taoism, along with its overt anarchistic ideal of a society free to run itself without interference, had an esoteric side that advocated a back-to-nature form of asceticism and various breathing exercises, dietetic disciplines, and regimens for sexual hygiene.[37] At the time when Ts'ui Shih wrote his book, practices of this kind were attracting a number of followers among the people of the countryside. He may not have been aware of this, but he keenly appreciated the basic incompatibility of his own activist beliefs with the quietism of the spiritual side of Taoism. This is proved by the following passage, in which he alludes to various procedures for "nourishing the vital principle," employing technical terms that go back to Chuang-tzu.

> "Rolling about like a bear, stretching oneself out like a bird" are perhaps suitable methods for prolonging life, but are no remedy for a chill. "Breathing in and out, spitting out and swallowing the breath" may well be the way (*tao*) to attain longevity, but is useless as an ointment for broken bones. In truth, laws that serve

36. *Tso-chuan*, Chao, 20th year.
37. On such practices see Maspero, "Les Procédés de 'nourrir le principe vital' dans la réligion taoïste ancienne," pp. 177 ff., and 353 ff.

the state are like medical treatment [*li,* "putting in order"] for the human body. If it is at peace, it is nourished; if it is sick, it has to have remedies applied. Now penalties and punishments are the medicines of disorder; virtue and education the daily nourishment of order. But attempting to get rid of troubles by means of virtue and education would be like attempting to cure sickness by prescribing a rich diet. Dealing with a peaceful situation by means of punishments and penalties would be like nourishing [a healthy body] with medicines.[38]

As an eyewitness of his times, Ts'ui Shih is as valuable a source as Wang Fu, although he does not provide such a full account. Several interesting passages fully corroborate some of the statements of the "hidden man." Ts'ui Shih sums up the anxieties of "men of judgment" under three heads. Human nature has a natural liking for well-being and luxury. Today, this tendency, instead of being restrained by the enactments of the law, is stimulated by displays of rare merchandise and the manufacture of luxury goods. Extravagant habits lead to a rise in the price of articles with no practical utility, but a reduction in the price of agricultural products. That is why the peasants abandon the plow and turn toward more lucrative occupations. "The granaries are empty and the prisons packed." [39] The extravagant display required by the funerary cult spells ruination. In order not to be left behind, in order to outdo one's neighbor, people willingly sacrifice the family fortune, then later are forced by poverty to become thieves. The effect of such customs is equally deplorable among officials and among the common people, for the latter have to take to brigandage because of the exactions demanded by the former. In these circumstances, it is hopeless to go on relying on old ways of doing things and refuse to undertake radical reforms. The only remedy is the method of Tzuch'an, father of all Legalists and a contemporary of Confucius: severe penalties and heavy punishments!

Ts'ui Shih also has an illuminating passage about the highhandedness of officials. If they make purchases at the market or order something to be made by a craftsman, they refuse to pay when the goods are delivered, or will not pay the price arranged, or delay payment for

38. *Hou-han shu* 82.16b. Cf. *Chuang-tzu* XV, 1 (*Ssu-pu ts'ung-k'an* edition, 6.1b).

39. *Ch'ün-shu chih-yao* 45.5a.

years. Often they return to a craftsman goods that have not yet been
paid for but have been used and are already beginning to show signs
of dilapidation—carriages, for instance, or caps of office. Naturally the
articles are no longer salable. The people, aware of these dishonest
practices, "regard officials as persons to be avoided; so they keep out
of their way, hide, and refuse to answer requests. Then they get arrested, intimidated, and forced to comply. But when no one puts his
heart into his work, the utensils manufactured are of poor quality, incidental expenses mount up, money is wasted, and prices bear no relation to cost." [40] That, he says in conclusion, is why there are so many
lawsuits.

On the other hand, there are many dishonest businessmen: for example, dealers in arms who supply weapons not fit for use. These
swindlers get into league with greedy armorers and untrustworthy officials, and they divide the profits between them. This reaches such a
pitch that the people on the frontiers have to forge their own weapons
if they want to hold their own against the barbarians. The mark of
manufacture—all goods were obligatorily marked with the name of
the manufacturer—is no guarantee so long as frequent amnesties and
the buying off of penalties allow malefactors to infringe the law. Again,
there is but one remedy: more severe laws. [41]

Ts'ui Shih brings his experience to bear on another theme dear to
reformers, the question of inadequate pay and frequent transfer of
officials, with the accompanying phenomenon of corruption. With admirable realism, and foreshadowing the attitude of Wang An-shih, he
says that "without nourishment men cannot exist. It is only after giving them something to clothe and feed themselves with that one can
teach them the rules of propriety and duty (*li* and *i*), or intimidate
them with penalties and punishments." [42] When an official sees that
his family is in need, he is capable of anything, especially as wealth is
within easy reach. And he quotes a saying we find again in the works
of Chung-ch'ang T'ung: "Thirsty horses are a guard on the water
supply, hungry dogs on the meat." [43] Formerly there was no competition between the administration and the people—another essential

40. Ibid., 6b–7a.
41. Ibid., 7b.
42. Ibid., 11b.
43. Ibid., 12a.

point in Legalist doctrine—because officials were given an adequate salary. How do matters stand at present? High officials, responsible for a district as large as the fiefs of former days, receive the salary of a clerk. They are allotted, in kind, 20 bushels of grain, and in money, 2,000 cash. Even if they do not possess any slaves, they at least require a servant, who will receive from his master 1,000 cash a month. Of the remaining 1,000 cash, half is spent on hay, fats, and meat, and half on firewood, charcoal, salt, and vegetables. The two men, the official and his servant, consume six bushels a month; the rest is only just enough for the horses. How then is it possible to pay for winter and summer clothing, the sacrifices of the four seasons, entertainment of visitors, and expenditure on relations, wife, and children? In these circumstances, corruption among officials is an unavoidable evil. Ts'ui Shih proposes that their salaries should be increased by at least 50 per cent.[44]

The question may be raised as to how much should be allowed for rhetorical exaggeration in the unfavorable picture of society painted by these moralists. For my part, I do not believe that they exaggerated in order to plead their case better. I am even convinced that their accounts fall short of reality, as we shall see when studying the "Sincere Words" of Chung-ch'ang T'ung.

CHUNG-CH'ANG T'UNG, OR THE "SINCERE WORDS" OF A MADMAN

Chung-ch'ang T'ung, perhaps the most attractive of the three moralists studied here, brings us to the threshold of the third century. He was born in 180—shortly after the persecution of the literati and on the eve of the revolt of the Yellow Turbans—in the south of present-day Shantung, not far from the native country of Confucius.[45] When he was twenty, he got to know the whole of North China, then in a state of turmoil, on the travels he undertook to complete his education, as was customary with most of the wealthy young men of his time. He was also, like the "wandering scholars" (*yu-shih*) of the third century B.C., in search of office, and during his wanderings he was frequently offered employment by local satraps who were as keen on learned discussions as their prototypes, the princes of the Warring Kingdoms,

44. Ibid., 12b.
45. In the principality of Kao-p'ing (*Kao-p'ing kuo*) in the commandery of Shan-yang (present-day Yen-chou-fu).

and who were even more eager to gain the additional prestige that would be conferred on them by having around them the most promising and brilliant young men from intellectual circles. During one of his journeys, Chung-ch'ang T'ung visited the nephew of Yüan Shao, at T'ai-yüan. This was a man named Kao Kan, who was governor of the prefecture of Ping (in present-day Shansi), and who, like his illustrious uncle, surrounded himself with young scholars from all over the country. The governor questioned Chung-ch'ang T'ung on the contemporary political situation; he, in spite of having been received with every courtesy, replied with a certain amount of frankness, not to say presumptuousness: "Sir, you have very high ambitions, but are lacking in talent. You like scholars, but you do not know how to select men for office. I must therefore give you a serious warning: take care!" This speech later contributed to the growing fame of Chung-ch'ang T'ung, because it was regarded as a sign of his foresight, for in 206 a revolt against Ts'ao Ts'ao, the sworn enemy of Yüan Shao's clan, put an abrupt end to the governor's ambitions.[46]

About 210, Hsün Yü (163–212), a great scholar, the director of the state secretariat, and an intimate counselor of Ts'ao Ts'ao, invited the young philosopher to join him on the intellectual general staff or "brain trust" which that great adventurer, Ts'ao Ts'ao, was clever enough to gather round him. Thus at thirty years of age, Chung-ch'ang T'ung, without being in any sense a careerist, had realized the ambition dreamed of by all men of his age group and education—that of playing an active part in the political events of the time, or at least of being able to follow them at close quarters by the side of the most important of all the politicians, the man who was the central figure in the struggles that lasted for a whole generation.

Chung-ch'ang T'ung was free and forthright in character, and frankly said what he had to say, coming straight to the point without being overpolite about it. His contemporaries sometimes called him "the madman" (*k'uang-sheng*), a term in current use at the time, and a good epithet for him. It originally meant a mad dog, but had come to mean a crazy fanatic, excitable and tempestuous, an extremist, a visionary. (The expression comes from *Lun-yü* XVII, 16.) Perhaps the best translation would be "nonconformist." And in fact, "every

46. *Hou-han shu* 79.11a; cf. *San-kuo chih* 21 (Wei *chih*), 21a–b and *T'ung-chien* 65 (year 206), 1a ff., where extracts from the *Ch'ang-yen* are also found.

time he was called upon to fill a post in a district or a commandery," we read in his biography, "he immediately excused himself on account of illness and never accepted. He always pronounced the opinion that all those who wander [in search of office] and visit kings and emperors have no other aim but to acquire celebrity by making a career. But renown does not last forever, and it is easy to lose one's life. One can, however, amuse oneself by happy wanderings here and there. One can choose a pure and spacious dwelling and thus fulfill one's aspirations." His reflections on the "desire for happiness" are contained in the *Lo-chih lun,* which has been preserved in his biography, and which I now translate in its entirety.[47]

Let the place where one lives have good fields and a large house set upon a hillside and looking over a river, surrounded by canals and bamboo-bordered pools. In front are laid out the threshing floor and the vegetable garden, and behind is planted an orchard of fruit trees. There are enough carriages and boats to ensure that one shall not have the trouble of walking or wading; there are enough servants to ensure that one shall not exhaust oneself with menial tasks. For nourishing one's family, the finest viands are at hand; wife and children do not have to bear the burden of doing any hard work.

When good friends pay a visit, they are served with wine and refreshments for their entertainment. When times are prosperous, on feast days a lamb or a suckling pig is roasted and served to them. There is enjoyment to be had between the fields and the garden, and sport to be had in the woods. There is bathing in clear water, or breathing in of fresh winds. One can fish for the darting carp, or shoot at wild geese on the wing. One can chant softly at the foot of the rain altar, or carouse up in the great hall.

One's spirits can be calmed in the interior apartments [the women's apartments], or one can meditate on the mysterious void of Lao-tzu, or make one's vital essence harmonious by practicing breathing exercises, in an attempt to become like the supreme men (*chih-jen*). With one or two initiates [*ta* combines the meanings of intelligent, penetrating, and free, untrammeled], the way

47. *Hou-han shu* 79,11a–b (cf. Forke, *Geschichte der mittelalterlichen chinesischen Philosophie,* pp. 173–74).

(*tao*) can be discussed and books explained. Upward and downward the Two Powers [Heaven and Earth] can be examined;
men and things can be analyzed and explored. The strings of the
lute can vibrate with the sublime song "The Southern Wind," or
a wondrous melody in the pure *re* mode can be sung.[48] In one's
transports all worldly affairs can be transcended, and from on high
what lies between Heaven and Earth can be contemplated. The
demands of one's times are left unheeded, and life can be prolonged for ever. In this way one can reach the firmament and
emerge into a region beyond space and time.

Why then should one be eager to be received by kings and
emperors?

This is a far cry from the austere, prosaic style of Wang Fu or Ts'ui
Shih. It is a poem in prose, a kind of philosophical confession of purely
Taoist inspiration. It abounds in the technical terms of *Lao-tzu* and
of the "Book of Changes" (*I-ching*), particularly those found in the
grand commentary on the *I-ching*, the *Hsi-tz'u-chuan*, which was held
in high esteem by the exponents of Taoist philosophy. The same is
true of the poems that have been preserved in the biography of Chung-
ch'ang T'ung in the *Hou-han shu*.[49] These poems contain all the
rapture of a spiritual journey, found in many of the poets of the
period, and akin to what is expressed in the following two lines by
Paul Valéry:

> Que l'univers n'est qu'un défaut
> Dans la pureté du non-être.

I have some scruples in giving here my very imperfect translation
of these four-character quatrains, for nothing remains of the flavor
of the original. But it is important to know something of the imaginative world and the realm of feeling that shines behind the hard prose
of political reality, of which we shall hear more presently.

48. The text—apocryphal—of the Song of the Southern Wind, the author of
which was the legendary Shun, is as follows (according to the *K'ung-tzu chia-yü*,
where it is quoted in the commentary): "The scent of the southern wind, oh! It
can carry away the hatred of my people, oh! The season of the southern wind,
oh! It can prosper the fortunes of my people, oh!" *Re* is the second string, the
pure string (*shang*).

49. *Hou-han shu* 79.11b–12a (cf. the translation in Forke, p. 174).

1.

The flying bird leaves behind the print of its claw
The emerging cicada sheds its skin
The rearing serpent quits its scales
The divine dragon loses its horns

The supreme man is able to change
The man who is free is detached from the commonplace
He rides the clouds without reins
He runs with the wind without feet

The falling dew is his curtain
The wide firmament his roof
The foggy vapors nourish him
The nine suns are his candles

The eternal stars are his shining pearls
The dawn sky his gleaming jade
In all the six directions
He lets his heart roam where it will

Let human affairs go by—
Why jostle and oppress each other?

2.

The Great Way is simple
But few are those who see the germs of it
Take things as they come without finding fault
Follow the trend without approving

From time immemorial thoughts turn and turn
Tortuous, sinuous, tedious
What good are all these thoughts
The supremely important lies in the self

I dispatch my anguish up to Heaven
I bury my sorrow in the Earth
In revolt I throw away the Classical Books
I annihilate and deny the Songs and the Odes

The hundred philosophers are obscure and petty
I'should like to set fire to them
My will mounts up high above the hills
My thoughts float far beyond the seas

The Original Breath is my boat
The light wind my rudder
I hover in the supreme purity
I let my thoughts dissolve.

The *Ch'ang-yen,* which might be translated as "Sincere Words" or "Frank Remarks," derives its title from the fact (so says the biography) that at every discussion on historical questions or political problems, Chung-ch'ang T'ung was always seething with indignation. The original book, a large volume of 100,000 words divided into thirty-four sections, was still in existence in T'ang times, but has since been lost. All we know of it are the three chapters quoted in the biography of the author, and a few fragments preserved in the *Ch'ün-shu chih-yao* and in other encyclopedias.[50]

The first chapter, entitled "Order and Disorder" (*Li-luan p'ien*), is a sort of balancing of historical accounts. It begins with a panegyric that contains lightly veiled allusions to Ts'ao Ts'ao. The other claimants to power have disappeared. Those who but a short time ago were our superiors or equals, who put us in prison and were planning to block our way so that they could make their fortune, have been defeated. They bow their heads and are content to be our tools. All the empire looks hopefully toward us, and all the power is concentrated in the hands of one man. It is a unique occasion, in which there is a conjunction of events so favorable that even a fool could scarcely help making successful use of it. Because of "his" exceptional situation, all the Dukes of Chou and Confuciuses in the world could not vie with "him" in wisdom. The "him" referred to is, of course, Ts'ao Ts'ao.

But Chung-ch'ang T'ung goes on to predict the fall of the new dynasty, because of the results of the continuous degradation power

50. *Ch'ün-shu chih-yao* 45.14b–28a; Ma Kuo-han, *Yü-han shan-fang chi i-shu* (fragments collected from various encyclopedias; Chi-nan-fu, 1874), 7, 6. The *Ch'ang-yen* was still in existence in T'ang times, as the authors of the Imperial Catalogue proved when discussing a commentary of the *Wen-hsin tiao-lung,* (*Ssu-k'u* 195, 4, 4351).

brings: dissipation, extravagance, the joys of the harem and the hunt, and emperors who have become the prey of women and flatterers. The greed of the bad shepherds drives the exploited people to revolt, and finally barbarian invasions bring about complete anarchy. "Everything crumbles and falls apart. And one fine day the dynasty is no more." This was a regular occurrence, according to Chung-ch'ang T'ung, who had evolved a theory of the cyclic disturbances in Chinese history by purely empirical methods, regarding them as resulting from the gradual decadence of dynasties. It must be admitted that at that time a more convincing explanation could not possibly be found. But however that may be, this prophecy was really an accusation made against the last Han rulers, a judgment arrived at through the bitter experience of half a century. It is among these reflections on grandeur and decadence in Chinese history that the passage of greatest interest, from a sociological point of view, occurs. After having reaffirmed the Legalist thesis that "the present is not like ancient times, and the further they are left behind, the greater the difference becomes," he goes on to say that numerous upstarts have been raised to important positions through sheer good fortune, while the intelligentsia, the literati, are struggling against the greatest material difficulties. He then continues as follows:

> The mansions of the great landowners stretch in rows by the hundred, their opulent domains cover the whole countryside, their slaves can be counted by the thousand, and their clients by tens of thousands. Dealers and merchants move about in their boats and carts in all directions, and the piled-up stocks of speculators fill the towns. The grandest houses are not big enough to contain all their jewels and gems; the hills and valleys are not wide enough to contain all the horses, oxen, sheep, and pigs. The splendid mansions are filled with ravishing boys and beautiful concubines; the halls within resound with the songs of singing girls and the music of courtesans. Guests attend the reception and dare not take their leave; carriages and horsemen jostle and cannot move forward. The flesh of domestic animals goes bad before it can all be eaten; the most carefully decanted wines get spoiled before they can all be drunk. [The master] has but to give a wink of the eye and his people obey him; he has but to give the least sign of pleasure or displeasure and his people follow his intimate wishes.

> Such are the ample pleasures of the nobility, such are the solid
> riches of the masters. This is what can be obtained by those who
> use guile and practice fraud! And once they have in fact obtained
> it, no one holds it against them as a crime! . . . What man
> would be likely to choose to follow the example of the literati
> who, in order to make a career, renounce fame and pleasure for
> destitution and poverty, exchange leisure and freedom for the
> servitude of duty? [51]

This chapter ends on a note of melancholy skepticism: the old will
not live to see again the better days they have known, and the young
will live just long enough to see a new period of decadence worse
than the one before. The existing situation, with towns in ruins and
whole areas of the countryside without a single living soul, seemed
much worse than the chaos that had reigned two centuries earlier
after the revolt of the Red Eyebrows. "I do not know what we are
coming to"—this is how his general survey, which is pessimistic
enough taken all in all, ends.

In the second chapter, bearing the title "Augmentation and Dimi-
nution" (*Sun-i p'ien*), Chung-ch'ang T'ung lays down what amounts
to a political program in eight sections, which may be summarized as
follows.

1. The program begins by stating the major theme of all reformers:
none of the old institutions must be retained except those suited to
the present situation; it is essential to change everything that is in
contradiction with modern times. What were the things that Chung-
ch'ang T'ung regarded as anachronistic? First and foremost, the power
of the aristocracy and particularly the preponderant political role of
the "external clans." He never tires of lashing out at the misdeeds of
these parasites who "live on their emoluments without ever moving a
finger." So, no aristocracy!—a stipulation which, like everything else in
the program, is clearly directed against the master of the hour.

2. The complaints against the nobility are similar in tone to those
expressed in the criticisms of Wang Fu and Ts'ui Shih. But Chung-
ch'ang T'ung draws a definite conclusion: the real reason so much
poverty exists is that "private property is not restricted (*fen-t'ien wu
hsien*). If the Great Peace is to be attained, it is necessary to re-estab-

51. *Hou-han shu* 79.13b–14a.

lish, once and for all, the old institution of the square fields divided into nine equal lots, arranged like the pattern traced by the character for the word "well." The question as to whether the famous *ching-t'ien* system ever existed is irrelevant here. For contemporaries, the term simply meant "equal distribution of land," and so we can interpret this second demand in more familiar terms as a demand for agrarian reform.

3. It is also necessary to re-establish the old penal code, which was of greater severity than the existing one. In answer to the objections of an imaginary critic who argues that the punishment of an innocent person would be unforgivable, Chung-ch'ang T'ung replies: "If good people had never suffered unjustly in earlier reigns, there would never have been the capital penalty for criminals. Your argument amounts to being indulgent to those who kill others, and merciless to those who punish others." [52] Nevertheless he proposed that the capital penalty should be used only for the three most serious crimes: murder, rebellion, and incest. His main interest was in jurisprudence: how to ensure that the code was administered efficiently, how to adjust disparities between rules of conduct and paragraphs in the code, between facts and terminology. We are already familiar with these ideas, which were common to the School of the Law and the School of Names.

4. This section contains proposals for practical government measures.

Basing himself on the *Hsi-tz'u-chuan,* the commentary on the "Book of Changes," Chung-ch'ang T'ung first of all lays down the principle that "the upper classes consist of a minority, the lower classes of the great majority . . . The foolish work for the wise, just as the branches of a tree stem from the trunk. This is an eternal law in the maintenance of order in the empire." [53] He also stresses the need for bringing the vast areas of uncultivated land under cultivation, and then makes the following sixteen proposals:

(1) The boundaries of administrative districts are to be rectified, allowing a maximum distance of 200 leagues between the administrative center and the circumference.

(2) Scrupulous exactness is to be used in compiling tax registers and census lists.

52. Ibid., 16a.
53. Ibid., 16b. Cf. *Hsi-tz'u chuan* IV, 3.

(3) The militia is to be reorganized into groups of ten and five.

(4) "Private property is to be limited so as to put an end to seizure of land," that is, an end to expropriation of the peasants by the large landowners.

(5) A fixed code is to be devised for the five punishments.

(6) The number of administrative authorities is to be increased.

(7) Agriculture and sericulture are to be encouraged in order to ensure adequate supplies (with the implication: for military purposes).

(8) Priority is to be given to the "fundamental occupation" over trade and crafts.

(9) Education is urgently needed.

(10) Good deeds are to be publicized, as a campaign for raising moral standards.

(11) A civil administration elite is to be selected.

(12) Military cadres are to be selected.

(13) Arms are to be overhauled and brought up to date.

(14) Severe rules and regulations are to be introduced for the prevention of abuses and shortages, along with absolute guarantees that rewards and punishments would be meted out.

(15) Sanctions are to be taken against vagabonds.

(16) Inquiries are to be made into exactions.

5. The next section develops the idea, so close to the hearts of the literati, of the selection of an elite. Chung-ch'ang T'ung's system for selection was a very simple one; it might be called a decimal system. Out of a population of ten million families, there were (in his opinion) at least a million men capable of filling minor posts, such as commanding a troop of militia. If no more than a tenth of these were selected, that would still provide 100,000 men who should have enough ability to occupy a position in the administration. The curious thing is that this harmless playing about with figures comes very close to the actual figures. According to my calculations, the number of personnel employed in the administration of imperial China must have been between 100,000 and 150,000, if we include everyone having any connection, close or remote, with the regular body of appointed officials. I shall quote from this section a passage containing a definition of social categories that is of more general interest. "Those who are

employed on account of the strength of their muscles are called men (*jen*). Among men, vigorous adults are what is required. Those who are employed on account of their talents and intelligence are called scholars (*shih*). Among scholars, what is valuable is age and experience." [54]

6. The sixth section, which is a very short one, consists of a justification of dictatorship. To those who might object on account of the principle of nonaction, Chung-ch'ang T'ung replies that everything depends on who applies the principle; the main thing is that the wolves should not be left to guard the lambs—this is his favorite image for the relations between officials and the people—nor the bandit Chih (a well known figure in *Chuang-tzu*) be appointed tax collector.

7. One might almost be listening to the voice of Wang An-shih when reading the preamble to the next demand. Increased salaries for officials was the only means for preventing corruption, for "the gentleman (*chün-tzu*) does not himself till the land or raise silkworms in order to eat or to clothe himself . . . It is only by awarding really substantial salaries that an end can be put to such bad practices as vexations, exactions, and haggling over prices." At present, poverty is regarded as a sign of probity, which is against the nature of things. "Among the best scholars there are few rich men and many poor men. If their salaries are not enough to live on, how can they help looking after their own private interests a little?" [55] The typically Chinese flavor of the last sentence is worth noting.

8. Finally, in the last paragraph of his program, Chung-ch'ang T'ung recommends an increase in taxation. He calculates that there should be a yield of three *hu* of grain per *mou* (the equivalent of 1.7 bushels per eighth of an acre), an amount appreciably higher than the traditional amounts given in the various sources, but exaggerating only slightly the level of productivity reached at that time. He proposes levying a land tax of one-tenth of the harvest, which he reckons would provide enough state revenue to meet the expenditure of any emperor, however full of extravagant whims. According to his account, taxes used to be heavy and are now too light: floods or a drought would be enough to upset all the budget calculations and cause a famine. Further, the levy of a twentieth, or, as at present, a thirtieth, is a bar-

54. *Hou-han shu* 79.17a–b.
55. *Hou-han shu* 79.17b and 18a.

barian custom. He therefore proposes that a tithe should be raised; that money payments in lieu of military service should be maintained; that where population is sparse and medium-quality land under cultivation, there should be restrictions on private property; and that uncultivated land should be brought under state ownership and given to those capable of tilling it themselves, for if such people were allowed to take possession of vacant land, fraudulent dealings would be the inevitable consequence.

The third and last of the chapters of the *Ch'ang-yen* known to us does not contribute any new ideas, but brings into prominence Chung-ch'ang T'ung's position as counselor to the dictator Ts'ao Ts'ao. In it he recommends that the government should be authoritarian, this being the only way to bring about the Great Peace, for sharing of responsibility results in a general feeling of irresponsibility and produces in practice a state of disorder. After renewed attacks on the "external clans" as being the real culprits, to blame for the whole chain of troubles, the chapter ends with a proposal that a chancellor be appointed who would be responsible for everything, and that he should be given full powers, for there was no need to have fears about excessive power being vested in one man.

This last point suggests the question: what possibilities were there for putting Chung-ch'ang T'ung's program into practice? Ts'ao Ts'ao, already in command of military operations in the north, had himself appointed chancellor (*ch'eng-hsiang*) in 208. This is no doubt what induced Ssu-ma Kuang to give the year 206 or thereabouts as the date of the "Sincere Words." But Ts'ao Ts'ao did not require any advice to take this step; and his program, which he was to carry out on a vast scale, was very different from the one recommended there. It consisted in bringing all abandoned cultivated land under state control and dividing it among his veterans. These were the famous military colonies (*t'un-t'ien*), which enabled Ts'ao Ts'ao not only to dispense with the increase in land tax proposed by Chung-ch'ang T'ung (since the tenant farmers on the state domains paid the state 50 or 60 per cent of their crops), but also provided the Kingdom of Wei with an economic base, so that the difficulties of provisioning his troops could be surmounted—and this, in the last analysis, was responsible for his final victory over his competitors. Chung-ch'ang T'ung was, incidentally, not the only person to recommend increased taxation; the idea was in the air.[56]

The mixture of cynical authoritarianism, Taoist poetry, and revolt against traditions, which characterized Chung-ch'ang T'ung, accurately foreshadows the main intellectual trends of the third century.[57]

56. See *San-kuo chih* 9.3a–b and 16.1b–2a; *Chin-shu* 26.3a; *T'ung-chien* 62.8a–b; cf. Yang Lien-sheng, "Notes on the Economic History of the Chin Dynasty," *Harvard Journal of Asiatic Studies,* 9 (1946), 128 and 172, and Chi Ch'ao-ting, *Key Economic Areas in Chinese History* (London, 1936), pp. 100 ff. On Wang Fu, Ts'ui Shih, and Chung-ch'ang T'ung, see an interesting article by Jung Chao-tsu, "Tung-Han chi-ko cheng-chih-chia ti ssu-hsiang," *Kuo-li ti-i Chung-shan ta-hsüeh yü-yen li-shih-hsüeh yen-chiu-so chou-k'an, 1,* 2 (November 1927), 1–9.

57. See Chapter 15 below.

NIHILISTIC REVOLT OR

MYSTICAL ESCAPISM

Currents of Thought in China

During the Third Century A.D.

I touch up, repaint, and varnish lines of old poems. This is Chinese and ridiculous, but it is traditional: in every terrible period of human history there is always a gentleman sitting in a corner cultivating his calligraphy and stringing together a few pearls of expression.—Paul Valéry, Letter to Albert Coste, 1915

There is an intimate sadness which comes to chosen souls simply from their consciousness of man's fate . . . This sort of sadness has always prevailed among intelligent Italians, but most of them, to evade suicide or madness, have taken to every known means of escape: they feign exaggerated gaiety, awkwardness, a passion for women, for food, for their country, and, above all, for fine-sounding words; they become, as chance may have it, policemen, monks, terrorists, war heroes . . . In order to escape even the contamination of evil, sensitive souls have no choice but to take refuge in poverty and renunciation; they must flee the world, flee even life itself . . . —Ignazio Silone, Seed beneath the Snow (trans. Frances Frenaye)

This chapter appeared originally under the title "Entre Révolte nihiliste et évasion mystique. Les courants intellectuels en Chine au III e siècle de notre ère," *Etudes Asiatiques,* 2 (1948), 27–55. The material was the theme of a lecture given on March 17, 1948, at the Institut des Hautes Etudes Chinoises in Paris (Sorbonne).

Before I discuss political and intellectual developments in the third century A.D. it might be appropriate to fill in the historical background of certain features that had their origin in late Han times.

The frenzied struggle for power at the end of the Han dynasty had first been waged between the old aristocracy and the nouveaux riches of the "external clans" (cliques grouped around the kin of the empresses), and later between the eunuchs—plebeians who were the tools of the despotic absolute monarchy—and the literati. The literati had organized themselves into a kind of political party, and had elaborated very effective methods of propaganda. But in the changed situation brought about by the revolt of the Yellow Turbans (A.D. 184), its ferocious suppression by the various strata of the ruling class (who had temporarily come to terms), and the ensuing civil war, the intellectuals found that the polemical weapons they had invented were now being used against them. They had steadily lost power during the whole sequence of events, and now had to resign themselves to dancing attendance on the military commanders[1] who were the new masters of the situation.

A curious text has survived that describes two men, both typical representatives, the one of the old gentry, the other of the new class of military adventurers. These were Yüan Shao, the man who had finally succeeded in exterminating the eunuchs, and Ts'ao Ts'ao, who founded a new dynasty. The text consists of a discourse given by a member of the "brain trust" that Ts'ao Ts'ao had been clever enough to gather around him to help in his career. Early in his rapid rise to power, when he was still no more than one claimant among many, Ts'ao Ts'ao received an arrogant and insulting letter from his opponent Yüan Shao (this was in A.D. 197) that incensed him so much that he felt the need of advice from his circle of intimates. The gem of rhetoric that follows is interesting from several points of view, and would be no less so if the whole thing were a pure invention. In any case, it contains portraits of the two most important politicians of the day, as seen with the eyes of a contemporary:[2]

1. See Chapter 13 above.

2. The speaker is Kuo Chia. The source is *Fu-tzu,* a lost work by Fu Hsüan (217–78), part of which is preserved in the *San-kuo chih* (*T'ung-wen* edition, 1884) 14.7b–8a. Cf. *Hou-han shu* (*Wang Hsien-ch'ien* edition, 1915) 100.18a and *Tzu-chih t'ung-chien* (Commercial Press edition, 1917) 62 (year 197), 11a–b. On Ts'ao Ts'ao, see above, Chapter 12, and D. von den Steinen, "Poems of Ts'ao Ts'ao," *Monumenta Serica, 4* (1939–40), 125–81.

Liu Pang and Hsiang Yü [the founder of the Han and his rival] were not equals, as you well know. It was only in intelligence that the founder of the Han was superior to Hsiang Yü. That is why Hsiang Yü, although stronger, was finally captured. After having thought it over carefully, I find that Yüan Shao has ten weaknesses against ten points in which you are superior to him. Yüan Shao cannot change this in spite of his military strength.

(1) Yüan Shao makes great use of rites and ceremonies. You rely on spontaneity. This is the first superiority, that of the way (*Tao*).

(2) Yüan Shao acts against the emperor, you make the whole empire follow you by espousing obedience. This is the second superiority, that of duty (*i*).

(3) Since the Emperors Huan (147–167) and Ling (168–189), the government has lost power through excessive leniency. Yüan Shao wants to remedy leniency with leniency, which is why he does not succeed in maintaining order. You set matters right by using severity, and superiors and inferiors alike respect the rules. This is the third superiority, that of order.

(4) Yüan Shao is outwardly generous and inwardly envious. He employs others, but distrusts them, and only allows his close kin to fill responsible positions. Outwardly you are rough and ready, inwardly, subtle and farseeing. You employ men without distrusting them and only if they have talent, and you do not seek to divide the near from the far. This is the fourth superiority, that of judgment (*tu,* "able to measure").

(5) Yüan Shao makes many plans without coming to a decision, and once he has acted is full of afterthoughts. Once you have come to a decision you carry it out immediately and adapt it to constantly changing circumstances. This is the fifth superiority, that of planning [of strategy].

(6) Yüan Shao is supported by a fortune inherited over several generations, is full of fine talk, and bows and scrapes in order to be paid compliments. Hence the literati, who like idle words and outward show, follow him in large numbers. You behave to others with complete sincerity, and do not indulge in empty formalities. You gain your followers by your simple manners, and you do not try to make bargains with those who have real merit. All sincere

and honest literati who have vision and are of solid worth want to serve you. This is the sixth superiority, that of virtue (*te*).

(7) When Yüan Shao sees a hungry man or one who is perishing with cold, his face wears an expression of pity. But what he does not see causes him no concern. This is what is called woman's compassion. But you, although you may occasionally be neglectful about little things, treat everyone well so far as important matters are concerned, and the favors you distribute always exceed expectation. Your solicitude extends to all, even those not known to you personally. This is the seventh superiority, that of human sympathy (*jen*).

(8) Yüan Shao struggles for power in the manner of a grand dignitary, and calumny introduces doubt and disorder among his followers. You direct inferiors by means of the *Tao,* and no calumnious insinuations are heard among your followers. This is the eighth superiority, that of enlightenment.

(9) Yüan Shao cannot distinguish between what is right and what is wrong. Those whom you regard as being in the right you treat with propriety (*li*), those whom you find to be in the wrong you correct with the law (*fa*). This is the ninth superiority, that of civil virtue (*wen*).

(10) Yüan Shao likes to make a vain display of force, but knows nothing about the essentials of military science. You win victories with few forces over a numerous enemy, and are inspired in the use of arms. Your soldiers respect you, your enemies fear you. This is the tenth superiority, that of military virtue (*wu*).

What interest does this discourse have for us, apart from the portraits of two of the protagonists in the civil war? It is an excellent illustration of the characterology that was so popular at the time. A few years before the occasion when the discourse was pronounced, Ts'ao Ts'ao himself had been characterized by the magnificent apothegm: "A vile bandit in times of peace, a heroic leader in a world of turmoil." This was a kind of horoscope he had got from the most sought-after physiognomist of the day, a certain Hsü Shao (150–195), after assiduously cultivating his acquaintance. Hsü Shao belonged to a curious circle that centered on the leader of the League of Literati. Its most celebrated member was Kuo T'ai (128–169), better known as Kuo Lin-tsung, the man who is regarded today as the originator of the "pure talk" (*ch'ing-t'an*). He was a giant of nearly six feet six inches tall, so poor that he had to hide the holes in his trousers with his hat, and ate only every other day. He was a great musician and a great traveler, and had a gift of gab that aroused the admiration of intellectual circles at the capital. He liked to exercise his lively mind by making witty remarks about his contemporaries; and his witticisms, which combined references to the science of physiognomy (*hsiang*), the categorization of human types (*jen-lun*), and the "criticism by the pure" or political comments of men of integrity (*ch'ing-i*),[3] became legendary.

Now, the whole history of third-century ideas, as far as moral and intellectual matters were concerned, is epitomized by the development that led from the "criticism by the pure" to "pure talk," which in turn became nothing but pure talk. It is therefore necessary to investigate the meaning of these terms a little more closely.

First of all, then, here are two examples of the criticism by the pure. One is an epigram on Ch'en Fan, a leader of the League of Literati: "Fearless before oppression, this is Ch'en Chung-chiu." The other was directed against a negligent official: "The [true] prefect of Nan-yang is Ch'en Kung-hsiao. Mr. Ch'en Chin of Hung-nung [the official prefect] only whistles his time away without doing anything." [4] It is not difficult to imagine the nature of the political situation that gave rise to such sallies as these, and it should be realized that it was this political climate that accounted for Kuo Lin-tsung's fervor, made 30,000 students acclaim him as their leader, and later brought him hundreds of private pupils. He himself was a deeply disillusioned man. In spite of his brilliant conversation and his interest in categorization of human types and the political application of the science of physiognomy, there was another side to his personality. He had an eremitic strain induced by the gloomy aspects of the century, which, he felt, forced the great

3. See the biography of Kuo T'ai in *Hou-han shu* 98.1a–3a, and the biographies of his friends and pupils Tso Yüan, Hsieh Chen, Pien Chang, Fu Jung, Hsü Shao, and others, ibid., 3a–8b. See also the epitaph for Kuo Lin-tsung written by Ts'ai Yung, *Wen-hsüan* 58.

4. *T'ung-chien* 55 (year 166), 13b–14a; cf. *Hou-han shu* 97.3a; 104A.1a; 109B.4b and 15a; *San-kuo chih* 9.21a; *Chin-shu* 45.1a.

men, the men of pure mind, to hide themselves, fall silent, and renounce all participation in public affairs.

Let us now turn to "pure talk." A whole collection of *ch'ing-t'an,* piously noted down and transmitted from generation to generation until collected by a prince at the beginning of the fifth century, has survived in the *Shih-shuo hsin-yü.* They consist of witty remarks— often quite impossible to translate—arising from a particular situation, and explained by an introductory anecdote.[5] It would be a mistake, however, to regard the *ch'ing-t'an* as nothing but a series of subtle, sophisticated witticisms, a game of idle repartee played by brilliant conversationalists. This was not so until a later stage, when, during the course of the third century, "pure talk" reached its apotheosis by becoming fashionable. Originally, "pure talk" was the name given to metaphysical discussions held by young out-of-work intellectuals. Being thoroughly disillusioned, they hoped by means of these discussions to detach themselves from mundane matters. They longed to escape from the miseries of a dangerous and uncertain life into the joys of nature, where everything was spontaneous, unspoiled, and untrammeled. This renunciation, this turning away from a world filled with crime and abominations, was initially a political gesture. We see this clearly if we follow the parallel development of that other branch of the activities of the "pure," the political comments of men of integrity *(ch'ing-i).* The propaganda procedure of classifying public figures into various moral categories, instigated by the fanatical literati of the League, had been put to quite a different use after the civil war, when the aristocracy adopted the idea and transformed it into an effective weapon

5. Cf. W. Eichhorn, "Zur chinesischen Kulturgeschichte des 3. und 4. Jahrhunderts," *Zeitschrift der Deutschen Morgenländischen Gesellschaft, 91* (1937), 451– 83. A Western analogy will give some idea of what the *ch'ing-t'an* were like. I recently came across a modern *ch'ing-t'an* in the *Figaro Littéraire* of February 7, 1948, published in an excerpt from Romain Rolland's diary concerning the death of Gandhi. Rolland speaks of the shameful way in which outstanding men like the philosopher Gentile kowtowed to authority in Mussolini's Italy, mentioning the Fascist oath that all officials had to swear, and relates how Umberto Zanotti-Bianco asked Gentile, who was then a minister, "Do you want to make these men sell their consciences, lose their souls?" Gentile replied ironically: "You know what the Gospels say: you must lose your soul in order to save it." This is a perfect example of *ch'ing-t'an,* and a moment's reflection on how difficult it would be to translate into Chinese makes it easy to understand why the *Shih-shuo hsin-yü* will remain untranslated for a long time to come.

against the intellectuals. This was the system of the "nine-grade classification" of candidates for office, operated by inspectors known as the "Impartial and Just" (*chiu-p'in chung-cheng*). These inspectors were supposed to be the guardians of public morality; far from being either impartial or just, they recommended only their kin, members of the high aristocracy, or sons of wealthy families, and in this way for a period of four centuries they prevented poor scholars from attaining high office and inaugurated an official system of protection that lasted until the T'ang re-established the more democratic system of selection by means of literary examinations.[6]

Thus we see that both the "criticism by the pure" and the transcendental talks arose out of the same political situation. They were originally interconnected, and although they later developed along different lines, there was still an interaction between them. The more the closed caste strengthened their hold upon all political activities, the more the intelligentsia tended to react by rejecting all traditional values. It would, however, be a grave mistake to follow Confucian moralists in failing to differentiate between the various manifestations of the nihilistic attitude found in all classes of Chinese society after the fall of the Han. A clear distinction must be drawn between the Taoist ideas that tinged the confused beliefs of peasant revolts, and the Taoist ideas discussed in certain intellectual circles. The mysticism of the peasant revolts concealed the realistic aim of attaining the Utopian ideal of a community having neither landlords nor officials; that of the intellectuals was often no more than a grotesque symbol, or a distant echo, of the convulsions taking place in society. Among the intellectuals, a further distinction must be made between those who were in revolt against a despotic state and expressed their intransigent and desperate opposition to it by this kind of renunciation, and those who merely wanted to be in the fashion—lordly and idle dilettantes who, between repasts washed down by copious supplies of wine, whiled away the time chatting about the vanity of this vile world.

But before discussing some representatives of the two categories of nihilistic revolt and mystical escapism—the libertarians and the libertines—I must give a brief account of general conditions in third-century China.

6. Cf. *Chin-shu* 45.2a and 48.6a, and *Nien-erh-shih cha-chi* 8.9a–b.

China at this stage in her history presented a picture of total desolation. Everything was in ruins: the towns destroyed, the countryside devastated, the population pillaged and massacred, their homes burnt down. In the vast disorder created by brigands and soldiers, by victims of disaster and refugees, there was a general atmosphere of panic, and everyone lived in a constant state of anxiety about what the morrow might bring. Out of this chaos there emerged a few islands of comparative security in places where the more fortunate landowners had with difficulty managed to bring their land under cultivation again. A widespread return to serfdom was the price the agricultural population had to pay for this security. The landowners, living in their fortified homes, directed the labors of the indebted peasants who had entered their service as tenant farmers, and of the refugees who worked for them as agricultural laborers. Their households were full of poor relations, who preferred being fed and clothed as domestic servants to being vagabonds, and sons of the less important neighboring families who had become their clients, men of arms, and flunkeys, and who lent prestige to their patron by forming a guard of honor when he went abroad. All the people of the household hoped to make their fortune through the protection, recommendation, and influential connections of their master.

The imperial government no longer existed, for the empire was divided into three parts, each with its own independent military governor. Each military governor entertained imperial ambitions, and the three capitals were centers of unceasing intrigue, where coups d'état were hatched in an atmosphere of mutual suspicion and recrimination. The Wei kingdom, founded by Ts'ao Ts'ao, had barely established its limited authority when the family of Marshal Ssu-ma seized power by means of a well prepared military coup. But no sooner had the Ssu-ma family succeeded in establishing their kingdom as the legitimate power in control of the whole empire, after crushing the rival kingdoms in the South and West by costly expeditions sent against them, than they too went down in a frenzied blood bath. The past twenty years had seen one coup d'état after another, all following a monotonous pattern like a square dance, and when the eight princes of the house of Ssu-ma finally destroyed each other in a mad fury of bloodthirsty revenge, the unity of China was finished and done with. Not only did the Chin dynasty of the Ssu-ma collapse, but the whole of China north of the Yangtze fell into the hands of the barbarians, who, manifestly superior, continued in control until the end of the sixth century. The South, which at the time of this debacle was no more than a colony, was all that was left to a succession of weak Chinese dynasties.

How was this state of affairs to be endured? For the intellectual who wanted to forget his plight and escape from a seemingly hopeless situation, little remained but dreams, alcohol, and the pleasures of the flesh; and if the search for artificial prolongation of life that was pursued at this time seems surprising, we must remember that many a man went in daily fear of having his head cut off. Longevity pills were nothing but the natural counterpart of severed heads. In their attempt to escape the calamities that fate held in store for them, Taoist intellectuals took to dreams, poetry, and music as if they were taking to drugs, whiled the hours away drinking and discussing the world's ills, and found occasional alleviation in the ecstasy of "distant excursions"—those spiritual voyages of Taoist meditation so eloquently described by Chuang-tzu. Their god was the *tzu-jan,* the "thusness-in-itself," an expression that combines the ideas of unspoiled nature, spontaneity, and the absolute. Their ideas gradually penetrated to all circles of society, thus preparing the way for the acceptance of the Buddhist faith, with its promise of salvation, either in a superterrestrial paradise or, for more exacting minds, by extinction in nirvana. The Taoist intellectuals were inclined to oscillate between the two extremes of affirming man's value as an individual and denying his value as a member of society; but they came to reject utterly the Confucian doctrine of the family with all that it implied of social duties, ethical beliefs, and decorous behavior, and by this rejection brought upon themselves the hatred of all right-minded people and persecution at the hands of the authorities. Their peculiar attitude should give us less cause for astonishment than the fact that it was reported by the chroniclers in no strong tone of censure.

The great wave of nihilism that broke over China as a result of the civil war swept into one section of society after another, or, to put it another way, bore along several consecutive generations in its wake. The men of the first generation belonged to Ts'ao Ts'ao's circle of intimates and were grouped round Ho Yen, the group forming a kind

of political center for nihilist leanings. Ho Yen was the son of one of
Ts'ao Ts'ao's concubines, and had been brought up in the household
along with the young princes, who treated him as an intruder. He was
an enigmatic figure. His biography depicts him as effeminate and nar-
cissistic, a debauched *bon vivant,* greedy and corrupt; but this source
is highly suspect, for it was written by the historians of the Chin dynasty, whose founder, the Grand Marshal Ssu-ma I, was the sworn
enemy of Ho Yen. The Marshal was a wily and unscrupulous old
man who was determined to supplant the Wei dynasty. He moved
toward this objective when the third Wei Emperor appointed him
regent and future executor of his will. But the Emperor also appointed
an influential member of the royal house to share these powers. Ho
Yen persuaded the royal regent to remove Ssu-ma I from power and
fill all the important posts with Ho Yen's friends. It is hardly surprising, therefore, that the Chin historians, bent on glorifying Ssu-ma
I, describe these people as "Ho Yen's gang," and make them out to
be monsters of depravity and dissipation, each more odious than the
next. Ho Yen managed to retain control over the choice of officials,
and stayed in power for ten years, from 240 to 249.[7] These ten years,
known under the reign-title of *cheng-shih,* may be regarded as the
apogee of the nihilist movement. The period ended in the coup d'état
of Marshal Ssu-ma I, which led to the execution of Ho Yen and his
friends and of their families to the third degree of kinship. It certainly
does look as if Ho Yen's memory had been purposely blackened by
his political enemies because of his attempts to prevent them from
coming to power, but it is difficult to discover what his motives were.
All we know is that his guiding principle was that of nonaction (*wu-
wei*), or rather of nonbeing (*wu*), which the Taoists held to be the
very essence of the universe and the underlying principle of both
nature and society.[8] Ho Yen and his young friend and protégé Wang
Pi (226–249), a precocious genius who died of the plague at the age of
twenty-three, are regarded as responsible for the general revival of
philosophic thought, particularly of nihilistic Taoism. Both wrote commentaries on the *I-ching* and on *Lao-tzu.*

7. The biographies of Ho Yen and his friends are appended to the biography
of the Regent, Ts'ao Shuang, *San-kuo chih* 9.15b–25a; cf. *T'ung-chien* 74 (year
239), 10a–b, and 75 (year 249), 7b–13b.

8. *Chin-shu* 43.6b; cf. *Chin-shu chiao-chu* 43.22b.

Wang Pi occupies a somewhat isolated position among the men of the second generation. According to recent research, he seems to have been less Taoistic than his protector, and less nihilistic too. Indeed, his attitude may be described as a positive one, for he was obsessed by the burning theme of the day: how to restore order to the world. In his view, order was to be found in the cosmic order expressed in the hexagrams of the "Book of Changes." [9]

The second generation of nihilists included men of letters, writers, poets, musicians, and several politicians. The famous circle of friends known as the "Seven Sages of the Bamboo Grove" (*chu-lin ch'i-hsien*) now provided a spiritual center for the movement, and may be described as the workshop of the new "mystical (or mysterious) doctrine" (*hsüan-hsüeh*). Around the middle of the century, these seven Bohemians, each more odd than the next, and all of them great drinkers, used to meet regularly in a bamboo grove at the home of Hsi K'ang, at Shan-yang, in the north of present-day Honan, where they drank, talked, wrote verses, and philosophized. Let us pause for a moment to look at these strange people, and to examine the attitudes —so characteristic of the times—that they adopted.

The most admirable of them, to my mind, was the poet Juan Chi (210–263), who was ten years old at the time of Ts'ao Ts'ao's death, and whose father was the high-ranking scholar responsible for the greater part of the written account of Ts'ao Ts'ao's deeds. Notwithstanding his father's position, Juan Chi belonged to the poorer branch of the family, and he lived with his nephew, Juan Hsien, who was also a member of the circle. Juan Chi's biography describes him in these terms:

> Handsome and imposing in appearance, and of open and far-ranging mind, Juan Chi was fiercely independent and did exactly

9. Cf. the thesis put forward by A. A. Petrov in *Wang Pi: Iz istorii kitajskoj filosofii* (Moscow, 1936), and the lengthy review of this work by A. F. Wright, *Harvard Journal of Asiatic Studies, 10* (1947), 75–88, which also contains a summary of recent Chinese works on Wang Pi; also T'ang Yung-t'ung, "Wang Pi's New Interpretation of the I Ching and Lun-yü," trans. W. Liebenthal, *Harvard Journal of Asiatic Studies, 10* (1947), 124–61. Cf. the discussion between Ho Yen and Wang Pi as to whether holy men (*sheng-jen*) have passions, as reported in the commentary on *San-kuo chih* 28.37a–38a. Ho Yen maintains that a saint has no human passions; Wang Pi says the saint has the same feelings as ordinary men, surpassing them only in spiritual power: "he responds to other beings, but is not attached to them."

as he pleased. Neither joy nor anger was ever expressed on his face. Sometimes he stayed shut up in his room studying books for several months on end, without ever going out; sometimes he went up into the mountains or to the waterside, forgetting for several days to return home. He read an enormous amount and had a special love for Chuang-tzu and Lao-tzu. He was a great drinker, an accomplished performer on the lute, and skilled in whistling. While he was following out a train of thought, he would quite forget about the outside world. His contemporaries often called him a madman.[10]

The expression for "madman" (*ch'ih*) was used to describe a simple-minded person—an idiot in the same sense as Dostoevsky's Prince Myshkin. "Madmen" frequently cropped up during the troubled periods of China's history—sages who feigned madness in order to escape the hate and envy of their contemporaries, the despotism of princes, and the follies committed by those in power. The buffoon or eccentric, often courted though never understood by princes, was, like the hermit, a type that appeared when times were bad. This is confirmed by the passage in Juan Chi's biography stating that "he had the inner intention of reforming the age, but belonged to the period between the Wei and the Chin when there were many difficulties and troubles, and few men of integrity among the well-known literati. That is why he did not take part in public affairs, and gave himself up to continuous drinking." [11] Juan Chi did indeed refuse every important official post that was offered to him, and in order to avoid having to accept the marriage alliance arranged for him by the dictator Ssu-ma Chao, son of Ssu-ma I, he remained dead drunk for sixty days. The only post he agreed to accept was a minor one in the administrative department of the infantry, but this was because the office building had a well furnished cellar, which probably enabled him to "allow the affairs of the world to fall into oblivion." The biography contains several anecdotes clearly showing how Juan Chi's free-thinking, amoral outlook shocked contemporaries with minds full of preconceived ideas, and also how, despite his prudence, his tirades earned him the vindictive hatred of the ritualists, the "men of the moral law" (*li-fa chih shih*). The most famous remark, often quoted, by which he shocked

10. *Chin-shu* 49.1a.
11. Ibid., 2a; cf. *Shih-shuo hsin-yü* 3A.37b.

contemporaries was made when someone read him a lecture upon finding him escorting his sister-in-law. "Surely you do not mean to suggest," he cried, "that the rules of propriety (*li*) apply to me?" We
cannot here describe all facets of Juan Chi's character or the characters
of his companions. In general, it might be said that all of them possessed great inner integrity and seriousness of purpose, yet for exhibi-
tionist reasons they gave the outward impression of being deliberately
nonconformist. Almost all of them had a curious propensity for "black"
(or "sick") humor, and they loved shocking people. I cannot resist
quoting the delightful piece entitled "Biography of Mr. Greatman"
(*Ta-jen hsien-sheng chuan*)—the most biting piece of lighthearted
satire against Confucianism since Chuang-tzu.[12]

> What the world calls a gentleman (*chün-tzu*) is someone who
> is solely concerned with moral law (*fa*), and cultivates exclusively
> the rules of propriety (*li*). His hand holds the emblem of jade
> [authority], his foot follows the straight line of the rule. He likes
> to think that his actions set a permanent example; he likes to
> think that his words are everlasting models. In his youth, he has
> a reputation in the villages of his locality, in his later years he is
> well known in the neighboring districts. Upward, he aspires to
> the dignity of the Three Dukes; downward, he does not disdain
> the post of governor of the nine provinces.
>
> Have you ever seen the lice that inhabit a pair of trousers? They
> jump into the depths of the seams, hiding themselves in the cotton
> wadding, and believe they have a pleasant place to live. Walking,
> they do not risk going beyond the edge of the seam; moving, they
> are careful not to emerge from the trouser leg; and they think
> they have kept to the rules of etiquette. But when the trousers are
> ironed, the flames invade the hills, the fire spreads, the villages are
> set on fire and the towns burned down; then the lice that inhabit
> the trousers cannot escape.
>
> What difference is there between the gentleman who lives
> within a narrow world and the lice that inhabit trouser legs?

The same images recur in the writings of that impenitent wag and
confirmed drunkard, Liu Ling (225?–280?), another member of the

12. *Chin-shu* 49.2a. This is only an extract. The complete version may be
found in the collected works of Juan Chi: *Han Wei liu-ch'ao po-san ming-chia
chi* (1892), Vol. 23, *Juan Pu-ping chi,* pp. 45a–57a.

Bamboo Grove circle. The inspired dithyrambs of his "Eulogy on the
Virtue of Wine" (*Chiu-te sung*)—the only poem he ever deigned to
publish, and well known through its inclusion in the anthology of literature, the *Wen-hsüan*—describe the power of alcohol to raise us
above the narrow world of reality, and the highly confusing sensations
experienced at an advanced stage of intoxication. On one occasion
some visitors came to see him, and, entering his room, were startled
to find him completely naked. His explanation illustrates the attitude
shared by the whole circle of friends, all of whom felt that they were
enclosed in a prison from which they longed to escape into the freedom of cosmic space. "Heaven and Earth are my dwelling," he said,
"and this room is my breeches. Who asked you, gentlemen, to come
inside my breeches? And where's the harm anyway?"[13]

Another of the boon companions was Hsiang Hsiu (230?–280?),
the first great commentator on the works of Chuang-tzu, and, according to tradition, the real author of the famous commentary which is
now known as Kuo Hsiang's commentary.

Hsiang Hsiu's closest friend was the host, Hsi K'ang (223–262).
Haughty, independent, with utter scorn for all outward formalities,
Hsi K'ang was an exacting but superb friend. He was a man of deep
religious feeling, but as well as being a fervent Taoist, he was both
an excellent writer and an incomparable virtuoso on the lute. His
favorite hobby was his forge, which he had set up under a big tree in
the middle of his garden, and Hsiang Hsiu often joined him when
he was carrying out experiments there. He did this partly for his own
amusement, but also in order to imitate the activity of the Tao, the
great smith.[14] Most of his time was devoted to the search for immortality. An ardent adept of the procedures for "nourishing the vital
principle," he was not one of those who contented themselves with
writing learned dissertations on the subject, but devoutly carried out

13. *Shih-shuo hsin-yü* 3A.37b; cf. *Chin-shu* 49.7b–8a. Cf. the translations of the
Chiu-te sung (neither of them entirely satisfactory) by G. Margouliès, *Le Kou-
wen chinois* (Paris, 1926), p. 124, and by Sung-nien Hsu, *Anthologie de la
littérature chinoise* (Paris, 1933), p. 124.

14. *Chin-shu* 49.6b; *Shih-shuo* 3A.49b. In spite of his poverty, he would never
accept payment for his work as a smith, and worked only for people he knew
well, accepting small presents (some chickens or wine) for his services. R. H.
van Gulik's book on Hsi K'ang, *Hsi K'ang and His Poetical Essay on the Lute,*
Monumenta Nipponica Monograph (Tokyo, 1941), unfortunately has not been
available to me.

the requisite practical steps, searching the mountains for the herbs needed to concoct the drugs, and discovering the caves where hermits lived who could impart the secret of longevity.

It is not, however, the religious beliefs or the artistic gifts of Hsi K'ang that I want to stress, but rather the political aspect of his work, and his tragic death. He might be described as a "conscientious objector," and on more than one occasion he expressed his innermost thoughts on his rejection of office. In his "Discourse on the Disinterestedness of the Superior Man" we find the following passage:[15]

He who may be called a Superior Man (*chün-tzu*) does not let his heart become attached to good and evil, and his actions are never opposed to the Tao. What is the explanation for this? It is because, when the soul (*ch'i,* "the breath") is calm and the mind empty, neither deference nor admiration remain in the heart; if the personality is steady, and the heart without shackles (*ta*), the passions do not become attached to worldly desires. If no respect or deference remains in the heart, a man can transcend the moral doctrine (*ming-chiao*), and place his trust in spontaneous nature. If his passions are not attached to worldly desires, he can judge impartially both nobles and common people, and enter into the passions of all living creatures. If he can enter harmoniously into the passions of all living creatures, the Great Way (*Tao*) is not disturbed. When moral injunctions (*ming*) have been transcended, and trust is placed in the heart, good and evil have no power over him. . . . Viewed from the standpoint of the Great Way, I no longer have an "ego" (*shen,* distinctive personality), so why should I feel anxious?[16] He who does not value life is best able to appreciate it. Explained from this point of view, it may be said that the Supreme Man (*chih-jen*) makes good use of his heart without ever having any attachments.

Hsi K'ang was even more explicit in the letter, written shortly before his death, in which he broke off relations with Shan T'ao (205–283), another member of the circle, who had not kept to his vow of

15. The title, according to *Chin-shu* 49.5a–b, is *Chün-tzu wu ssu lun,* but cf. the collected works, *Hsi Chung-san chi* (*Ssu-pu ts'ung-k'an* edition) 6.1a–5a, where the title is given as *Shih ssu lun,* "Explanation of private (selfish) feelings."
16. Cf. *Lao-tzu* 13.

uncompromising integrity, and who, after accepting a high post, had even dared to suggest that Hsi K'ang should become his assistant. Hsi K'ang, full of violent indignation, threw the offer back in his face, saying abruptly that his aspirations were not of this world, and explaining with much eloquence what Flaubert somewhere in his letters has expressed in the lapidary formula: *Les honneurs déshonorent, le titre degrade, la fonction abrutit.* Hsi K'ang enumerates seven points demonstrating the dismal, insupportable boredom of official life, and explains why he prefers strolls in the country, music, and contemplation of nature to the servitude, imposed by the rules of propriety and moral law, that has to be endured at court. He loathed the hypocrisy of mourning, intercourse with vulgar people, and all the formalities, hurly-burly, gossip, and affectations of social life. Moreover, he had nothing but contempt for all the most revered heroes of Confucianism, and, not being at all diplomatic, liked to express his unshakable convictions openly. All of this would have been quite unpardonable in an official. In order to express his determined resistance to all attempts to tame him, he used to compare himself to a doe, or to the young phoenix in Chuang-tzu's metaphor.[17] "All I want now is to remain in my old hut, bring up my children and grandchildren, take a stroll from time to time with old friends, talk about life, drink a glass of wine, play a melody on the lute. That is the sum of my ambition." These were the closing words of the impetuous letter[18] that was to seal Hsi K'ang's fate. For it so happened that the all-powerful Duke of Chin, who was shortly to dethrone the Wei and found a new dynasty, took in bad part the allusions that were obviously aimed at him. He was probably predisposed to do so, because his favorite, a certain Chung Hui who was a member of the high aristocracy, could not forgive Hsi K'ang for the affront offered him on the occasion when he had gone to visit the poet-smith. Hsi K'ang had carried on with his work at the anvil, and had not addressed a single word to his grand visitor until the latter, offended by the very impolite reception he had met with, was on the point of leaving. But an opportunity for revenge soon offered itself when Hsi K'ang testified to the innocence of a

17. *Chuang-tzu* XVII; James Legge, *Texts of Taoism* (Oxford, 1891), *1*, 391; L. Wieger, *Les Pères du système taoïste* (Hsien-hsien, 1913), p. 347.

18. *Wen-hsüan* 23; *Hsi Chung-san chi* 2.5b–9a; *Chin-shu* 49.5b–6b; *Chin-shu chiao-chu* 49.19b–21b.

friend who had been unjustly accused of lack of filial piety.[19] Both he
and his friend were accused of plotting against the state, and were
imprisoned and executed in 262. In prison, Hsi K'ang, then thirty-nine
years of age, expressed his poignant longing for survival and his indignation at such base behavior in some farewell verses entitled "Black
Exasperation" (*Yu-fen*).[20] The petition for his reprieve, signed by
three thousand students, was rejected by the Grand Marshal, the Duke
of Chin. On his way to execution, Hsi K'ang played his lute, and
watched the shadows cast by the setting sun on the faces of his friends
and followers.

My reason for dwelling at such length on the tragic circumstances
of Hsi K'ang's death is that it illustrates the dangers that lay in store
for those who got caught up in the mesh of politics. And if such a
fate could befall the most inoffensive of dreamers that ever lived, how
much more perilous was the position of men whose aim was to achieve
the Utopian ideal of creating a community free from restrictions, and
with neither lords nor slaves.

The histories say nothing about the men who had Utopian ideas
of this kind. Fortunately, however, an important text survives, probably dating from the end of the third century or the very first years
of the fourth century, which translates the Utopian ideal into political
terms. It is the treatise to which the Taoist alchemist Ko Hung (253–
333) devotes a whole chapter of his lengthy work.[21] In refuting it, he
had the happy idea of reproducing the whole text. Its author is a

19. This affair concerned a quarrel between two brothers, friends of Hsi K'ang,
over adultery and subsequent revenge. The relevant documents are collected in
Chin-shu chiao-chu 49.21b–22b.

20. *Wen-hsüan* 23; *Chin-shu* 49.6b; *Hsi Chung-san chi* 1.4b–5b. For the meaning of the expression *yu-fen*, cf. the letter from Ssu-ma Ch'ien to Jen An, *Han-
shu* 62, trans. Chavannes, *Les Mémoires historiques, I*, ccxxxiv, and, in particular,
the eulogy of Ssu-ma Ch'ien by Pan Ku (ibid.): "When he had undergone the
supreme punishment (i.e. castration), he breathed out his exasperation in prison
(*yu erh fa-fen*). His letter gives proof of this." The famous letter reaches its
climax in expressing Ssu-ma Ch'ien's theory of aesthetics—namely, that master-
works are produced out of exasperation by men who have been mortified and
humiliated, and are a cry of indignation (*fa-fen*) that expresses, and compensates
for, their impotence.

21. *Wai-p'ien*, section 48 (*Ssu-pu ts'ung-k'an* edition), 1a–3a; cf. A. Forke,
Geschichte der mittelalterlichen chinesischen Philosophie (Hamburg, 1934), pp.
224–26.

certain Pao Ching-yen, of whom nothing is known except that "he had a predilection for the books of Lao-tzu and Chuang-tzu, and was a powerful dialectician"—the remark with which Ko Hung introduces him to his readers. The treatise shows Pao Ching-yen to have been China's first political anarchist, a daring thinker who went well beyond the vague Utopianism of popular Taoism by placing his argument firmly on the political level, and describing in a matter-of-fact way the struggle against despotic absolutism. The boldness of his thought is remarkable for the age in which he wrote, and is to my mind in no way lessened by his having been unable to free himself from the usual retrospective Utopianism typical of all Chinese social thinking. He had to project his golden age, not into the future, as was done in the West, but into the remote past, so that it could wear an air of venerable tradition and be acceptable to the various schools of thought. He was of course very much influenced by Taoism, especially by Chuang-tzu, who is quoted several times. But if some of his ideas are borrowed from Taoism, the social interpretation he gave them was his own, and it is this that distinguishes him so sharply from his forerunners. His motto, "neither lord nor subject," is often referred to in modern literature, and his philosophy seems to me of sufficient interest and social significance to warrant a complete translation of the balanced but powerful phrases of his short treatise.

The Confucian literati say: "Heaven gave birth to the people and then set rulers over them." But how can High Heaven have said this in so many words? Is it not rather that interested parties make this their pretext? The fact is that the strong oppressed the weak and the weak submitted to them; the cunning tricked the innocent and the innocent served them. It was because there was submission that the relation of lord and subject arose, and because there was servitude that the people, being powerless, could be kept under control. Thus servitude and mastery result from the struggle between the strong and the weak and the contrast between the cunning and the innocent, and Blue Heaven has nothing whatsoever to do with it.

When the world was in its original undifferentiated state, the Nameless (*wu-ming,* i.e. the Tao) was what was valued, and all creatures found happiness in self-fulfillment. Now when the cinnamon-tree has its bark stripped or the varnish-tree is cut, it is not done at the wish of the tree; when the pheasant's feathers are plucked or the kingfisher's torn out, it is not done by desire of the bird. To be bitted and bridled is not in accordance with the nature of the horse; to be put under the yoke and bear burdens does not give pleasure to the ox. Cunning has its origin in the use of force that goes against the true nature of things, and the real reason for harming creatures is to provide useless adornments. Thus catching the birds of the air in order to supply frivolous adornments, making holes in noses where no holes should be, tying beasts by the leg when nature meant them to be free, is not in accord with the destiny of the myriad creatures, all born to live out their lives unharmed. And so the people are compelled to labor so that those in office may be nourished; and while their superiors enjoy fat salaries, they are reduced to the direst poverty.

It is all very well to enjoy the infinite bliss of life after death, but it is preferable not to have died in the first place; and rather than acquire an empty reputation for integrity by resigning office and foregoing one's salary, it is better that there should be no office to resign. Loyalty and righteousness only appear when rebellion breaks out in the empire, filial obedience and parental love are only displayed when there is discord among kindred.

In the earliest times, there was neither lord nor subject.[22] Wells were dug for drinking-water, the fields were plowed for food, work began at sunrise and ceased at sunset; everyone was free and at ease, neither competing with each other nor scheming against each other, and no one was either glorified or humiliated. The waste lands had no paths or roads and the waterways no boats or bridges, and because there were no means of communication by land or water, people did not appropriate each other's property; no armies could be formed, and so people did not attack one another. Indeed since no one climbed up to seek out nests nor dived down to sift the waters of the deep, the phoenix nested under the eaves of the house and dragons disported in the garden pool. The

22. Cf. the description of "paradise" in *Lieh-tzu* 5, where *pu chün pu ch'en* occurs (A. C. Graham, *The Book of Lieh-tzu* [London, 1960], p. 102, translates "no one is ruler or subject"), and of Utopia, *Lieh-tzu* 2 (translated by Graham, p. 34: "In this country there are no teachers and leaders; all things follow their natural course")—tr.

ravening tiger could be trodden on, the poisonous snake handled. Men could wade through swamps without raising the waterfowl, and enter the woodlands without startling the fox or the hare. Since no one even began to think of gaining power or seeking profit, no dire events or rebellions occurred; and as spears and shields were not in use, moats and ramparts did not have to be built. All creatures lived together in mystic unity, all of them merged in the Way (*Tao*). Since they were not visited by plague or pestilence, they could live out their lives and die a natural death. Their hearts being pure, they were devoid of cunning. Enjoying plentiful supplies of food, they strolled about with full bellies.[23] Their speech was not flowery, their behavior not ostentatious. How, then, could there have been accumulation of property such as to rob the people of their wealth, or severe punishments to trap and ensnare them?

When this age entered on decadence, knowledge and cunning came into use. The Way and its Virtue (*Tao te*) having fallen into decay, a hierarchy was established. Customary regulations for promotion and degradation and for profit and loss proliferated, ceremonial garments such as the [gentry's] sash and sacrificial cap and the imperial blue and yellow [robes for worshiping Heaven and Earth] were elaborated. Buildings of earth and wood were raised high into the sky, with the beams and rafters painted red and green. The heights were overturned in quest of gems, the depths dived into in search of pearls; but however vast a collection of precious stones people might have assembled, it still would not have sufficed to satisfy their whims, and a whole mountain of gold would not have been enough to meet their expenditure, so sunk were they in depravity and vice, having transgressed against the fundamental principles of the Great Beginning. Daily they became further removed from the ways of their ancestors, and turned their back more and more upon man's original simplicity. Because they promoted the "worthy" to office, ordinary people strove for reputation, and because they prized material wealth, thieves and robbers appeared. The sight of desirable objects tempted true and honest hearts, and the display of arbitrary power and love of gain opened the road to robbery. So they made weapons

23. *Chuang-tzu* IX; cf. James Legge, *Texts of Taoism, 1*, pp. 278 and 280.

with points and with sharp edges, and after that there was no end
to usurpations and acts of aggression, and they were only afraid
lest crossbows should not be strong enough, shields stout enough,
lances sharp enough, and defenses solid enough. Yet all this could
have been dispensed with if there had been no oppression and
violence from the start.

Therefore it has been said: "Who could make scepters without
spoiling the unblemished jade? And how could altruism and righteousness (*jen* and *i*) be extolled unless the Way and its Virtue
had perished?" Although tyrants such as Chieh and Chou were
able to burn men to death, massacre their advisers, make mince-
meat of the feudal lords, cut the barons into strips, tear out men's
hearts and break their bones, and go to the furthest extremes of
tyrannical crime down to the use of torture by roasting and grill-
ing, however cruel they may by nature have been, how could
they have done such things if they had had to remain among the
ranks of the common people? If they gave way to their cruelty
and lust and butchered the whole empire, it was because, as rulers,
they could do as they pleased. As soon as the relationship between
lord and subject is established, hearts become daily more filled
with evil designs, until the manacled criminals sullenly doing
forced labor in the mud and the dust are full of mutinous thoughts,
the Sovereign trembles with anxious fear in his ancestral temple,
and the people simmer with revolt in the midst of their poverty
and distress; and to try to stop them revolting by means of rules
and regulations, or control them by means of penalties and punishments, is like trying to dam a river in full flood with a handful
of earth, or keeping the torrents of water back with one finger.

Libertarian anarchism like Pao Ching-yen's, however, was against
the general trend of nihilistic thought, and remained an isolated phenomenon. The men of the third generation, born about the middle of
the century, were already veering toward libertinage, and by the end
of the century the intellectual atmosphere had changed completely.
The principal aim was now not so much to seek spiritual liberation
from social bondage as to find individual escape from obligations and
responsibilities. It was then that "pure talk" reached its final stage. It
was taken up by the gilded youth—"the brothers and sons of the idle

aristocracy" (*kuei-yu tzu-ti*), in the stock phrase of the Chinese historians—and became fashionable, whereupon the attempt made by the politicians of the first generation and by the artists of the Bamboo Grove to break free from social conventions degenerated into moral breakdown. What had been, with men like Juan Chi or Hsi K'ang, a high state of tension that was part of a serious effort to transcend human limitations, relapsed into mere abandonment of the ordinary decencies of life. The frenzied attempt at emancipation had turned to wanton frivolity, the cry of revolt to cynical acceptance, liberty to libertinage.

I should like here to make a short digression on liberty in China. I doubt whether sufficient attention has been paid to the fact that this idea has always been foreign to the Chinese, and that no word for it exists in the Chinese language.[24] All the circumlocutions used by the writers of the time to convey the notion of liberty carry a sense of laxity, of license, even of depravity. When they spoke of liberty, it was something negative they had in mind—the idea of letting go, or of letting slide, or of not being bound.[25] And this was only natural, for in a despotic, strictly hierarchical society, every step toward freedom from the tyranny of the ritualistic prescriptions that dominated everyday life was certain to be regarded as a dangerous transgression of the moral code and would inevitably meet with opprobrium and create a scandal. Anyone who had been provoked into making some sort of protest not only appeared to be arrogating authority to himself; he was in fact doing so.

The biographies of the libertines[26] all reveal the same decadence beneath the picturesque details of their public and private lives, no matter who they might be—the minister Wang Jung, his cousins, the Grand

24. Cf. Max Weber, "Die Wirtschaftsethik der Weltreligionen. 1. Konfuzianismus und Taoismus," *Gesammelte Aufsätze zur Religionssoziologie, 1*, 435–36: "On the other hand, there was no sanction in natural law for any kind of individual freedom. The very language lacked a word for 'freedom.' The historical background, and the fact that the State was based on a patrilineal system, supply a full explanation for this."

25. The key words that constantly occur, in various combinations, are: *fang, tsung,* and *jen,* "to let go," "to let slide," "to loosen," "to relax," "to permit," "to tolerate"; *pu-chü,* "without restriction," "without restraint"; *pu-chi,* "unreined," "unfettered," "uncontrolled"; *ta* and *t'ung,* "communicating," "penetrating without hindrance."

26. Some are collected in *Chin-shu* 43, most in *Chin-shu* 49.

Constable Wang Yen and the high dignitary Wang Ch'eng, or their friends, the nudists Hu-wu Fu-chih, Hsieh K'un, Pi Cho, or any others. All were men of high position who accepted important posts only in order to neglect their duties, and made it a point of honor to scorn the moral code, but whose flirtation with nonconformism never went beyond drunkenness and debauchery. When they were not drunk, they were intoxicating themselves with abstruse conversation and fine phrases. A witty remark made in a tavern, and pronounced with the right air of self-assurance, could open the way to a career for one of the elegant young men in chic circles at the capital.

Wang Jung (234–305), who in his youth had taken part in the debates of the Seven Sages of the Bamboo Grove, was one of the biggest landowners of his day.[27] He pushed meanness to the point of removing the stones from his plums before selling them, so that no one else could cultivate the same variety; and he economized on food, although he had more money than could be counted. A contemporary was of the opinion that Wang Jung indulged in avarice as if it were a narcotic drug, and perhaps this was so. Certainly this trait distinguished him from the rest of his circle, who considered it good taste to adopt an attitude of pretending to despise money;[28] and since he was involved in several corruption scandals he was despised by the "pure."

His cousin, Wang Yen (256–311), was the acknowledged leader of the gilded youth. A brilliant talker, he had enjoyed discussing political strategy (*tsung-heng chih shu,* "the art of alliances") in his younger days, but soon lost interest in public affairs and became absorbed in the "mysterious void" (*hsüan-hsü*). As he let fall from his lips sibylline oracles that were regarded as the very summit of the art of *ch'ing-t'an,*

---

27. He was also "an important patron of the early water-mill technologists"; Needham, *Science and Civilisation in China, 2,* 157.

28. Wang Yen, appalled by the vulgar acquisitiveness of his wife, who was a princess, never spoke about money. When his wife put him to the test by having money piled up round his bed, he gave his slave the following order: "Take *that* away!"; see *Shih-shuo hsin-yü* 2B.40b; *Chin-shu chiao-chu* 43.23b–24a. On Wang Jung, cf. *Chin-shu* 43.4b–6a (*Chin-shu chiao-chu* 43.13b–20b); *Shih-shuo hsin-yü* 3B.31b and 3B.2a, where the following characteristic anecdote may be found: Wang Jung, always late for the meetings of the Bamboo Grove circle, once heard himself thus apostrophized by Juan Chi: "Is this boor once again going to wreck our train of thought?" Whereupon the young Wang Jung, with great presence of mind, replied: "Is it as easy as all that to wreck your train of thought, Sir?" (Cf. *Chin-shu chiao-chu* 43.15a.)

he held in his pale hands a feather-duster with a jade handle, with which to sweep away, symbolically, the dust of this vile world—a practice that spread rapidly. Perhaps Wang Yen is more easily understood if we remember that twice in his life he had to feign madness—the first time, in order to avoid marriage with the daughter of Yang Chün, the all-powerful head of the "external clan" then briefly in ascendancy; and later, to escape the resentment of one of the eight bloodthirsty princes. When captured by Shih Lo, one of the leaders of the Hun invasions, he is said to have spent several days explaining to the unlettered barbarian his doctrine of detachment and his profound disgust with life. Shih Lo, furious, is said to have replied, before having him assassinated: "Your fame stretches over the four seas, and since your youth you have occupied the highest positions. How can you pretend, now that your hair is white, never to have taken part in the events of the century? The fall of the Empire: *that* is *your* crime!" It is of course more than likely that the Confucianist historian speaks through the mouth of the innocent barbarian in order to pronounce his judgment, and it is probably also he who speaks when reporting the dying words of Wang Yen: "Ah! Even although we were inferior to the men of antiquity, yet if we had not been so fond of frivolous vanities, and had applied our energies to defending the Empire, this day might well never have arrived!" [29]

His younger brother, Wang Ch'eng (269–312), considered by many Wang Yen's superior in the art of conversation, was strangled by his kinsman Wang Tun, another leading light of the day. Wang Ch'eng excelled himself in profligacy, and took active part in the drinking bouts and licentious activities of the circle of nudists known as "The Untrammeled" (*ta*).

Let me complete this portrait gallery of the libertines by quoting the famous remark of Yüeh Kuang, another great talker who perished in the troubles arising from the coups d'état of the princes. When Yüeh Kuang (250?–302?), at that time prefect of the capital, learned of the scandalous goings-on of Wang Ch'eng's young friends, he said, with a smile indulgent rather than shocked: "What is the use of all that? There is plenty of pleasure to be found while keeping within the moral doctrine (*ming-chiao*)." [30]

29. *Chin-shu* 43.7a–b; *Chin-shu chiao-chu* 43.25a–b.
30. *Chin-shu* 43.10a; *Chin-shu chiao-chu* 43.35a; *Shih-shuo hsin-yü* 1A.7b.

Faced with so much weakness or so much strength (depending on whether it was a question of the libertines or the libertarians), the Confucianists were bound to take action of some sort, since both libertines and libertarians, in transgressing the moral code, profaned the most sacred tenets of Confucianism. But it was a sign of the profound change that had taken place that the most vigorous attack, at least on the plane of ideas, did not come from the old-fashioned ritualists, who had by now either disappeared or lost influence, but from the "pure talk" circle itself. There were several positive spirits, particularly some Legalists, who, trained in the school of philosophical dialectics, handled their logical weapons brilliantly, and, with youthful ardor, turned them against nihilism. Their spokesman was P'ei Wei (267–300).

P'ei Wei came of a family of high officials and jurists. At the age of thirty he was made chief assistant of the state secretariat, and he was involved in the critical political events at the end of the century, finally losing his life in the first coup d'état of the eight princes because he was related to the Empress Chia. As son-in-law of Wang Jung and friend of Wang Yen, he was intimately acquainted with the frivolous circle of conversationalists, taking active part in their debates, and was even one of the leading spirits. This redoubtable dialectician, whose logic was impeccable and who was never short of arguments, was known by his contemporaries as "the man who stabbed the talkers in the back." [31] Sickened by the emptiness of the nihilistic ideas then in fashion, he set out to refute such a socially pernicious philosophy in two dissertations on "the pre-eminence of being" (*ch'ung-yu*), a term designed to contradict the term "excellence of non-being" (or nothingness, *kuei-wu*) in use by the nihilists. The two dissertations, which were ardently discussed at the time, date from 297; combined into one treatise, they are preserved in the "History of Chin." We should not let the extreme subtlety of P'ei Wei's metaphysics, which makes him very difficult to translate, eclipse the pragmatic value and the purely utilitarian side of this work, which he undertook for political reasons.

31. For P'ei Wei's biography, see *Chin-shu* 35.3b–6a (*Chin-shu chiao-chu* 35.12b–18b); cf. *T'ung-chien* 82 (year 297), 18a–b, which gives extracts from his treatise. His memorial on jurisdiction is in *Chin-shu* 30.9a–b (*Chin-shu chiao-chu* 30.25b–27b); cf. *T'ung-chien* 83 (year 299), 4b–5a; *Shih-shuo hsin-yü* 1A.27a; 1B.12a; 2A.27a and 49a; 2B.20a–b and 22a; 3A.8a and 39a; 3B.32a and 47a; and, in particular, 1B.12a–b; cf. *San-kuo chih* 23.18b.

If evidence of his reasons is required, I need only quote the passage from his biography introducing the treatise:

P'ei Wei was profoundly distressed by the slackening (*fang-tang*) of moral standards in his day. Confucianism was no longer venerated. Ho Yen and Juan Chi had a widespread reputation among the generation who held talks on frivolous vanities (*fou-hsü*), did not observe the moral law (*li-fa*), and, only interested in the salary and favors brought by office, neglected their duties. Later Wang Yen and his set achieved a celebrity far beyond their deserts, held high positions, and had considerable influence. They were not interested in the affairs of this world, and, when this attitude became fashionable, morals and doctrines were jeopardized. In order to deliver people from this evil, P'ei Wei wrote the "Discourse on the Pre-eminence of Existence" (*Ch'ung-yu lun*).

To give some idea of P'ei Wei's metaphysical ideas, I should like to quote the main definitions with which his treatise begins:

The mingling of all origins in chaos, this is the Way (*Tao*) of the Supreme Principle. The localization following upon the diversity of species, this is the classification into categories. Differentiation of forms and of phenomena is the essential basis for the existence of all creatures. The alternation of the influences is the origin of orderliness (*li*). While the various species are established by classification, their natural disposition inclines that way. The inclination is not sufficient in itself; that is why it depends on external matter. Thus whatever might be regarded as reason in life itself is called orderliness. The substance (*t'i*) of orderliness is called existence (*yu*). That on which existence depends is called matter (*tzu*) . . . [etc.] [32]

Having thus found a metaphysical argument for establishing the division of society into categories on an existential basis, P'ei Wei first extols such social virtues as individual effort, moderation, respect, frugality, loyalty, and fidelity, and then turns upon the licentiousness and depravity of the libertines. "Such behavior," he says, "might be

32. *Chin-shu* 35.4b; cf. Forke, pp. 226 ff.

described as a way of losing one's life by the very enriching of it." And so he arrives at the main part of his argument, which I should like to quote in full.

> When one examines [in the discussions] the evil caused by depravity and the good brought about by simplicity and restraint, [these libertines] start discussions on the value of Nothingness (*kuei wu*) and build theories on the baseness of existence. But if one despises existence, one must necessarily place oneself outside empirical reality (*hsing,* "physical forms"); if one places oneself outside physical reality, one must necessarily neglect the rules; if one neglects the rules, one must necessarily disdain the prohibitions and if one disdains the prohibitions, one must necessarily forget about the proprieties (*li,* "the rites"). But if proprieties and rules no longer exist, *there is then no means of governing left.*[33]

It is the duty of the sovereign to see that everyone keeps his place, is assigned his own particular task, and earns his living by peacefully following one of the four professions, which should not trespass on each other or interfere with each other. Then P'ei Wei continues his argument:

> It is possible to moderate excessive desires, but it is not possible to suppress them out of existence. It is possible to restrict extravagant expenditure, but it is not possible to declare the pre-eminence of Nothing-at-all. These accomplished talkers do indeed enumerate the causes of existence and of empirical reality with great profundity, and they praise with emphatic fervor the beauties of the Void and of Nothingness. But the causes of physical reality can be proved, whereas the meaning of the Void and of Nothingness is difficult to examine. Their phrases of sophisticated subtlety may in fact be sheer nonsense, and their plausible analogies may lead to error. The crowd is confused by what it hears, but is eager to adopt ready-made opinions. There are, however, many points on which people disagree with the views expressed, and since there is no help to be derived from the words that express them they stick to the ideas with which they are familiar. That is why one can never get the better of those who argue the merits of the

33. *Chin-shu* 35.5a.

Void and of Nothingness. The song they sing finds an echo; but
many who go in that direction never return. As a result, they
neglect the business of keeping the world in order, despise the
making of arduous efforts, exalt futile occupations, and deprecate
the merits of men of solid worth.

It is a foible of human nature to be particularly eager for fame
and profit. Hence those who are good at expressing themselves invent fine phrases, and those who express themselves with difficulty
admire their efforts. Finally the crowd is infected. So they invent
sayings based on the Void and on Nothingness which they call
"mysterious and marvelous" (*hsüan-miao*). If someone holds an
official post, he takes no share in administrative duties, and calls
his inactivity "noble distance" (*ya-yüan*). In their private lives,
people forsake frugality and restraint, and call that "being untrammeled" (*k'uang-ta*). As this attitude gradually becomes a
habit, it leads to complete decadence. This accounts for the way
in which the libertines (*fang-che*) rebel against the conventions
of what is proper and improper, and despise the outward formalities of behavior. They profane the rules concerning the distance
between generations, and sow confusion in the distinctions of rank
between commoners and nobles. The worst of them go so far as
to walk about naked, and play all sorts of pranks, forgetting the
proprieties, and regarding an attitude of carefree nonchalance as
something magnificent.[34]

P'ei Wei thus fully clarifies the Confucianist attitude toward the
destructive ideas of nihilism. We see here that permanent trend in
Chinese philosophy which I stressed earlier—namely, the social basis
of metaphysical thought. But the Confucianist attack on what were
only the symptoms of the organic disturbances undermining third-
century society were doomed to ineffectiveness. Nor was the belated
attempt of others who, feeling that they were on the brink of an abyss,
tried to rethink things out and arrive at a more positive outlook, any
more fruitful. The jurists vainly attempted to prevent the fall of the
empire by recasting the Han and Wei codes, hoping to maintain the
rigid state hierarchy by providing it with a legal basis. Their immense
labors produced the monumental Chin code, promulgated at the be-

34. Ibid., 5a.

ginning of 268. It contained 2,926 paragraphs of statutes on every imaginable crime, and, including laws and decrees, ran to 60 volumes containing 126,300 characters—30 volumes more than the preceding codes.[35] But while the jurists were delighting in their quibbles, convinced that they had foreseen everything and had regulated everything according to cast-bronze laws, the ruling class for whose benefit they had legislated publicly displayed its hopeless weakness, and, what was worse, did so in full view of the petty border tribes who were awaiting the opportunity to swoop down on the fertile Chinese plain. Even while P'ei Wei was dissecting nihilist ideas with the surgical skill of a subtle dialectician, barbarian fists, clumsy yet efficient in their own way, were already hammering down the gates of the empire.

Confucianism eventually profited—though indeed very much later —from the intellectual currents of the third century. The manner in which "pure talk" was conducted stimulated philosophical debate and doctrinal discussion, and thus contributed materially if indirectly to the renewal of orthodox teaching and the study of the classics. But what profited most from the ensuing breakup of the empire into a host of rival states was Buddhism, the new light that dawned upon the scene of unrelieved chaos and hopeless poverty presented by the country as a whole—the salvationist religion that reigned supreme for three centuries.

35. *Chin-shu* 30.6b. Cf. *Chin-shu* 49.3a: "At this time, the Emperor (Yüan, 317–22) already employed the methods of Shen Pu-hai and Han Fei-tzu [i.e. severe punishments, as recommended by the Legalists] in order to save the world, but it was not yet possible to get rid of men like Juan Fou." Juan Fou (280– 328) was a grandnephew of Juan Chi, and a great libertine.

THE FIRST

CHINESE MATERIALIST

The history of Buddhist thought has made remarkable advances during the last two centuries. There has been a fundamental change of view on the importance of the Mahāyāna, and the outlines of Chinese Buddhism are gradually becoming clearer. But the interconnections are lost because the total picture still exists in a vacuum. Buddhism is still regarded as an isolated phenomenon, a thing in itself, detached from the historical circumstances in which it arose and unrelated to outside events. At the most, cursory treatment is given to its inner development, to questions such as the proliferation of sects and the increasing sophistication of basic tenets. Yet if historical circumstances are not taken into account, the beginnings of Indian Buddhism are as incomprehensible as are its spread and further development on Chinese soil. And when I urge that "history" should be taken into account, I do not mean a mere listing of names, bibliographies, translations, and commentaries. Unless it is recognized that a struggle was taking place between the upholders of two opposing world views, the ideas of the protagonists will remain colorless and devoid of significance.

The fifth century was decisively important for the spread of Buddhism in China: China was at that time not only partitioned, but also torn by social contradictions and innumerable and unbridgeable differences of opinion, and full of a desperate longing for salvation. There were two centers of Buddhism, which were at the same time the two political centers of the country, divided as it was between the Northern and the Southern dynasties, and they had an ever-widening circle of

This article originally appeared under the title "Buddhistische Studien. Der Philosoph Fan Dschen und sein Traktat gegen den Buddhismus," *Sinica*, 7 (1932), 220–34.

influence, like two stones dropped into the waters of the Chinese sea of thought. This was a period of adaptation. The foreign words were feverishly taken over and transcribed, and the unfamiliar thoughts busily assimilated to Chinese traditional ways of thinking. When Buddhist ideas were expressed, they were larded with thousands of quotations from the classics and steeped in analogies, in order to make them more palatable to minds brought up on a mixture of Confucianism and Taoism. But it was also a period of ideological battles and terminological disputes, of endless discussions and debates. The propaganda activities of Indian missionaries and Chinese monks brought a breath of fresh air into Chinese ways of thinking, and in the fight against this new world view, Chinese minds became more agile, more flexible, more elastic.

Behind these lively intellectual battles can be discerned the emerging campaign conducted by the Chinese bureaucracy—mainly Confucianist —against monasticism and the growing temporal power of the church. Ever louder became the accusations made against Buddhism: that it was antisocial, unproductive, and parasitical, and prevented the people from carrying out their economic tasks. The condition of the peasantry and the political power of the state were the issues at stake.[1]

It was this hostile attitude toward Buddhism that gave rise to one of the most interesting works produced by medieval Chinese philosophy: the materialist tract *Shen-mieh lun,* the complete text of which is preserved in the biography of Fan Chen in the annals of the Liang dynasty.

Fan Chen came of an impoverished scholar-official family, and must have been born around 450 in the south of present-day Honan.[2] At that time, the fame of a Confucian teacher from Anwhei called Liu Huan (ca. 434–489) had spread far and wide throughout the South.[3]

1. To cite one example among many, in Wei, in 506, the Censor Yang Ku wrote a memorial saying that vague and fruitless theoretical discussions about agriculture must cease, and unprofitable expenditure on Buddhist monks must be curtailed; see *Tzu-chih t'ung-chien* 146.7b.

2. For the biography of his younger cousin Fan Yün (451–503; see below), who came from the same district, see *Liang-shu* 13.1a–4b. All other biographical details, unless a specific reference is given, are from the biography of Fan Chen, *Liang-shu* 48.4a–10a.

3. See *Nan-Ch'i shu* 39.1a–4a; *Nan-shih* 50.1a–5a; *Chung-kuo jen-ming ta-tz'u-tien,* p. 1494.

The intelligentsia at the capital were all sending their sons to him to be taught, and the young Fan Chen also became one of this distinguished band of pupils. Because of his brilliant gifts, he soon became one of the master's favorite pupils, and, as a mark of special favor, the master personally placed the cap of manhood on his head at the capping ceremony. Fan Chen remained at Liu Huan's school for several years, and "acquired a comprehensive and thorough knowledge of canonical literature, being particularly well versed in the three manuals of ritual (*Chou-li, Li-chi,* and *I-li*)"; he then returned home to his family.

The terse description of his character in the annals is revealing: "He went about on foot through the streets, always in straw sandals and clothes of coarse cloth [a sign of poverty]. There were many landowning and aristocratic people among Liu Huan's pupils, but Fan Chen felt no shame in their midst. . . . He was simple and upright in character, and loved making bold statements and discussing serious matters. His fellow-pupils and his friends felt unsure of themselves in his presence." In other words, Fan Chen was a brilliant polemicist whom people hesitated to attack. According to the testimony of his cousin, Hsiao Ch'en (478–529)—the only person with whom he was on truly friendly terms—he is said to have "declared that he could get the better of all opponents in discussion, and that he was daily able to convert thousands of people to his point of view." [4]

Fan Chen entered upon his official career as a scribe, as was then customary, and was posted to the military prefecture known as the "Pacification of the Man barbarians" (*Ning-man fu*). He soon mounted the ladder of promotion to reach the post of secretary in the state chancellery. After 489, friendly relations were re-established between the Wei dynasty in the North and the Ch'i dynasty in the South, and the ambassadors despatched by Ch'i were for the most part able young literati. Thus it was that Fan Chen, along with his two cousins, Fan Yün and Hsiao Ch'en, came to visit Wei.

In the eighties of the fifth century, one of the intellectual centers in the South was the court of Prince Hsiao Tzu-liang (460–494). The chief pride and boast of this great Maecenas was the guests he entertained. A lover of literature and art and himself a writer and art collector, and an ardent Buddhist who wrote a number of Buddhist

4. *Hung-ming chi* 9.29a. On Hsiao Ch'en, see *Liang-shu* 26.6a–8a and *Chung-Kuo jen-ming ta-tz'u-tien,* p. 1653.

works, he gathered around him all the best known literati and celebrated monks. His Western Palace, in the Chi-lung-shan mountains to the north of Nanking, was filled with all kinds of antiques. Here he provided special occasions for his illustrious guests, organizing learned debates in which he took part personally, without regard for the rules of propriety. In addition to these activities, he supervised the copying of the best works of Chinese literature, and still found time to fulfill his official duties, being the occupant of several high posts.[5] Everyone of any note took part in the entertainments he provided, which offered both corporeal and spiritual enjoyments; among the participants were Shen Yo (441–513), Hsieh T'iao (466–501), Jen Fang (460–508), Wang Jung (467–493), and Hsiao Yen, later Emperor Wu Ti of the Liang dynasty. The prince had an intimate circle, known as the "Eight Friends," to which Fan Chen's cousins, Fan Yün and Hsiao Ch'en, belonged, so naturally Fan Chen could not fail to belong as well. Visits to the luxurious palace of a prince who regarded benevolence and charity as the highest tasks of a Buddhist, where one could mix with learned and glib-tongued monks, could not fail to exercise a considerable influence on Fan Chen the polemicist, who loved above all "making bold statements and discussing serious matters." This is where his materialist ideas were formed, and this provided the stimulus for the *Shen-mieh lun.*

A conversation between the prince and his guest, which I should like to quote in full, is preserved in the *Liang-shu*:[6]

> During the time of the Ch'i dynasty, Fan Chen often waited upon the Prince of Ching-ling, Hsiao Tzu-liang. Tzu-liang was a firm believer in the Buddhist faith, but Chen openly announced that the Buddha never existed. Tzu-liang posed the question to him: "If you do not believe in the evidence of facts, how then do you explain the fact that the world contains both rich and high-born people, and poor and ordinary people?" Chen replied: "Man's life

5. Hsiao Chih-liang nearly came to the throne as successor to his father, but the plot failed because of the hotheadedness of his brilliant protégé, Wang Jung, who was forced to commit suicide in prison, in 493, before his powerful protector was able to rescue him. Hsiao Chih-liang fell into disgrace and died a year later. See *Nan-Ch'i shu* 40.1b–11a; *Nan-shih* 44.5a–9a; *Tzu-chih t'ung-chien* 136.1a ff.; 138.5a ff.; 139.7b; *Chung-Kuo jen-ming ta-tz'u-tien,* p. 1642.
6. *Liang-shu* 48.5a–b.

is like the blossom of a tree. The branches all grow at the same time, and together the sprays of blossom burst into bloom. But the blossoms fall where the wind blows them. One will be blown against the woven bamboo of a screen, and will sink to the ground on the soft matting. Another is driven against a bamboo hedge and falls into a dung-hole. Those which sink on to soft matting are high dignitaries such as Your Highness. Those which fall into a dung-hole are like me, subordinate officials. High-born and low-born certainly go different ways, but what has the evidence of facts got to do with it?" Tzu-liang could not convince him, and was full of admiration.

After the death of Hsiao Tzu-liang, the next stage of Fan Chen's career found him in Hupeh, where he was prefect of present-day Ching-chou-fu. But he had to give up this post almost immediately because of the death of his mother, which meant that he had to spend the mourning period in his native Honan. Meanwhile, Hsiao Yen was busy preparing the downfall of the short-lived Ch'i dynasty. Rebel troops were gathering throughout the country. The "Righteous Army" came through Honan on their march to Chien-k'ang (present-day Nanking), and Fan Chen, to the great joy of his old acquaintance Hsiao Yen, went to meet them wearing his black mourning bands: this action indicated that he was in support of the cause of righteousness and wanted to take up arms before the three-year mourning period was over. When Chien-k'ang was captured after a short blockade in 501 and the new Liang dynasty was proclaimed, Fan Chen had good hopes that the way to high office would be opened to him, along with most of his old acquaintances from the Western Palace days, through former friendship with the new emperor. In fact, however, Wu Ti gave him only a provincial post, although it was an important one. He was made prefect of the commandery of Chin-an (now Min-hou-hsien, or Fuchow, the capital of Fukien). For four years (501–505) Fan Chen looked after the affairs of this province, and the annals praise him for being "honorable and moderate and living only from his of-ficial salary"—already at that time an exception proving the rule of official corruption.

From Fukien, Fan Chen was called to the capital to take up the post of first secretary in the state chancellery, and he might have become chancellor had it not been for his fateful friendship with a former head of the chancellery, Wang Liang. Wang Liang, having failed to attend a New Year's audience on the plea of illness, was banished from the capital and degraded to the rank of commoner. So Fan Chen, in any case disillusioned and dissatisfied with the new regime, felt that the most urgent thing for him to do upon arrival at the capital was ostentatiously to visit his old friend now fallen into disgrace, and to offer him a gift; and at the first opportunity he said openly to the emperor that he could not understand His Majesty's behavior. Wu Ti, indignant at such bluntness, begged him to explain himself, but Fan Chen stuck to his opinion. Thereupon the censor Jen Fang accused him, in a long-winded memorial, of disrespect, ignorance, heretical opinions, being in the pay of Wang Liang, and so on and on, and begged the emperor to remove Fan Chen from office and banish him.[7] Wu Ti accepted the recommendations of the memorial, and Fan did penance for his political presumption in the traditional banishment province of Kuangchow (Canton), probably in the farthest South.

It is not certain how long he remained in exile, and the year of his death is also uncertain. The annals give only the following cursory account: "Fan Chen remained for several years in the South, and then returned to the capital. On his arrival in the capital he was appointed as a secretary in the chancellery and as a Master of the National Academy (*Kuo-tzu po-shih*). He died in full enjoyment of honors and of office." It is safe to assume that Fan Chen died sometime around the year 515.

The *Shen-mieh lun* was a tract written by Fan Chen during the time when he was engaged in the debates at the court of Prince Hsiao Tzu-liang, in answer to the pressing need for an effective theoretical weapon against Buddhism. The intention behind the tract is made quite clear by Fan Chen himself in the last paragraph, in which he discusses the application of the theory he has been expounding. The very title contained an unmistakable attack. Two surviving essays of

7. See the biography of Wang Liang in *Liang-shu* 16.1a–4a, and *Chung-Kuo jen-ming ta-tz'u-tien*, p. 104. Wang Liang was reinstated in 509 after a three-year mourning period and died a year later while holding high office. This indicates that Fan Chen must have been banished in 505 or 506.

the time are entitled "On the Immortality of the Soul" (*Shen pu-mieh lun*)—one by the celebrated founder of the Lotus School, Hui-yüan (333–416), the other by a certain Cheng Tao-tzu.[8] So the *Shen-mieh lun*, "Essay on the Extinction of the Soul," maintaining that the spirit did not survive and the human soul was not immortal, was to some extent an answer to them.

Until the spread of Buddhist thought in the Middle Ages, the problem of immortality had never played as great a role in Chinese philosophy as it did in the West. The practical Chinese mind, concerned with the things of this world, was inclined to dismiss the question as unimportant. Confucius had given the agnostic position its classic formulation in the often quoted passage in the Analects: "While you do not know life, how can you know about death?"[9] This attitude went very well with ostentatious funeral ceremonies, with ritualistic display as an end in itself. Mo Ti was the only person to preach survival after death, and he did so precisely because of his opposition to the wasteful extravagance of Confucian funeral customs, which would be rendered entirely unnecessary by the existence of a life beyond the grave. To the Taoists, life and death were merely transitional states of being. Chuang Tzu's metaphor of the firewood coming to an end while the fire mysteriously goes on burning was susceptible to several interpretations. The Buddhists saw in it (at a much later date, it is true) a belief in immortality, but probably Chuang Tzu himself would have repudiated this with an ironic and forgiving smile. Prior to Fan Chen, the only person to argue consistently against a belief in immortality was the skeptic Wang Ch'ung (27–97).

It was only after the introduction of Buddhism into China that men became concerned with the problem of the immortality of the soul. When that happened, complicated theories requiring a high degree of training in speculative thought were simplified into religious doctrines of salvation, the metaphysical idea of a chain of being was popularized into the moral doctrine of reincarnation, and the void of Buddhist epistemology was solidified into a concrete heaven. The "Pure Land" school founded by Hui-yüan was the chief example of the trend toward religious beliefs that would harmonize both with existing popular beliefs and with the religious needs of the great mass of the com-

8. *Hung-ming chi* 5.
9. *Lun-yü* XI, 11.

mon people, while at the same time answering to the pessimistic escapist mood of the ruling classes. This trend reduced the abstruse theories of the Mahāyāna to their lowest common denominator: salvation. It was against this popular form of Buddhism encouraged by the court that Fan Chen set out to do battle.

His short tract is written in dialogue form—a form that had already been adopted by Mou Tzu, the first apologist for Buddhism in China, and that had been in favor since the fourth century. Fan Chen asks himself the kind of questions that any average Buddhist of the time might have asked, and replies in the capacity of "host" to the questions put by the "guest" (these being the descriptions of the debating partners given in the Chinese text). The thirty-one questions fall into five sections.

The first section (questions 1–13) contains metaphors concerning the problem of the relations between body and soul, for which a materialistic, monistic solution is found. The materialist view, strongly reminiscent of Lucretius, is summed up in the thesis: "The body is the soul's material basis; the soul is the functioning of the body." Fan Chen meets his imaginary opponent's arid, mechanistic way of thinking with dialectical arguments stressing developmental factors. In the second section (questions 14–24), the problem of the soul as function is viewed from another angle. The opponent asks about the location of the soul, and Fan Chen replies according to the deep-rooted convictions of his time. The heart had always been regarded by the Chinese as the seat of thought, in just the same way as Aristotle held that the central psycho-physical organ was not the brain, but the heart. The argument here, however, depends upon a differentiation between thought on the one hand, and feeling and perception on the other. Like the ancient philosophers, Fan Chen did not distinguish between *perceptio* and *sensatio*. This results in his arriving at a solution with a very modern ring to it: thought is differentiated from feeling only by degree of intensity.

While the first two sections are purely philosophical, the next two enter into the realms of religion and mythology. The style matches the content. Instead of sharp, clear, and concise definitions, we find the habitual indulgence in "historical" quotations from the classics. It was customary in the tracts of the time to prove everything by biblical sayings. The Buddhists themselves were fond of relying on biblical authority as a heavy defense weapon against their Confucian opponents. Section 3 (questions 25–27) treats of the like quality of spiritual power in the holy sages of antiquity, the argument being conducted in somewhat unconvincing metaphors. Finally, in the fourth section (questions 28–30), Fan Chen attempts to come to grips with the problem of the relation between human and supernatural beings, a problem that arises from the double meaning of *shen:* "soul" or "spirit," and "spirits" in the sense of supernatural beings. But he gives confused and evasive answers to the opponent's questions, the opponent having meanwhile been converted to the belief in the mortality of the soul. On the one hand Fan argues that the ancestral cult has a merely educative value—a point of view that comes very close to Confucianism in its original form—and uses the same arguments as Wang Ch'ung against ghost stories about evil spirits, while on the other he acknowledges the existence of dark spirits and only denies the possibility of men changing into spirits. This is the contradiction —whether conscious or unconscious is an open question—upon which Fan's materialism founders.

The last section is no longer a discussion. The opening question on the application of the mortality theory is merely a prelude to the great peroration on the harmfulness of Buddhism. Fan Chen here expounds his own beliefs, which combine Taoist naturalism and Confucian social views. He states his preference for the well-being and happiness of the human family on earth over salvation in the next world. To be contented with one's lot and resigned to one's fate are what maintain the upper and lower parts of society in a permanent state of balance.

The *Shen-mieh lun* had a powerful effect on Fan Chen's contemporaries. "When this essay appeared, voices were raised at court and among the people, and Hsiao Tzu-liang assembled monks to raise objections, but they could not convince (Fan Chen)." [10] This discussion, which, according to the *Tzu-chih t'ung-chien,* took place in 484, gave rise to two anecdotes that throw light on the character of the argumentative materialist. According to the first, a certain "Wang Yen of T'ai-yüan wrote an essay in which he mocked at Fan Chen as follows: 'O-ho Master Fan! You do not even know where the spirits of your ancestors are!,' thinking that Chen would find this unanswerable. But Chen replied: 'O-ho Master Wang! You do know where the

10. *Liang-shu* 48.10a.

spirits of your ancestors are, yet fight shy of committing suicide in order to join them.'" It is characteristic of materialists everywhere and in all periods that they go into the attack against their opponents. Fan Chen's sharp and witty comment on the believers in immortality is reminiscent of a saying of the Indian materialists (the *Cārvāka*): "We do not believe in Heaven and salvation nor in the soul's existence in another world . . . If the animal that is slaughtered enters into Heaven, why does the sacrificer not dispatch his own father into the better world?" [11]

The second little story, no less characteristic than the first, runs as follows: "Wang Jung went to Fan Chen on Hsiao Tzu-liang's behalf and asked: 'Sir, you have such outstanding capabilities, why do you worry unnecessarily lest you should not obtain a post as secretary in the Chancellery? But it is unfortunate that you should have written this essay out of sheer contrariness. You ought to destroy it immediately!' Chen replied with a loud laugh: 'If Fan Chen could be persuaded to give up his opinions as the price of obtaining office, he would have been Chancellor and minister long ago. Why is he now only secretary in the Chancellery?'" [12]

Two polemical essays of counterargument, apparently also composed at Hsiao Tzu-liang's court immediately after the appearance of Fan's tract—around the year 490—and used in the first discussion, are fortunately preserved in the *Hung-ming chi*. Sometime after 507, Seng-yu (died 518) collected together the objections raised by Fan Chen's opponents and added them to the earlier version of this work of his that is of such inestimable value for the history of Buddhism.[13] The two pamphlets, which bear the same title, "Objections to the Essay on the Extinction of the Soul by Fan Chen" (*Nan Fan Chen Shen-mieh lun*), occupy most of the ninth chapter of the *Hung-ming chi*. The first is the work of Hsiao Ch'en, Fan Chen's cousin; the second is by a certain Ts'ao Ssu-wen, of whom nothing is otherwise known. Hsiao Ch'en's objections are particularly valuable, because ahead of each objection, the full text of the *Shen-mieh lun* is given paragraph by paragraph, thus enabling us to emend and amplify the

11. Paul Deussen, *Die nachvedische Philosophie der Inder* (Leipzig, 1894–1920), p. 202.

12. *Tzu-chih t'ung-chien* 136.2a.

13. Cf. P. Pelliot, "Meou-tseu ou les doutes levés," *T'oung Pao, 19* (1920), 270 f.

version given in the annals. Whether the version in the *Liang shu* goes back to this text is difficult to establish, for the variations in the two texts are almost negligible, and moreover the collected works of Fan Chen were still extant in early T'ang times (the compilation of the Liang annals was completed in 633).[14] The objections of Ts'ao Ssu-wen also contain a valuable supplement to the *Shen-mieh lun,* namely, some of Fan Chen's replies to these objections, in which he further clarifies his position with regard to the classical books.

The inclusion of this polemic in the *Hung-ming chi* was a result of the second discussion, inaugurated by Wu Ti himself. The tenth chapter of the *Hung-ming chi* contains the edict calling for the discussion and the replies of sixty-two high officials. As Pelliot has already established, the names and titles of these officials enable us to fix the date of the discussion. It took place in 507. In all probability Fan Chen was by that time in the far South, and perhaps it was his banishment that prompted the Emperor to open up the question of the immortality of the soul once again. The official replies are without exception brief exercises in literary style condemning the tract as heretical, and most of them conclude with a devout Buddhist greeting formula.

These happenings, which led to a new upsurge of Buddhism, suffice to demonstrate what an influential work the *Shen-mieh lun* was. Because of historical circumstances, it had precisely the opposite effect to that originally intended. But the importance of Fan Chen as a materialist thinker goes far beyond the contemporary debates about Buddhism. His philosophical definitions have a value of their own, and in spite of containing many of the contradictions and prejudices of his time, which he himself was unable to transcend, his tract is the work of a powerful mind. There is every justification for maintaining that no history of Chinese philosophy should fail to include the name of Fan Chen.

14. In the bibliographical treatise of the Sui history (*Sui-shu* 35.17a) they are listed as "Collected Works of the First Secretary of the State Chancellery of the Liang Dynasty, Fan Chen, in Eleven Chapters." According to the biography, there were only ten chapters. There is no mention of the work in later bibliographies.

ESSAY ON THE EXTINCTION OF THE SOUL[15]

I

(1) *Someone asked me:* You say the soul becomes extinguished. How do you know it becomes extinguished?

Answer: The soul and the body are identical. Therefore while the body survives the soul survives, and when the body perishes the soul is extinguished.

(2) *Q.* "Body" refers to something that lacks consciousness, "soul" to something that has consciousness. Consciousness and lack of consciousness[16] are two different things, therefore soul and body cannot reasonably be treated as one. I have never before heard it said that body and soul are identical.

A. The body is the soul's material basis; the soul is the functioning of the body. Consequently, since "body" refers to the material basis and "soul" to the functioning, body and soul cannot be regarded as separate.[17]

(3) *Q.* But since admittedly the soul is not the material basis and the body not the functioning,[18] where is the sense in saying that they cannot be regarded as separate?

A. These are separate names referring to a single object.

(4) *Q.* Since the names are separate, how can there be only one object?

A. The soul is to the material basis as sharpness is to a knife; the body is to its functioning as knife is to sharpness. "Sharpness" does not name knife nor "knife" sharpness. Nevertheless, without sharp-

15. The text used is that of *Liang-shu* 48.5b–10a, but the *Hung-ming chi* version (*Kyoto Tripiṭaka* XXVIII, 1.29a–31a) has also been consulted. I numbered the questions and divided the essay into sections. (It is difficult to translate *shen.* In the German version it appears as *Geist.* "Spirit," "mind," and "consciousness" are possibilities, but "soul" has been chosen—in spite of the fact that it differs in connotation from *shen*—because it is usual to speak of the immortality of the soul.—tr.)

16. Here *chih* and *wu chih* must be translated as "consciousness" and "lack of consciousness," although later the same terms undoubtedly mean "sentient" and "insentient." See note 23 below.

17. *Chih,* "matter"; *yung,* "use," "function." Cf. the similar formulation in Lucretius, III, 168–69, 175, 325–26, 554–62, 798–99.

18. The *Liang-shu* text is corrupt here: "the soul is not the functioning" obviously does not make sense, whereas the *Hung-ming chi* version, which I have used, does.

ness, there is no knife; and without a knife, there is no sharpness. I have never heard of sharpness surviving the destruction of the knife; how then can we allow that the soul survives after the body has perished? [19]

(5) *Q.* It may be admitted that the relation of knife to sharpness is as you explain it, but the relation of body to soul cannot be interpreted in this way. How shall I put it? Wood is made of insentient matter, man of sentient matter.[20] That is to say, that although man is made of matter just as wood is, yet man also has sentience, which distinguishes him from wood. Is it not plain, therefore, that wood consists of one thing and man of two things?

A. That is a strange way of putting it! If it were true that man were made of matter, as wood is, and that this constitutes his body, while he also had sentience, which wood has not, and this constituted his soul, then your argument might hold. But the matter man is made of is sentient matter, whereas wood is made of insentient matter. That is to say, man and wood are not made of the same kind of matter. So how can you say that man is made of matter just as wood is and yet in addition has sentience which distinguishes him from wood?

(6) *Q.* Supposing, then, that the only thing that differentiates the matter man is made of from that of wood is that it is sentient, what difference is there between a man and wood if the man happens to be unconscious?

A. The matter man is made of is never insentient, just as wood never has a sentient body.

(7) *Q.* B t surely you would not maintain that a dead man's skeleton is not insentient matter?

A. This is not the matter man is made of.

(8) *Q.* If that is the case, that would seem to confirm my argument that man is made of matter as wood is, and is distinguished from wood by having sentience.

A. The dead are like wood, being without the sentience that

19. The extract in *Tzu-chih t'ung-chien* 136 (year 484), 2a, stops here. It follows the conversation between Fan Chen and Hsiao Tzu-liang quoted above, which is given almost in full. Both the extract and the conversation were handed down, via the *T'ung-chien kang mu* (28.1a), to de Mailla, *Histoire générale de la Chine, 5,* 161 ff., and Wieger, *Textes historiques, 2,* 1194 f. De Mailla adds some baseless inventions of his own.

20. See note 16 above.

distinguishes them from wood. The living have sentience that distinguishes them from wood, being made of matter which is not the same as that of wood.

(9) *Q*. Is not the skeleton of a dead man the same as the bodily frame of a living one?

A. That a living body is different from a dead body and a dead body from a living body is obvious in the extreme. How is it possible to have, at one and the same time, the bodily frame of a living man and the skeleton of a dead man?

(10) *Q*. If the bodily frame of a living man is not the same as the skeleton of a dead one, then the skeleton of a dead man does not derive from the bodily frame of the living one; if it does not derive from the bodily frame of the living man, where then does the skeleton come from?

A. The bodily frame of the living man changes into the skeleton of the dead man.

(11) *Q*. But surely, even if the bodily frame of the living man does change into the skeleton of the dead man, this only means that death has occurred to something that was alive? So that we can assume that the dead body and the living body are substantially the same? [21]

A. The change is analogous to that when the wood of a growing tree changes into the wood used for building material. You would scarcely maintain that wooden building material is substantially the same as the wood of a growing tree?

(12) *Q*. But when the wood of a growing tree has changed into lumber, it must still be made of the same wood the tree was made of, just as when raw silk turns into silk thread, the thread is the same silk as the raw silk was made of. How could it be different?

A. If wood were the same when it is part of a growing tree as when it is lumber, then a tree could be withered while it is growing, and lumber could bear fruits. Moreover, the wood of a tree could not change into lumber, for if the two are the same, there is no possibility of changing from one state to the other. If the two were really the same, why can the wood not begin by being lumber and then be part of the growing tree? How is it that it must first be part of the growing

21. *T'i* combines the meaning "body," "form," "object" with "substance," so that when the Chinese says the dead *t'i* is like the living *t'i*, it means they are the same in substance.

tree and then lumber? The analogy of the raw silk and the silk thread can be refuted on the same ground.[22]

(13) *Q.* When life departs from the living body, the end might be expected to come suddenly. What is the reason for the process of decay being such a gradual one?

A. The reason is that the change from a living state to one bereft of life inevitably follows a certain sequence. For what has suddenly come into existence must perish suddenly, and what has gradually come into existence must gradually perish. The whirlwind is an example of something that comes suddenly into existence. Animals and plants are examples of things that come gradually into existence. That there should be both sudden and gradual ways is simply a law of nature.

II

(14) *Q.* If the body is identical with the soul, are separate parts of the body, such as the hands, likewise identical with it?

A. They are all parts of the soul.

(15) *Q.* If all are parts of the soul, then since the soul can think, the hands and other parts must likewise be able to think?

A. The hands and other parts can have sensations of pain and touch, but cannot have thoughts about right and wrong.[23]

(16) *Q.* Do sensations and thoughts belong to one category or two?

A. Sensations and thoughts belong to the same category. When superficial, they are sensations; when deep, they are thoughts.[24]

(17) *Q.* In that case, they must be two different things?

A. Since man has only one body, how can his soul be twofold? [25]

(18) *Q.* If his soul cannot be twofold, how then are there sensations of pain and touch and in addition thoughts about right and wrong?

A. Just as hands and feet, although different, both form part of

22. This is the first place where the two versions diverge in meaning (elsewhere they have differed in minor grammatical points only). In the *Hung-ming chi* version, this last sentence runs: "The similarity of raw silk and silk thread is not a valid comparison."

23. Here it is quite clear that *chih* means "sensation" or "awareness." *Shih fei,* "right and wrong," could also be translated "what is true and what is untrue."

24. Thought and sensation differ only in degree of intensity.

25. *T'i* is again used here (cf. note 21 above). It might be better to translate: "man's body is of one substance."

one single person, so do thoughts of right and wrong and sensations of pain and touch, although also different, form part of one single soul.

(19) *Q.* Thoughts about right and wrong have no connection with hands and feet then; with what part of the body are they connected?

A. Thoughts about right and wrong are ruled over by the heart.

(20) *Q.* This heart is the same as the heart which is one of the five viscera, is it not? [26]

A. That is correct.

(21) *Q.* But is there any such difference between the five viscera as would explain why the heart alone has thoughts about right and wrong?

A. There is just as little difference between the seven openings,[27] yet their functions are not the same.

(22) *Q.* Thoughts have no extension; how then do you know that they are ruled over by the heart?

A. If the heart is sick, then thoughts become bad.[28] Each of the five viscera has its function, but none (except the heart) has the capacity for thought. That is why the heart is held to be the root of thought.

(23) *Q.* How do you know that they do not have their seat in parts of the body such as the eyes?

A. If thoughts had their seat in parts of the body such as the eyes, why then should not the eyes[29] have their seat in other parts of the body, such as the ears?

(24) *Q.* The substance of thought has no roots, that is why it could be seated in a part of the body such as the eyes. The eyes however do have roots, and so could not possibly be seated in another part of the body.

A. Why should the eyes have roots and yet thoughts not have

26. The five viscera (*wu tsang*) are: heart, liver, lungs, spleen, and kidneys.

27. Eyes, ears, mouth, and nose (*ch'i ch'iao*).

28. This is where the second important difference between the two versions occurs. The first sentence of the reply (which fits in logically with the argument) is found only in the *Hung-ming chi,* the second only in *Liang-shu.*

29. The fuller version of the *Hung-ming chi* has been used here. At first sight, the *Liang-shu* version seems more likely to be correct: "If thoughts had their seat in parts of the body such as the eyes, why should they (i.e. thoughts) not just as well have their seat in the ears?" But the next question makes it quite clear that the *Hung-ming chi* version is correct.

any roots? If they really had no roots in one's body and could have their seat in any place anywhere, then it would be possible for the feelings of Chang Someone-or-other to have their seat in Wang Some-one-else, and the characteristics of Li Someone-or-other to dwell in the personality of Chao Someone-else. Is it so? No, it is not so.

III

(25) *Q.* The body of the sage is similar to the body of ordinary men, yet there is a difference by which the sage is distinguished from ordinary men. From this it can be inferred that body and soul are different.

A. Not at all. Pure gold glitters and unwashed gold does not. Pure gold that glitters surely cannot be made of the same unglittering material as that of unwashed gold. How much less, then, can the soul of a sage be lodged in a vessel such as the ordinary man? Nor would it be possible for the soul of an ordinary man to dwell in the body of a sage. Therefore Fang Hsün is depicted as having eyebrows of eight colors, and Ch'un Hua eyes with double pupils,[30] Hsien Yüan as having the face of a dragon and T'ai Hao the mouth of a horse;[31] all of which are outward bodily signs of their exceptional nature. All the seven openings were found in the heart of Pi Kan,[32] the gall bladder of Po Yüeh was as big as a fist,[33] which shows that their inner organs were unusual. Thus we know that certain parts of the bodies of sages are quite out of the ordinary, and that sages are not only superior to ordinary human beings, but also surpass all other creatures in bodily

30. The sage rulers Yao and Shun are also known in the *Shu-ching* as Fang Hsün (the Meritorious) and Ch'ung Hua (Doubly Glorious). The legends about the eyebrows of eight colors and the eyes with double pupils come from Han times and are contained in a number of works; cf. P. Pelliot, *T'oung Pao, 19* (1920), 355 ff.

31. Hsien Yüan is another name for the Yellow Emperor, Huang Ti, who is supposed to have been born in the place of this name in Honan; T'ai Hao (Great Brilliance) is used for the legendary ruler Fu Hsi. It is possible, though, that the reference is to Kao Yao, another legendary figure. Cf. R. Wilhelm, *Li Gi* (Jena, 1930), pp. 281 ff.

32. The tyrant Chou Hsin had his uncle Pi Kan put to death because he had been so often reprimanded by him for immoral behavior, and had the heart torn out of the body, saying: "I have heard that the holy sages have seven openings in the heart." See Chavannes, *Les Mémoires historiques, 1,* 206.

33. Po Yüeh was the given name of Chiang Wei, one of Chu-ko Liang's generals who fell in battle in 263; the anecdote about his gall bladder is told in the commentary on his biography in *San-kuo chih* 44.11b.

form. Whether ordinary men and sages are made of the same substance or not is a question I would not dare to attempt to answer.

(26) *Q*. You say that the bodies of sages are always different from
those of ordinary men. May I therefore put the following question:
Yang Huo resembled Chung Ni, and Hsiang Chi was like the great
Shun.[34] What is the reason for Shun and Hsiang, K'ung and Yang,
being different in wisdom yet alike in body?

A. Alabaster is similar to jade, but it is not jade. A cock resembles a phoenix, but it is not a phoenix. Since such relations obtain
among created things, they cannot but obtain among men as well.
Hsiang and Yang had only an outward resemblance (to Shun and
K'ung), but not an inner one. If the inner organs are not the same,
outward resemblances are meaningless.

(27) *Q*. Let us admit that the difference between sages and ordinary
men is that their bodies and organs are not the same. But the sage is
absolutely perfect, so there cannot reasonably be more than one kind,
and yet Ch'iu and Tan differed in appearance and T'ang and Wen
were unlike in build,[35] which is a further indication that soul and outward appearance do not tally.

A. Sages have the same kind of heart, but do not necessarily
have the same bodily appearance, just as horses may have different
kinds of coat, but all are fleetfooted, and precious stones may be of different colors, but all are beautiful. That is why the precious stones of
Ch'ui Chi of Chin and of Pien Ho of Ch'u both had the value of
several cities,[36] and the chestnut Hua Liu and the black horse Lü Li
could both go a thousand miles.[37]

34. Yang Huo (or Yang Hu) was steward to one of the three great families
who seized power in the state of Lu, and is mentioned in *Lun-yü* XVII, 1. His
resemblance to Confucius—Chung Ni being the given name of K'ung-tzu—is
referred to in *Mou-tzu*: see Pelliot, *T'oung Pao, 19* (1920) 318. Hsiang Chi is
Hsiang Yü, leader of the feudal lords and main opponent of the founder of the
Han dynasty. In his biography, Ssu-ma Ch'ien says: "Shun had eyes with double
pupils. I have heard it said that Hsiang Yü also had double pupils." Chavannes,
Les Mémoires historiques, 2, 322.

35. Ch'iu and Tan are the personal names of K'ung-tzu and the Duke of
Chou; T'ang the Completer was the founder of the Shang dynasty, Wen Wang
of the Chou dynasty.

36. In *Tso-chuan*, Hsi Kung second year, the following story is told: "Hsün
Hsi of Chin begged his prince to allow him to offer the horses from Ch'ü and
the precious stones from Ch'ui-chi to gain passage through Yü in order to attack
Kuo. The prince replied: 'These are our most precious possessions.'" The small

IV

(28) *Q*. I have now accepted your argument that body and soul cannot be regarded as separate. It is certainly reasonable to conclude that upon the death of the body the soul is extinguished. But may I ask what it means when the canonical writings say: "They prepare the ancestral temple [to receive the tablets of the departed] and there present offerings to the disembodied spirit"? [38]

A. This is a manner of speaking adopted by the sage for educational purposes, whereby the hearts of pious sons are strengthened and frivolous thoughts kept under control. It is to this that "understanding by spiritual insight" refers.

(29) *Q*. Po Yu appeared in a coat of mail, and P'eng Sheng appeared as a wild boar.[39] Surely these events were not recorded in the sacred books merely for educational purposes?

---

state of Yü lay between Chin and Kuo; Ch'ui-chi is an old place name. (Cf. James Legge, *The Chinese Classics*, 5, 135; S. Couvreur, *Tch'ouen Tsiou et Tso Chuan* [Ho kien fou, 1914], *1*, 234.) Pien Ho lived during the eighth century B.C. in the state of Ch'u. He found a precious stone in the mountains which he offered first to Prince Li, then to Prince Wu. The stone was thought to be a fake, and as punishment Pien Ho had first the left foot and then the right cut off. At last, under the third ruler, Prince Wen, the stone was recognized to be genuine, and called "the precious stone of Ho." The story comes from *Han Fei-tzu* 4.7a ff. It was not until the third century that the famous stone came into the possession of the state of Chao, and the ruler of Chin offered fifteen towns in exchange; see *Shih-chi* 81.1b.

37. Two of the famous horses belonging to King Mu of Chou.

38. *Hsiao-ching* 18 (Legge, *The Sacred Books of China*, *1* [Oxford, 1879] 488). The terms *kuei* and *shen* have double meanings. In the classics, the compound *kuei-shen* simply means "the departed," "the ancestral spirits." The dualistic theory of the soul (it is not known when it arose) adds to *shen* the meaning of the spirit into which the bright *Yang* part of the soul (*hun*) changes after death, and to *kuei* the meaning of the ghost into which the *Yin* part (*po*) changes.

39. Liang Hsiao, whose given name was Po Yu, was a grandson of Duke Mu of Cheng. He wanted to force the high dignitary Kung-sun Hei to go as ambassador to Ch'u. (Legge, *The Chinese Classics*, 5, 551). Kung-sun Hei refused, knowing that the embassy would mean certain death for him, and he attacked the family of his opponent. Po Yu took flight and found refuge in the neighboring state of Hsü. The high dignitaries then met and made a covenant against him, whereupon Po Yu attacked the capital of Cheng and was killed in battle (see *Tso-chuan*, Hsiang Kung 30th year; Legge, *The Chinese Classics, 5, 553, 557*; Couvreur, *Tch'ouen Tsiou et Tso chuan, 2,* 550 f.). Ten years later Po Yu appeared to someone in a dream, clad in a coat of mail, and foretold the death

A. There is an endless number of stories about the supernatural, some of which get preserved and some not. Many people have come to a violent end without a single one of them turning into a ghost,[40] so why should P'eng Sheng and Po Yu be the only ones capable of doing so? It cannot have been an exclusive prerogative of a prince of Ch'i or of Cheng to be a man one moment and a wild boar the next. (30) *Q.* In the *I-ching* it is said: "Hence we know how it is with the outgoing and the returning spirits. Insofar as man is thus similar to Heaven and Earth, he will not come into opposition with them." [41] There is also mention there of "a carriage full of ghosts." [42] What is the meaning of these sayings?

A. The difference between birds and beasts is the difference be-

---

of his murderers. The prophecy came true on the very day foretold, and the ghost of Po Yu became the terror of the people of Cheng. At last, the minister Kung-sun Chiao (Tzu Ch'an) reinstated Po Yu's son as his father's successor, and the ghost ceased to haunt the people (Legge, *The Chinese Classics, 5,* 613, 618; Couvreur, *Tch'ouen Tsiou et Tso Chuan, 3,* 140 ff.). The fame of this passage is mainly due to the principle contained in the answer given by Tzu Ch'an when asked whether Po Yu could have become a ghost: "Yes," he said, "when a man is born, the soul of the first stages of development is the *po.* Once the *po* has come into being, its bright side is the *hun.* The psychological faculties increase along with growing experience of the material world, and the two souls *hun* and *po* become stronger, until the psychological faculties become so vigorous that they may even show true spiritual power. When the ordinary man or woman dies a violent death, their *hun* and *po* souls may still hang around people in the form of an evil apparition; how much might this be expected of someone like Liang Hsiao, a descendant of our former ruler Duke Mu." Kung-tzu P'eng-sheng, the half-brother of Duke Hsiang of Ch'i, was to accompany the ruler of Lu on his homeward journey from the feast Ch'i had given in his honor. In the carriage, however, he killed the Duke of Lu, and was subsequently punished by death. Later when the Duke of Ch'i went hunting, there suddenly appeared a boar that looked human, and in which the attendants recognized P'eng Sheng. The Duke shot an arrow at it, and the boar raised itself on its hind legs and gave forth human sounds. See *Tso-chuan:* Legge, *The Chinese Classics, 5,* 69, 81; Couvreur, *Tch'ouen Tsiou et Tso Chuan, 1,* 126, 143.

40. This argument against the existence of ghosts had already been put forward by Wang Ch'ung; see A. Forke, *Lun-heng* (Berlin, 1907), *1,* 193, 208.

41. *I-ching, Hsi-tz'u chuan* I, 4. I have retained Wilhelm's translation, in *I Ging* (Jena, 1924), *1,* 222 f. (here translated into English), because it conveys both the philosophical background and the etymological factors (*shen,* "to stretch," "to move outward"; *kuei,* "to return home") that colored the Chinese conception of the soul (although here the reference is to the dualistic soul theory).

42. *I-ching,* Hexagram 38.

tween flying and walking, and the difference between men and ghosts is the difference between the dark and the light. Whether men become ghosts after death or not, or the other way around for that matter, is something beyond our comprehension.

V

(31) *Q.* What is the practical application of the belief in the extinction of the soul?

A. Distressed by the political harm caused by the Buddhists, by the undermining of morals brought about by the Sramana [monks], and by the way in which they continue on their whirlwind course or creep over the country like a rising mist, I pondered how to prevent this calamity from overwhelming us.

Now why do people donate all their wealth to monasteries and become monks, or ruin themselves in worshiping the Buddha, without thought for kith and kin and without pity for the poor and needy? It is because they are full of feelings of self-regard and lacking in concern for others. Thus a stingy look passes over the face of someone who gives a trifle to a poverty-stricken friend, whereas his whole countenance lights up with joy when he contributes a thousand bushels of grain to a rich monk. Surely this is a case of great expectations when the monk is given a large amount of grain, and no hope of reward when the friend is given a mere handful?[43] Deeds of charity are not so much aimed at helping the needy as at making sure of gaining virtue for oneself.

Furthermore, because they have been deceived by vague, dark sayings that threaten them with the torments of everlasting hell,[44] or enticed by meaningless, extravagant statements that promise them the delights of the highest heaven,[45] people discard the wide-sleeved scholar's robe and don monastic garb, lay aside the square and the round sacrificial vessels and take up the bottle and the begging-bowl, each and all of them forsaking their nearest and dearest and cutting themselves off from their descendants. And this has occurred to such an extent that the ranks of the army lack competent soldiers, govern-

43. The expressions *to tu* and *i ping* come from the *Shih-ching,* Sung I, ii, 4, and Hsiao Ya VI, 8.

44. *A-pi (avīci)*, the last of the eight hells, where sinners everlastingly die and are born again.

45. *Tou-shuai (tusita)*, the heaven where Bodhisattvas are reborn.

ment offices are emptied of clerks, grain stocks are used up in feeding lazy vagrants [the monks], and money is all squandered on monastic buildings and images. Thus it is that these rascally monks have become an insuperable nuisance, and Buddhistic songs of praise rise up everywhere.

The reasons I have put forward are the sole reasons that account for the ceaseless spread of this sect and for the boundless harm that results.

But if it is believed that everything in the universe[46] follows its own natural law and develops according to its own nature, spontaneously springing into being and then later coming to an end, so that its arrival cannot be controlled nor its departure retrieved, then everything will find its own completion in following its natural bent. The common people will be happy tilling their fields and the ruling class will be able to lead a life of leisure. And when there is no shortage of food, because there are plowmen to produce it, and no lack of clothing, because there are silkworm-tenders to provide the material, then the lower orders will have a surplus for offering [as tax] to their superiors, and the ruling class will not be obliged to impose harsh laws on their inferiors.

If this belief is put into practice, everyone can be assured of a livelihood,[47] the country put in order, and the ruler restored to full authority.

46. The expression *t'ao-chen* comes from the favorite metaphor of the potter's wheel upon which all things are molded. Cf. *Ch'ien-Han shu* (Wang Hsien-ch'ien edition) 51.10b.

47. The *Hung-ming chi* version adds here: "parents can be cared for, one can do something for oneself and for others."

A FORERUNNER

OF WANG AN-SHIH

Even at the time the Sung dynasty was founded, it was already infected with the germs of the disease to which it was bound to succumb sooner or later, and from which it eventually died. The only cure would have been to attack the diseased condition with deep surgery, for the nidus in China's body politic could not have been removed by mere application of plasters and ointments. The lesions incidental to the diseased condition brought out all the more sharply the underlying constitutional weakness, so that the best doctors were forced to grope their way toward discovering what was basically wrong with Chinese society. In the long list of these "doctors" or reformers, the best known figure is Wang An-shih, the most radical of them all. But others before him had arrived at the same diagnosis as he, though most of them did not get beyond pronouncing it in writing, whereas it was Wang An-shih's distinction to pass from word to deed and put his theories into practice. One of his immediate forerunners was Li Kou,[1] a contemporary who came from the same part of the country.

The founder of the Sung dynasty wanted to eradicate the ill that had caused the great T'ang dynasty and its five small successor states to totter, and was determined to prevent the reappearance of those all-too-powerful provincial military satraps (*chieh-tu-shih*) who, with their garrisons (*fan-chen*), had had the whip hand over the central government and had been able to defy or dethrone emperors as they

1. Hu Shih is responsible for having rescued this eleventh-century reformer from oblivion. See "Chih Li Kou ti hsüeh-shuo," *Hu Shih wen-ts'un erh-chi 1*, 43–73.

This chapter originally appeared under the title "Ein vorläufer von Wang An-schï," *Sinica, 8* (1933), 165–71.

pleased. He thought that, by weakening military strength in the provinces and establishing a strong army of mercenaries at the capital, he had made the throne safe for the ruling house for centuries. But it was precisely this weakening of military strength that brought about the fall of the dynasty. The army of mercenaries, composed of riffraff from the towns and landless victims of floods, poor harvests, and famines, was militarily incompetent and weak in morale, and was shifted from one place to another under a constant change of command until it was unable to stand up to the assaults of the Ch'i-tan and the Hsia-hsia. This meant that the drain on state finances caused by its upkeep was all the greater and the more unavoidable. Taxes were screwed up to the highest possible level, yet by the middle of the eleventh century, China, as a result of the tribute her military weakness obliged her to pay to the barbarians, was faced with immediate bankruptcy.[2] Reform was inescapable in these circumstances, but it was at the same time impossible to carry out, because those upon whom the task of altering circumstances fell would themselves have had to be reformed. The officials—for the most part effete, and trained solely in the literary arts—were "indifferent, and chiefly concerned with lining their own pockets. Confucian pacifism, which tried to make up in cultural self-conceit what it lacked in practical ability and a sense of responsibility, had already crippled the national will."[3] Wang An-shih was almost alone in seeing a clear need for this particular reform, but even he was unable to put it into effect, because, as Professor Franke so trenchantly remarks, "the weight of tradition, and the vested interest of those concerned in maintaining the existing state of affairs, were far too strong to be overcome in so short a time."[4]

Hence the main planks in the platform of all reformers under the rule of the absolute bureaucratic state, from Chia I right up to K'ang Yu-wei, were: increase of wealth, strengthening of military power, and selection and training of officials.

These were also the questions handled by Li Kou—who was never in office, but for that very reason influenced his generation all the more

2. Cf. Liang Ch'i-ch'ao, *Wang Ching-kung chuan,* pp. 15 ff.

3. Otto Franke, "Der Bericht Wang Ngan-Schïs von 1058 über Reform des Beamtentums," *Sitzungsberichte der Preussischen Akademic der Wissenschaften, Philosophische-historische Klasse, 13* (1931–32), 265.

4. Ibid., 266.

as writer and teacher[5]—in his two most important works. The Chinese tradition of backward-looking Utopianism always required that original thoughts should be clothed in historical garb. It is therefore not surprising that the first work (written in 1039) bears the pregnant title "Thirty Plans for Enriching the Country, Strengthening Military Power, and Satisfying the Needs of the People" (*Fu-kuo chiang-ping an-min san-shih ts'e*), while the second (written in 1043) makes reference to the *Chou-li* in dealing with contemporary problems, and is entitled "The *Chou-li* Leads to General Well-being" (*Chou-li chih t'ai-p'ing lun*). That these titles illustrate a general trend is confirmed by the judgment on Wang An-shih's commentary on the Chou-li found in the Imperial Catalogue:

> Since everyone knew that the *Chou-li* was not applicable to later times, Wang An-shih himself can hardly have failed to be aware of it. His real intention was to advocate wealth and power in order to amend the current weakness of the Sung. But since he feared that the Wealth and Power theory (*fu-chiang chih shuo*) would meet with strong opposition from the Confucian literati, he advocated it under cover of sayings from the classics in order to stop the mouths of the Confucians. In reality, he did not truly believe in the possibility of practical application of the *Chou-li*.[6]

5. Li Kou (T'ai-po), 1009–59, came from Nan-ch'eng-hsien in the southeast of present-day Kiangsi. He led an uneventful life amid his books and his pupils. He wrote his first book when he was 22, and went to the capital for the first time in 1036. The following year he called upon the most famous statesman and scholar of the day, Fan Chung-yen, with whom he struck up a close friendship. (Fan Chung-yen, who is usually regarded as a conservative, is described by Liang Ch'i-ch'ao [*Wang Ching-kung chuan,* p. 39] as a premature Wang An-shih!) In 1041, when he was 33, he paid another visit to the capital in order to sit for the state examination. He did not pass, and returned home, where he took over the direction of the district school. He was repeatedly recommended for promotion by Yü Ching and Fan Chung-yen, and it can be seen from the letters of recommendation that Li Kou was by now (1050) regarded as one of the most outstanding scholars (*fei-ch'ang ju*) in the country. He was appointed first as assistant, and then (1058) as professor, at the National University. He died at the age of 50. Cf. *Sung-shih* 432 (*ju-lin chuan*) and the *nien-p'u* (biography arranged according to years) which prefaces his collected works, *Chih-chiang Li hsien-sheng wen-chi,* 41 chapters, in the *Ssu-pu ts'ung-k'an.* (The original title was *Hsü-chiang chi;* see Imperial Catalogue 153). Hereafter cited as *Works.*

6. *Ssu-k'u* 19 (*Chou-kuan hsin-i*). See also Franke, "Der Bericht Wang Ngan-

Li Kou's main thesis is expressed in the opening sentences of the *Fu-kuo ts'e:*

> As far as I can see, the essays of Confucian scholars seldom fail to prize righteousness and despise profit, and never a word is said that does not contain moral uplift. Yet, of the eight methods of government in the "Great Rule" (*Hung-fan*), the first concerns food, and the second money,[7] and K'ung-tzu said that "the requisites of government are that there be sufficiency of food, sufficiency of military equipment, and the confidence of the people in their ruler." (*Lun-yü,* XII, 7.) Thus the very core of good government is that it must be based on efficient administration of the country's finances . . . That is why enlightened rulers and capable statesmen give priority to the enrichment of the country.

But enriching the country did not mean levying excessive taxation, but rather "strengthening the foundation (the peasantry) and cutting down expenditure, so that below there is no one who does not have enough, and there will be a surplus for those above."[8]

In the second chapter, Li Kou deals with the question of the much-needed land reform. Basing his argument on the "system of maximum exploitation of land" advocated by Li K'uei,[9] he traced the cause of low agricultural productivity to the unfair distribution of land: on the one hand, vast estates with an inadequate supply of labor, on the other, landless peasants. "The cunning ones among the poor take up the lesser occupations and become superfluous consumers (for this expression, see below). Those who are incapable of doing this have no option but to become day laborers on other people's land."[10] And

Schi̇s von 1058 über Reform des Beamtentums," p. 273: "The fight against the literati would have been rendered quite pointless if it had entailed giving up their common cultural heritage." It is interesting to find that Li Kou, in a letter to Fan Chung-yen, emphasizes the real nature of Kuan Chung's and Shang Yang's reforms, and quite consciously borrows from them the two expressions *fu-kuo* and *chiang-ping* (*Works,* 27.28b).

7. Or "objects of value"; the term in the *Hung-fan* is *shih-huo,* which later became the title of the economic treatises in the histories.

8. *Works,* 16.1.

9. See O. Franke, "Staatssozialistische Versuche in alten und mittelalterlichen China," in *Sitzungsberichte der Preussischen Akademic der Wissenschaften, Philosophische-historische Klasse, 13* (1931–32), 227.

10. *Works,* 16.4b.

where there are vast estates and too few agricultural laborers, the work
is not done properly. Moreover, however willing, the laborers have
no incentive to work hard, since the land does not belong to them.
The remedy: to bring peasants who have taken flight, and who are
now in secondary occupations or working as agricultural laborers,
back to the land, and to restrict the size of estates. The argument
deserves to be quoted in full:

> When the peasants who have taken flight are brought home and
> the snatching up of land has been stopped, then the price of land
> will certainly go down. Once the price of land has gone down,
> then land will be easily obtainable. If land is easily obtainable, and
> the trend toward taking up secondary occupations and enjoying
> the status of superfluous consumers is thus ended, then the peas-
> ants will wholeheartedly devote their energies to agriculture. If
> their energies are devoted wholeheartedly to agriculture, then the
> land can be exploited to the full.[11]

Thus productivity takes first place, and equal distribution of land
comes second.

Li Kou also maintains that there would be an adequate supply of
precious metals and silk if consumption were not so extravagant
(third chapter). Then follows a passage I should like to quote in full,
because it provides a lively picture of the social conditions of the time,
under the slogan: "Down with social differentiation, back to a natural
economy!" Li Kou first explains two expressions used above. The
"secondary occupations" are crafts and trade, the "superfluous consumers" are people who do not fit into any of the traditional class
categories. Then, after stating that formerly simple natural products
were made into articles of use and exchanged, he goes on to say:

> Nowadays licentiousness and extravagance are beyond all bounds.
> People dazzle each other with curiosities and swagger about in
> the latest fashions. Craftsmen regard the mere use of natural
> products as beneath them, and compete in making ingenious con-
> traptions. Merchants regard handling natural products as com-
> monplace, and compete in dealing in unusual luxuries. Sometimes
> an article that has taken months to make will be ruined in a day,

11. Ibid., 5a.

sometimes an article that has come from ten thousand miles away will be dropped on the floor and smashed. The articles are of no practical utility, but the profits are immense. Hence the people prefer this kind of occupation, and the number of craftsmen and merchants grows daily.[12]

Who are the superfluous consumers? The wealthy Buddhist and Taoist monks who, without doing any work, have the most fertile lands, the finest houses, and the best food; the servants, runners, and clerks, and all those who hang around government offices, who, insatiable as thieving dogs or greedy caterpillars, suck the very lifeblood of the people; the quacks, soothsayers, and magicians, who are up to all sorts of tricks to entice money out of people's pockets; the musicians, actors, dancing girls, and singing girls, who are supported by others. There must be a "return to natural simplicity and a stop to vain artificiality." By forbidding the building of monasteries and the taking of monastic vows, riddance can be made of both the black and the yellow monkish garb. Careful selection of officials would remove the possibility of corruption. Li Kou finally stipulates that entry into the medical profession should be limited and that there should be a strict qualifying test, and recommends the complete suppression of all sorcery and soothsaying, and of festivals where there are music and theatrical performances.

The next chapter deals specifically with monasticism. Buddhists and Taoist monks (see above) must be proceeded against with caution, because draconic measures might cause too much unrest among the people. Li Kou then discusses ten disadvantages—with a paragraph devoted to each—from which the state would suffer if monasticism were allowed to continue, together with the corresponding advantages if it were abolished.[13]

12. Ibid., 7b.
13. Ibid., 9b–11b. The disadvantages were: (1) the monks are clothed and fed by the peasants without doing any work themselves; (2) they are celibate but lead unchaste lives; (3) they avoid corvée labor; (4) the lay population pays out money to them; (5) none of them supports his dependents; (6) they take possession of fields and wastelands; (7) they take up the peasants' time with building monasteries and (8) raise the price of building materials, while the people lack even a hut to live in; (9) their luxurious tastes make crafts and trade prosper; (10) lazy people and rascals take refuge with them. The advantages consist in doing away with the disadvantages.

Next comes the question of grain prices. Whether the price of grain is high or low, the peasant always gets the worst of the deal and the merchant always makes a profit. The speculator takes advantage of the shortage of grain at sowing time and sells to the peasants at exorbitant prices, while after the harvest the peasant has to sell at a low price.

> The peasant would rather part with his life than with his grain. When he cannot go on any longer without selling it, there are reasons for this. Lesser reasons are the need for clothing and for utensils, greater reasons the need to provide for weddings and funerals, and to meet government tax demands and repayment of private loans.[14]

Hardly is the first crop ripe than he is daily having to take his grain to market. Supplies are plentiful and the price is low. Before very long his meager stocks are used up. In spring, when he has no seed corn and no food supply left, he has to go again to the merchant, but this time in order to buy at high prices. There is only one proven remedy for this: state regulation of grain prices by means of the leveling granaries.[15] (Sixth chapter.) Why is this system not working today? (1) An insufficient amount of grain is bought up. (2) The distances from the prefectural granaries are too great. For the peasants in outlying villages either the transport costs are beyond their means, or it is not worth while making the long journey. (3) The employees in charge are corrupt, and make a profit for themselves out of an arrangement which originally had a charitable purpose.

For times when the harvest is bad there are the public granaries (*i-ts'ang*). (Seventh chapter.) But the old system of graded quotas did not work, because the wealthy people who contributed the largest quantities of grain usually still had some in stock when times were bad. This was equivalent to having to pay an unfair tax. Li Kou then makes a remarkable proposal that the contributions of wealthy people should be entered in a ledger, and when after several years the amount had reached a certain quantity, the contributor should be given a title.

14. Ibid., 12a.
15. See Franke, "Staatssozialistische Versuche," pp. 220 ff., and Balazs, *Beiträge zur Wirtschaftsgeschichte der T'ang-Zeit,* pp. 158 ff.

He adds that this system would be quite distinct from the normal purchase of official appointments.

Li Kou's money theory (eighth chapter) is the usual one. To prevent a shortage of cash he recommends that bronze statues should be melted down and the use of copper for industrial purposes prohibited, and also advises that watch should be kept on the export of cash through barbarian channels. He also recommends that bad coins should be called in against reimbursement to prevent false coinage.

The last two chapters are in direct contradiction of the views condemning trade expressed in the preceding ones. Li Kou is against state monopolies in salt and tea and supports trading by license, because the state would derive more benefit from the regular income from licensing fees than from conducting the trade itself, since unavoidable corruption ends in deflecting the profits into private pockets.[16]

The second main section of the work, on the strengthening of the army (*Chiang-ping tse*), also contains ten chapters, in which Li Kou, making frequent use of historical examples, lays down the following axioms, which testify to his conversance with the military side of political problems as well as indicating (if taken in their reverse sense) the actual state of affairs.

1. *Political strategy is more important than military strategy.* "If the army is not strong, the sage ruler cannot govern the common people."[17] The Confucians say: only goodness and righteousness. The generals say: only cunning and strength. Both views are one-sided. For in a land with a good and just government, no enemy arises. On the other hand, the best of armies will be of no avail in a state that levies unjust taxation and where the people are poor and oppressed.

2. *No wars of conquest should be conducted; the frontiers should be protected by military agricultural colonies.* The empire is likened to a body: the Chinese are the heart, the barbarians the extremities. If the heart is not in order and efforts are made to control the extremities, then before the extremities have been attended to the heart will have succumbed. The barbarians are like wild animals, entirely without civilization. Therefore the best strategy is to have military colonies (*t'un-t'ien*) that can supply themselves with enough grain

16. The *Chou-li chih t'ai-p'ing lun* (in 50 chapters) contains virtually identical ideas. The most striking passages are quoted by Hu Shih, pp. 50 ff.

17. *Works*, 17.1a.

on the frontiers. The soldiers are well fed and always in readiness. If the enemy comes, they can repulse him in strength. If he flees, they do not give chase. Why do we not have enough military colonies? Too little cultivated land, no soldiers who know how to plow. The civilian population on the borders should be removed to the interior at the state's expense, and redundant workers from the towns, both outlaws and volunteers, should be recruited for the military colonies, given instruction in agriculture, and provided with tools.

3. *Agricultural colonies should supply the regular army. In the interior, a village militia should be set up.* The state derives little benefit from publicly owned land, since it is mostly leased out to large landowners. Instead, the state should itself till this land with specially recruited agricultural laborers under technically trained overseers. There should be a trained militia (civilian army) to guard against robbers and bandits at home. Civil officials do not know anything at all about the use of arms. They should be given some training in military matters to ensure the efficiency of officers and men in the militia.

4. *Not racial characteristics, but military training is what counts.* It is usually said that only in the North are strong, hardy, tough soldiers to be found. In the South men are supposed to be weak, soft, and unreliable. This is true, with the qualification that training is more important than natural endowments. A thorough training in strategy and cavalry warfare can make good soldiers out of men from all parts of the empire.

5. *Arms must be of good quality.* The provinces supply arms of poor quality that have not been properly tested. There should be state manufacture of arms under the supervision of specialists, with a carefully chosen labor force maintained on a highly nourishing diet, and using the best and costliest materials.

6. *Generals must be independent.* The ones that win are those without interference from the central government.

7. *Generals should not be constantly changed.* Success in warfare requires a feeling of solidarity between leadership and troops. There is no point in punishing a man simply for being defeated. It is his capabilities that matter. Sometimes a defeated general will be the most invincible of fighters because he wants to wipe out the disgrace.

8. *No extravagant rewards should be bestowed for victories.* For

generals who have had honors, titles, and lands heaped upon them, and who have been able to benefit all their kin, victory can have no further interest.

9. *Make use of everyone according to his abilities.* The secret of waging war is to make full use of everyone's abilities and qualities. Nowadays ability is not demanded, but mistakes are reprimanded. People should not be irritated by constant nagging.

10. *It is not enough simply to study strategy; what is required is to be a born strategist.* Theoretical knowledge is less important than having a genius for strategy and tactics.

The last ten of the "thirty plans," the *An-min ts'e,* contain fewer original ideas, but the way they deal with the central theme—the bureaucracy—is entirely on a par with Wang An-shih's famous report of 1058. The standpoint of both is the same: officials are not properly educated; instead of being trained to become energetic, practical men, they are snowed under with bookish learning quite unrelated to life and quite useless. The teachers concern themselves with verbal quibbles instead of with moral training, so that when the literati are faced with the realities of existence, and can no longer rely on their classics and their writing brushes, they are completely at a loss.[18] The examination system is valueless. It consists of tests concerning words, whereas deeds are what is required. The official with his purely literary training is nevertheless let loose among his fellow men. The special knowledge he requires can be acquired only after he has started doing his job. But since he only begins his studies in administration on the day he is appointed, nothing much of value can be learned. Institutes for training should be founded, where the abilities and character of the candidates can be constantly watched over and tested.[19]

Li Kou is not sparing in his censure of the Confucian literati of his time, although he himself was a convinced Confucian. When he was only twenty-two he had already protested: "The words of K'ung-tzu fill the whole empire, but the way of K'ung-tzu is not yet followed . . . Nourishment is sought from what is dead, not from what is alive. His words are followed, not his way. That is why those who have got hold of his words are rich and of high estate, while those who have

18. Ibid., 18.3a–4b.
19. Ibid., 4b–6b.

got hold of his way are left to starve. How sad!" [20] And later he became perhaps sharper still, when in one passage he gives a pertinent
description of how the literati harm the present with their perennial
worship of the past.

> Do Confucians have an influence on order and disorder? Yes.
> Does order reign when they are in office and disorder when they
> are not? No. There have been times when Confucians were in
> office and order reigned, but also times when Confucians were in
> office and disorder reigned. If the Confucians are the right sort
> of men, then they bring good fortune. If they are not, then they
> are like bandits. When those made of the material of inferior men
> are clothed in the outer garments of holy sages, it is just as if a
> tiger had been given wings and attacked all the people in the
> town with its claws.
>
> There are many stories from the past, some of which apply to
> existing circumstances and some not. All have a for and an against.
> If persons of inferior quality try to apply them, then one side is
> stressed and the other suppressed in order to mislead the emperor
> and promote their own private interests. [There follow examples
> of how it is possible to find in history a convenient justification
> for any project.] Ah! When the activities of Confucians come to
> such a pass as this, there is something to be said for the burning
> of the books by Ch'in! [21]

Li Kou's anti-Buddhist views, the political and economic aspects of
which were discussed above, had also a philosophical side which was
no less important. Li Kou, who has been acclaimed by Hu Shih as
the founder of Sung philosophy,[22] saw perhaps more clearly than any
other Chinese that Confucianism failed to satisfy religious and metaphysical needs. For this reason, he sought to replace Buddhism, which
then reigned supreme, by a new version of the all-embracing Confucian code of behavior (*li*, "custom").

> The Confucians grumble against Buddhism because it ensnares
> the world, but why this should be so they do not explain. The

20. Ibid., 20.6a (closing words of the *Ch'ien-shu*).
21. Ibid., 21.5b–6a (from the *Ch'ing-li min-yen*, written in 1043).
22. Hu Shih, p. 44.

Buddhists are very good at extolling their own doctrine, and although within it is false, without it is strong. In youth and in age, in petty and in lofty matters, no day goes by without depending for something on the Buddha. Because of this, people accept the faith and deeds get performed. Not so with the Confucians. Those who have not yet got what they want use Confucianism in order to raise themselves. When they have attained what they wanted, they then say that politics and literature are two different things, concentrate their efforts on finding themselves a post, and look on their past as if it were a skin that has been sloughed off. Then when they become oppressed by the existence of evil, feel compassion for the victims of crimes and sickness, want to understand about life, they do not realize that our Confucianism has its own answer to such problems, but turn to Buddhism and seek it there.

I have traveled for many a day south of the Chiang and the Huai, and many of the places there have schools. If I visited a place and asked: Are the rooms in good order? I often got the answer: They are used as a dwelling for a retired official. Is the full complement of utensils there? Answer: They fill the kitchen of the prefectural office. Is the prefect there? Answer: He is meditating in such-and-such a courtyard, or listening to lectures in such-and-such a monastery.

Ah! Buddhism has been with us for a long time now. When I first became acquainted with it, I was in doubt about it. Then when I acquired a taste for its words I saw that what had appealed to me in them did not in any way surpass various sayings in our *I-ching, Hsi-tz'u, Yüeh-chi,* and *Chung-yung.* And if these should not supply it, then it can be found in the books of Lao-tzu and Chuang-tzu. Why then should one tear the cap off one's head and crawl before the barbarians? [23]

In the same year he wrote a letter giving his reply to a scholar who had misunderstood his argument:

I have been fighting against Buddhism for a long time now. Everyone has read what I have to say in my *Ch'ien-shu* and *Fu-*

23. *Works,* 23.6b–7a, "Note on the Endowment of Land for the School in Shao-wu-chün" (Fukien), written in 1047.

kuo ts'e. How, when nearing forty, an age when one's character becomes more and more set, could I have suddenly changed my opinions? It is only that you, Huang Han-chieh, have not quite understood what I said. All I did was to censure the Confucians strongly; I paid no homage to the Buddhists.[24]

The earlier Confucians did really lead the people, the letter goes on to say, if a summary is made of the various points raised. Thus the people had no time to run after heretical doctrines. Later, when Confucianism had left the people leaderless, they could no longer resist the temptation to give themselves up to Buddhism.

Yet Li Kou had no desire to create a new Confucian metaphysic to put in the place of the Buddhist one. In contradistinction to the leading spirits of the Sung School, who allowed Buddhist theories that had earlier been openly disputed to creep in unnoticed by the back door of *I-ching* speculations, he attacked mystical and cabalistic interpretations of the "Book of Changes."[25] Man occupied the central position in his utilitarian conception of the universe, and he considered man's feelings to be an entirely natural phenomenon. The *li* did not seem to him a moral prison, for he held that the rules of propriety did not contradict man's nature; on the contrary, they made possible the free unfolding of his natural endowments. This positivist Weltanschauung of Confucianism, which in the eighteenth century, was worked out and given a deeper meaning by the Ch'ing School, headed by Tai Chen, rounds off the picture of the reformer Li Kou and points toward the connection between philosophy and history that was to appear in later times.[26]

24. Ibid., 28.26a.
25. Hu Shih, pp. 56 ff.
26. *Works* 28.20b–22a.

CHRONOLOGY

CHRONOLOGY

DYNASTIES	SIGNIFICANT EVENTS	SOCIAL AND CULTURAL DEVELOPMENTS	IMPORTANT PERSONS
B.C.			
500		Age of the Philosophic Schools	
400		Confucianism School of Tao School of Mo-tzu The Legalists	
	403–221 Warring States		
300			
221 ⎱ Ch'in 206 ⎰	221 Abolition of feudalism Beginning of united empire		
200			
Former Han			c.179–c.104 Tung Chung-shu c.145–c.90 Ssu-ma Ch'ien 141–87 Han Wu ti
		Adoption of Confucianism as state idology	
100			
A.D.			
8 Hsin			r. 9–23 Wang Mang
	18 Red Eyebrows Rebellion		
25 Later Han			c. 90–c.165 Wang Fu

Period	Events		Persons
100	100 Invention of paper	Introduction of Buddhism	c.110–c.170 Ts'ui Shih
			128–169 Kuo Lin-tsung
200 Later Han		Onset of social and intellectual crisis: Ch'ing-t'an, Neo-Taoism, Neo-legalism	155–220 Ts'ao Ts'ao
220 Three Kingdoms	184 Yellow Turban Rebellion		180– ? Chung-ch'ang T'ung
265 Western Chin			223–262 Hsi K'ang
300		Refeudalization	226–249 Wang Pi
317 Eastern Chin	317 Non-Chinese invasions Division into North and South		
400		Rapid spread of Buddhism	
420 Liu Sung		446 First suppression of Buddhism in North China	c.450–c.515 Fan Chen
479 S. Ch'i	485 Equalization of land (Chün-t'ien System)		
500			
502 Liang			
557 Ch'en			
589 Sui	589 Reunification of North and South Invention of block printing	Examination system 610 Grand Canal completed	
618			

293

DYNASTIES		SIGNIFICANT EVENTS	SOCIAL AND CULTURAL DEVELOPMENTS	IMPORTANT PERSONS
618			Use of "flying money" 661-721 Liu Chih-chi	735-812 Tu Yu
800	T'ang	756 An Lu-shan Rebellion 780 Fiscal reform		768-824 Han Yü 772-846 Po Chü-i
900 906 960	Five Dynasties	868 Printing of Buddhist Sutras	841-45 Buddhism persecuted Rise of manors	
1000	Northern Sung		Increasing urbanization Revival of Confucianism Proto-banks	1009-1059 Li Kou 1018-1086 Ssu-ma Kuang 1036-1101 Su Tung-p'o
1100 1127		1127 Division of China		
1127 1200	Southern Sung	Sung Dynasty in the South 1131 China's first port-capital at Hangchow		1104-1162 Cheng Ch'iao 1130-1200 Chu Hsi 1250-1325 Ma Tuan-lin 1260-1294 Khubilai Khan 1275-1292 Marco Polo in China
1279				

Date	Dynasty	Political Events	Cultural / Intellectual	Figures
1279	Yuan	1279 Mongol conquest of S. Sung; Use of non-Chinese officials	1313 Adoption of Neo-Confucianism as state ideology	
1300				
1368	Ming	1368 Restoration of Chinese rule		1368–1398 Ming Ta'i-tsu (Chu Yüan-chang) 1403–1424 Yung-lo Emperor
1400		1421 Ming Capital moved to Peking	Flowering of Intuitionist Neo-Confucianism	
1500			Jesuit Missions	1472–1529 Wang Yang-ming
1600		1644 Manchu conquest	School of "Han Learning"	
1700	Ching		State-sponsored encyclopedic compilations	1716–1798 Yüan Mei 1724–1777 Tai Chen 1736–1796 Ch'ien-lung Emperor
1800		Taiping Rebellion; Boxer Rebellion		1858–1927 K'ang Yu-wei 1891–1961 Hu Shih
1900		1912 Abdication of Manchus 1927 Establishment of Nationalist Government 1949 Foundation of People's Republic of China	1919 May Fourth Movement	1887– Chiang K'ai-shek 1893– Mao Tse-tung

INDEX

Administrative practice, guides to, 137–38

Agrarian policy, 103, 106, 122–23. *See also* Land regulations; Reform, agrarian

Agriculture as the "fundamental" occupation, 40, 153, 199, 201

Alcoholic liquor, sale of, 97

An Lu-shan 安祿山, rebellion of, 117, 119

Ancestor worship, 18, 155, 263

Aristocracy, 7, 40, 105, 188, 202–03, 204, 220, 227, 231, 232; tribal, 107, 114, 123. *See also* Feudal nobility

Aristotle, 262

Arms, manufacture of, 212, 285

Artisans, 16, 39, 40, 56, 67, 72, 90, 151, 153

Asiatic society, 15, 20, 36–37

Astronomy (*t'ien-wen* 天文), treatises on, 137

Bailiffs, employment of, 119–20, 124

Bamboo Grove circle, 236–42, 247, 248

Bibliographical monographs (*ching-chi* 經籍 or *i-wen chih* 藝文志), 138

Bibliographies, 138–39, 146, *147*

Bodde, Derk, 28

"Book of Changes." See *I-ching*

Bourgeois revolution, 8, 37

Bourgeoisie, 23, 24, 30, 33, 66; the Chinese, 12, 36, 37, 39, 42, 44, 53. *See also* Merchant class

Bribery. *See Corruption*

Buddhism, 254, 255, 257–59, 261, 265; Fan Chen's tract against, 260, 262 ff.; hostile attitude toward, 256, 262, 287–89; spread of in China, 255–56. *See also* Monasteries; Monks

Bureaucratic society: China as a, 13–27, 28, 29; feudalism within, 7; in modern times, 12, 14, 24. *See also* Officials; Regulations; Scholar-officials; Society

Bureaucratic state centralism, 31

Byzantine Empire, 65

Calendar, 8, 16; treatises on the (*lü-li chih* 律曆志), 137

Cambaluc (Peking), 74

Canals, 60, 83; in Hangchow, 87. *See also* Waterways

Capital: accumulation, 51–52; investment, 52, 53

Capital punishment, 6, 209

Capitalism, 21, 23, 25, 29, 31; absence of, 35; birth of, in China, 34 ff., obstacles to research on, 36–39; buds (seeds, germs) of, 23, 29, 30, 31, 35, 44; Chinese form, 39, Mao's definition of, 36; development of Chinese, 34, 52–53, impediments to, 32–33, 52, 53; expansion of Western, 34–35, 160; industrial, 31, 39, 53; mercantile, 23, 31; state, 24, 54, 168; tendencies toward, 30, 31; thrift and early, 51–52

Cattle, land allotted for, 109